FREEDOM AT LAST

HEALING THE SHAME OF CHILDHOOD SEXUAL ABUSE

BEVERLY ENGEL

Prometheus Books
Guilford, Connecticut

(PB) Prometheus Books

An imprint of Globe Pequot, the trade division of The Rowman & Littlefield Publishing Group, Inc.
4501 Forbes Blvd., Ste. 200
Lanham, MD 20706
www.rowman.com

Distributed by NATIONAL BOOK NETWORK

British Library Cataloguing in Publication Information Available

Library of Congress Cataloging-in-Publication Data

Names: Engel, Beverly, author.
Title: Freedom at last : healing the shame of childhood sexual abuse / Beverly Engel.
Description: Lanham : Prometheus, 2022. | Includes bibliographical references and index. | Summary: "In this groundbreaking book, leading psychologist Dr. Beverly Engel reveals the truth about how childhood sexual abuse affects victims, dispels common myths surrounding this type of abuse, explains the nuances behind the emotion of shame, and teaches readers how to develop more self-awareness about how shame has manifested in their lives along with powerful and effective shame-reduction strategies"—Provided by publisher.
Identifiers: LCCN 2022014953 (print) | LCCN 2022014954 (ebook) | ISBN 9781633888043 (paperback) | ISBN 9781633888050 (epub)
Subjects: LCSH: Child sexual abuse—Psychological aspects. | Adult child abuse victims—Mental health. | Self-help techniques. | Shame in children. | Sexually abused children.
Classification: LCC RC560.C46 E5397 2022 (print) | LCC RC560.C46 (ebook) | DDC 616.85/83—dc23/eng/20220715
LC record available at https://lccn.loc.gov/2022014953
LC ebook record available at https://lccn.loc.gov/2022014954

∞™ The paper used in this publication meets the minimum requirements of American National Standard for Information Sciences—Permanence of Paper for Printed Library Materials, ANSI/NISO Z39.48-1992

CONTENTS

ACKNOWLEDGMENTS

I would like to express my heartfelt appreciation for my agent, Tom Miller. Thank you for your consistent support of my projects, your diligence, your patience, your insightful feedback, but mostly for your unwavering faith in me. I am truly blessed to have you on my side. A special thanks to the helpful staff at Prometheus, especially Jake Bonar and Jessica Kastner. A special thank-you to all my readers, many of whom have been with me from the beginning, providing feedback and gratitude all along the way. You are the reason I continue to write.

INTRODUCTION

Shame is a sickness of the soul.
—Silvan Tomkins

Child sexual abuse (CSA) is not only an assault on the body—it is an assault on the mind and the spirit. It is an insult to the integrity, the self-esteem, the very being of the victim. The damage to a victim's life can be enormous. According to a systematic review comprising 270,000 participants from 587 separate studies (Maniglio, 2009), CSA survivors have a significantly higher risk of medical, psychological, behavioral, interpersonal, and social difficulties. Systemic reviews have also specifically established that CSA is a risk factor for depression, anxiety, post-traumatic stress disorder (PTSD), dissociative patterns, sexual problems, relationship problems, sexual exploitation, intimate partner violence, suicidality, substance abuse, eating disorders, and educational difficulties.

But all those effects and risk factors pale in comparison to one particular consequence of child sexual abuse—shame. Many psychotherapists agree that shame is among the most damaging aspects of child sexual abuse, if not *the* most damaging. The humiliation a child feels when violated in this way can be absolutely devastating, creating wounds that can last a lifetime.

Although research shows that depression is the most common long-term effect among survivors of CSA, this depression tends to originate with shame. Survivors have difficulty externalizing the abuse, which causes them to blame themselves. This self-blame leads to feelings of worthlessness, a clear by-product of shame. Further, years of negative self-thoughts cause survivors to feel worthless and to avoid others because they believe they have nothing to offer.

Most important, the shame of child sexual abuse creates an *internalized core belief* that one is worthless, unlovable, or bad. Changing this core belief is one of the most difficult tasks a former victim can encounter.

Shame has been examined extensively during the past decade. We have learned from a range of clinical and empirical literature, alongside recounts of survivors' lived experience, that shame following CSA can be intensely painful, disempowering, deeply distressing, and potentially destructive to one's sense of self and place in the social and relational world. This is why healing this shame warrants an entire book.

HEALING STRATEGIES

This book will provide effective strategies for not only healing the negative effects of abuse-related shame but also overcoming the shame that keeps you from reaching out to others or seeking help.

My proprietary shame-reduction program is based not only on my extensive experience working with CSA victims but on sound research. This research highlights the importance of addressing shame in order to achieve recovery. Qualitative studies have found that the following strategies reduce shame:

- self-compassion
- discussing and externalizing shame and blame
- connecting with others and engaging in helping others

My proprietary shame reduction program includes all these recommended strategies plus other important avenues for change, including:

Education. This includes busting the myths and lies concerning child sexual abuse that keep former victims stuck in shame.

Strategies and permission for emotional release. This includes teaching former victims how to release the pain, fear, and anger associated with the trauma.

Learning to practice self-compassion. Compassion and self-compassion have both proven to counter and heal shame. I take readers step-by-step through the process of learning this scientifically proven strategy for healing shame.

Encouragement and strategies for being freed from a secret. Secrets create shame, and holding the secret of child sexual abuse is especially shaming. My program offers readers encouragement, strategies, and suggestions about who is the safest person to tell and how to safely tell their secret.

Teaching former victims self-forgiveness. Self-forgiveness can be extremely important yet extremely difficult for victims of CSA. Through the process of self-understanding, I will help readers learn why they have behaved the way they have and in turn, come to a place where they can forgive themselves for the harm that they have caused others, as well as themselves.

Eliminating shame-causing behaviors. Former victims of CSA are notorious for taking on unhealthy, shame-inducing behaviors as a way of coping with their trauma. They need help in learning how to identify and eliminate these behaviors.

Removing the shame from unhealthy sexual behaviors and attitudes. Former victims tend to behave in unhealthy ways regarding their sexuality, everything from pornography addiction to passively accepting aggressive and abusive behavior from their partners. I identify these behaviors; help readers make a connection between these behaviors and their victimization; and offer alternative, healthy sexual behaviors to replace the unhealthy ones.

Not only is shame considered by many to be the most devastating, debilitating after-effect of child sexual abuse, but it is the most difficult after-effect to alleviate. Unless the shame that childhood abuse caused is addressed and healed, former victims will continue to be plagued by it. Not only will it continue to affect your self-esteem, your body image, your sexuality and your very identity, but it will motivate you to sabotage any success, happiness, or love you manage to experience. Worse yet, unhealed shame will cause you to repeatedly return to the trauma in an attempt to gain mastery of it. Many will continue to attract abusive partners or reenact the abuse in various ways, whereas others will attempt to undo what was done to them by becoming abusers or perpetrators themselves, physically, emotionally, or sexually.

Women who were molested in childhood experience an extremely high rate of revictimization, primarily due to the amount of shame and self-blame they experience. And men who were sexually abused as children tend to re-enact the abuse by engaging in dangerous sexual practices—often culminating in rape and humiliation.

In addition to revictimization, the debilitating shame of child sexual abuse needs to be addressed and healed for still another important reason: addictions. A strong correlation has been found between child sexual abuse and every type of addiction, whether it be alcohol and drug abuse, sexual addiction, or eating disorders. At the core of all these addictions is shame. Former victims plagued by shame will be far more likely to turn to a substance or activity that will help them to hide from their shame. In short, many of the most troubling issues we face today are caused by the shame of childhood sexual abuse.

I have specialized in working with victims of child abuse for more than forty years. During the course of those years, I came to realize that, in my opinion, the shame caused by child sexual abuse is the most profound wound any victim can experience. This discovery is what has motivated me to write this book. As a survivor of child sexual abuse, I fully understand the horrendous damage the shame experienced by being violated in this way can cause a person. Like many victims of CSA, my life was radically changed by the sexual abuse I experienced. More specifically, just as it is with so many other victims of child sexual abuse, I can say that my life was shaped by the shame I felt as a consequence of the abuse. It affected my self-esteem, my core beliefs about myself, my body image, my ability to protect and care for myself, my relationships with men, my relationship with my mother, and my sexuality, among many other aspects of my life.

I had to work hard to overcome my shame. In fact, I can say that I worked harder to reduce my shame than any other aspect of my abuse recovery. I tried many avenues of healing: individual therapy, group counseling, Reichian therapy, sex therapy, Jungian therapy, and cognitive behavior therapy. Due to the work I did in these therapies, I became less depressed, my self-esteem improved, and I resolved some of my sexual issues. But because none of these modalities and none of the therapists I worked with addressed my shame, I continued to suffer from self-blame, an eating disorder, alcohol abuse, reenactments of the abuse, and self-sabotaging behavior—all as a result of the shame I experienced.

I started therapy when I was sixteen years old because of a suicide attempt. After telling the psychiatrist my story (unlike many survivors, I did not block the memories of my abuse), he told me, "You know the reason for your problems, and you are an intelligent, strong, and resilient young girl. You don't need my help."

That statement from the psychiatrist should have offered me relief and hope, but it didn't. My heart sank as I realized that I had just fooled the psychiatrist. I knew I needed help, but my ability to appear strong and to be articulate got in the way. As I was to discover in my work, many former victims put up a defensive wall just as I did. This defensive strategy may protect them from further shaming, but it also prevents them from being open to the help they need.

It wasn't until many years later, when I found a book called *Shame: The Power of Caring* by Gershen Kaufman, a pioneer on the subject of shame, that I realized that it was the shame from the sexual abuse I had suffered that was damaging my life in so many painful ways. I set out to learn more and more about shame and how I could help both myself and my clients to address it and heal it. Further research led me to Kristin Neff's research on the benefits of self-compassion, which proved that it is the antidote to shame. This information helped me make a major breakthrough in my own healing, as well as offering me an effective strategy for clients.

I started applying the information I gleaned from Kaufman and other experts on shame, as well as that conducted by Neff, to my work with clients. Clients reported feeling more understood because of the information I passed on to them, as well as reporting that the proprietary processes I created helped them tremendously. At the same time, I focused on healing my shame in EMDR sessions, as well as in somatic therapy sessions, both very effective in helping me decrease my own shame.

In this book I offer the information I gleaned from my reading and research, along with what I learned from my own therapy experiences and in working with clients. I offer this in hopes that the information and strategies that I share will help you to address the role shame plays in your life and that you don't waste precious time either hiding from your shame or not recognizing it.

USING THE TERM "FORMER VICTIM" INSTEAD OF "SURVIVOR"

As you may have already noticed, I use the word "former victim" instead of the word "survivor" when describing someone who was sexually abused as a child. Many people think of the word victim as a dirty word, synonymous with weakness or being a "loser," but the actual definition of victim is "a person harmed, injured or killed as a result of a crime, accident, or other event or action."

In our victim-hating and victim-blaming culture, the term victim has become more an insult than an accurate identifier indicating that a person has endured a trauma at the hands of another person (or persons). We have bastardized the word to the point that it is used to diminish, discredit, and disparage anyone who has endured the worst of humanity.

I use the word victim deliberately because I want to counter this tendency to make victim a dirty word. And I want to help you come out of denial about the fact that you were, in fact, a victim of child sexual abuse. I don't want to minimize the feelings of shame, pain, fear, and betrayal you have experienced. I don't want to minimize the damage that was done to you. At this point, you are, in fact, a victim and all that implies. In admitting that you were a victim of child sexual abuse, you are taking the first step toward healing. You can't heal what you don't acknowledge.

It has become politically correct to use the word survivor instead of victim when describing someone who was sexually abused and survived the experience. The argument is that this term is more empowering than the word victim, and I completely agree. But I also believe that the word survivor can paint a misleading picture of victimhood and healing. It encourages victims to "get over" it and "move on," instead of addressing and having compassion for their suffering, an important step in healing.

Over the years I have received feedback from many clients who are offended when someone calls them a survivor, especially when they are just beginning to heal from the abuse. They feel that by being called a survivor, their victimization is being glossed over—that the word survivor makes other people more comfortable than admitting that the person was victimized. They have shared with me that they want to be the one to decide what they call themselves and that the word survivor doesn't fit for them until they have experienced some substantial recovery. For the most part, I will use the phrase former victim to describe those adults who were sexually abused as a child. It's not that I don't want you to feel empowered, because the word survivor can certainly empower people. And it's not that I don't give you credit for surviving horrific abuse.

If you have a strong reaction to the word victim, I ask you to question why that is. Is it possible that you are still struggling with the fact that you were, in fact, victimized? Is it because deep down inside you still blame yourself? Is it that you hate the idea that someone could overpower you and make you feel like a victim?

TRIGGER WARNING AND SUGGESTIONS FOR SELF-CARE

This is not your typical "trigger" warning. I'm not going to warn you that certain words, phrases, or examples are likely to trigger you. You need to know going in that this entire book may trigger you. Yes, there absolutely will be words and phrases of a sexual nature that you may find uncomfortable, and many of the examples may remind you of your own trauma. But being reminded of your own abuse is not necessarily a negative thing. This is because many former victims are in so much denial that being reminded of what happened to them can help them get out of denial, a major problem for many former victims. The more you can face the truth about what happened to you, the healthier you can become.

WHAT TO EXPECT AS YOU READ THIS BOOK

You can expect to have any number of reactions as you read this book. First, you may find that you feel tremendous relief as you realize that you are not alone—that other people have experienced similar abuse and feel the same way you feel, and that it is normal to have the feelings and reactions you have had. For example, it can feel tremendously validating to discover that other victims are also afraid to tell anyone about the abuse.

You may also find that some of what you read will upset you. You may read statements about child sexual abuse that cause you to feel a range of emotions, including sadness, anger, fear, shame, or guilt. You may read stories of other victims that may remind you of your own story; this may catapult you back into the past, making you feel as if the abuse is occurring right now. In other words, information and stories may indeed trigger you, causing you to react strongly. For this reason, make sure that you take care of yourself while reading the book.

Here are some suggestions that will help you get the benefits of the book without traumatizing you or feeling like you need to stop reading:

1. Read the book slowly. It is best to read one chapter at a time and then allow yourself to absorb the information.
2. Don't force yourself to read a particular section or chapter. If you become too upset, put the book aside for a while.
3. Choose a time to read the book when you feel somewhat safe and secure, versus reading the book when you are upset, afraid, or insecure.
4. Start a journal so that you can write about your reactions, feelings, and thoughts.
5. Remind yourself that the abuse is no longer occurring and that you are safe now (if, in fact, this is true). For example, you can tell yourself, "I am safe now," or "I am no longer being abused," or "I am safe from my perpetrator; he is no longer around me."
6. Provide yourself with self-care and self-soothing while reading the book and afterwards (holding yourself, stroking your cheek or your arm, cuddling with a stuffed animal, listening to soft music, taking a warm bath, watching a favorite movie).
7. Stay connected to your body and your emotions.

PART I

UNDERSTANDING THE SHAME
ASSOCIATED WITH CHILD SEXUAL ABUSE

ONE

WHY CHILD SEXUAL ABUSE IS SO SHAMING

Shame is the most disturbing experience an individual will ever have about themselves; no other emotion feels more deeply disturbing because in the moment of shame the self feels wounded from within.

—Gershen Kaufman

IF YOU WERE SEXUALLY ABUSED as a child or adolescent, you undoubtedly suffer from shame. Your shame may come from the fact that the things that were done to you or the things you were forced to do made you feel dirty, contaminated, or damaged. Your shame may come from the fact that you blame yourself for the abuse, either because you feel you tantalized your abuser in some way, or because you were someplace you weren't supposed to be. It may come from the fact that you felt some physical pleasure. Or it may come from you continuing to go back to the abuser because you were lonely, or you felt unloved, and the abuser paid attention to you. Finally, you may feel shame because you never told anyone, and your perpetrator went on to abuse other children.

As you will discover while reading this book, for many reasons former victims of child sexual abuse (CSA) are often overwhelmed with shame—in fact, they are haunted by shame. One major reason is the way that victims are perceived and treated in our culture.

- Being perceived as a victim is synonymous with being seen as weak or a loser, and we tend to despise weakness in any form. This is especially true for male victims.
- In our culture (and virtually every culture in the world) we blame victims for their own victimization. An implied (and often verbalized) belief is that no one is a complete victim—that they must have played a role in their own victimization. We don't want to recognize that someone can be a victim through no fault of their own. This is because if we recognize

that someone can be a true victim, this would remind us that we are all vulnerable—that we can also be a victim at any given time—or that, in fact, we have ourselves been a victim in the past.

- We don't want to admit to ourselves that at times we have no choice—times when we have to take the mistreatment that others are putting on us. We prefer to believe that if we are strong enough, we can get out of any situation, and that if we can't, it means we are weak.

In addition to feeling shame because you were a victim of childhood sexual abuse, you may feel shame because you haven't been able to move past it. We not only ignore and blame victims, but we expect them to recover from their adversity in record time. In our culture, we are supposed to "get over" adversity and "move on," and many people don't have much tolerance or patience for those who don't.

The truth is, it takes time to recover from adversity, especially one such as childhood sexual abuse. Most victims did not receive the help they needed when they were children or adolescents. In fact, most victims don't seek help for the abuse until many years after the abuse ended, and many never recognize that they need professional help. Even when victims begin to receive professional help, no "quick fix" exists. It takes many years for most former victims to heal from the multitude of effects of childhood sexual abuse. They aren't malingering, they aren't just trying to get attention, and they shouldn't be shamed because they are still suffering.

THE DAMAGE THAT SHAME CAUSES

Shame, and the consequences of shame, are among the most destructive and debilitating of the many negative effects of sexual abuse. Victims often suffer from the following as the result of the shame they experience after having been sexually abused:

- low self-esteem
- self-loathing
- self-destructiveness (engaging in dangerous activities such as unprotected sex, reckless driving)
- self-harm
- disgust and hatred of the body or certain parts of the body
- neglect of the body
- self-sabotaging behavior

- extreme fear of criticism, judgment
- isolating and withdrawing behavior
- addictions, including alcoholism, drug addiction, food addiction, and sexual addiction
- defenses such as putting up walls, need to be in control
- perfectionism
- reenactments (continuing to be victimized, either emotionally, physically, or sexually); getting involved with people who are replicas of one's abuser
- rage and abusive behavior (emotional, physical, or sexual)
- relationship problems, including negative patterns, difficulties with intimacy
- sexual dysfunction, sexual anorexia, compulsive sexual behavior, and fantasies
- suicide ideation

Take a good look at that list and see if you suffer from any of these problems. If you do, the chances are very high that these feelings and behaviors are the result of the shame you experienced due to the sexual abuse you suffered. For many people, making this connection can feel like a relief because it explains their behavior—behavior they may have been feeling terribly ashamed about. Making this all-important connection between the sexual abuse you suffered and the negative behaviors you practice can be the first step toward healing your shame.

Many of you reading this book are keenly aware of your shame. You suffer from it every day. You are plagued by self-doubt, self-criticism, a fear of negative judgment from others, a sense of being "different" from others. Most significant, you suffer from feelings of worthlessness, self-loathing, self-condemnation and failure, along with a sense of being "less than" others, a feeling of being damaged, unworthy, bad, and unlovable.

For many former victims, the memories of the abuse and the shame they feel as a result of it are never far from their thoughts. This is what my client, Robin, told me about her situation:

> I feel dirty inside—like damaged goods. Like no one could possibly love me if they knew what I have done—who I really am.

And this is what another client, Avery, told me when he first began therapy:

I carry my shame around like an albatross around my neck—proof of my sin. I go to confession every week. Of course, I don't talk about the sexual abuse with the priest—I wouldn't want him to know just how much of a sinner I am. But nothing helps—no amount of penitence or absolution can take away the horrible feeling of shame I carry.

Still another client, India, described her experience with shame like this:

I take my shame with me everywhere I go. It lies dormant, just waiting to be triggered by a look, by a comment someone makes. I might as well have a scarlet A on my forehead. I assume everyone can see who I am, what I've done.

MAKING THE CONNECTION

Although some former victims of CSA are keenly aware of the reasons they feel shame, others suffer from shame without making the connection between the sexual abuse they endured and the shame they feel. If you are one of these people, you likely have a powerful inner critic that monitors and chastises you relentlessly. You may feel uncomfortable around other people, constantly fearing that they are judging you. You may be critical of the way you look, and you may suffer from body image issues. You may constantly compare yourself with others and end up feeling inadequate or like a failure.

Many suffer from shame without realizing it—without calling it shame. For example, my client Rene described a problem she was having with her husband:

I love my husband very much, but I constantly push him away. We'll have a good night together, I'll allow myself to get close to him and even have sex, but the next day I start an argument with him. I accuse him of not loving me, or being unfaithful to me, when I really don't believe either of those things. I don't know why I can't allow him to get close to me.

Rene was describing self-sabotage—a behavior based on the inability to take in anything good that comes your way—whether it is love, success, even beauty. When you are filled with shame, you don't believe you deserve good things. No matter how much someone tells you he or she loves you, you can never really believe it. No matter how successful you are in your career, you have an overwhelming feeling that you don't deserve it and fear that it will all be taken away from you at any time, and so you may sabotage it in some way (e.g., you say something cruel to someone you care about, you start showing up late for work).

Closely connected to self-sabotage is the "imposter syndrome." No matter how many accolades or awards you receive, you continue to believe you are inadequate and firmly believe that you are just fooling everyone. This is what my client Tom recently shared with me:

> I always feel like I'm deficient in some way. I act like I'm confident, but inside I feel like I'm going to be exposed for being the imposter that I am.

DEFINING SHAME

Shame is at the core of the intense emotional wounding victims of childhood sexual abuse (CSA) experience. But what is shame exactly? Shame is a painful self-conscious emotion typically associated with a negative evaluation of self; a desire to withdraw or isolate oneself, and feelings of distress, exposure, powerlessness, and worthlessness.

This is how various experts describe shame: Shame is characterized by feelings of *self-condemnation* and the *desire to hide* the damaged self from others (Lewis, 1992; Tangney, 1995). It is conceptualized by clinicians as an intense and painful emotional experience resulting from an evaluation of the self as *defective or fundamentally flawed* (De Young, 2015; Lewis, 1992). In its extreme shame, as is experienced in cases of CSA, the victim can develop an *internalized idea of self as defective, defiled, and unlovable and unworthy.*

The Fear of Exposure

The word shame originates from the Teutonic root word "skem," which means "to cover oneself." This makes sense, because a significant aspect of shame is *an intense fear of exposure*—of having one's badness or inadequacy seen by others. This fear of exposure prevents the person from feeling "a part" of life and creates a deep sense of *loneliness* and *isolation*. Many former victims live in fear of "being found out"—of those around them finding out about the sexual abuse. This is what my client Gary shared with me:

> I'm always afraid someone's going to figure it out and then turn on me. I act like I'm comfortable with my sexuality when I'm really not. I make sure to laugh at sexual jokes like everyone else, but I'm really uncomfortable with them. I'm even uncomfortable in the locker room at my gym, because I don't like people looking at my naked body.

The secretive nature of child sexual abuse and the likelihood that you probably kept the abuse a secret only adds to your shame. This is how my client
Markus describes it:

> I've never told anyone—not even my wife—that I was sexually abused by my
> grandfather when I was kid. I know that if people around me knew about it,
> they would see me for what I am—a damaged and sick human being. I've
> thought about telling my wife many times, especially because she accuses me
> of not opening up with her, but I'm afraid that if I told her, she'll get turned
> off to me or even repulsed.

A Cluster of Feelings, Experiences, and Beliefs

As you can see, shame is not one feeling or experience, but a cluster of feelings,
experiences, and beliefs. These include:

The feeling of being humiliated. We tend to feel humiliated whenever we
become conscious that we are involved with wrong or foolish behavior. Sexual
abuse almost always has an element of humiliation to it, because it is a violation
of very private parts of the body. There is a "knowing" on the child's part that
incest and/or sex between a child and an adult is taboo. (This is true in nearly
every culture in the world with the exception of a few obscure tribes in Africa
where sex with an adult is considered a rite of passage.)

The feeling of impotence and helplessness. When a child comes to know that
he can't do anything to stop the abuse, he feels powerless, helpless, impotent.
This can also lead to always feeling unsafe, even long after the abuse has stopped.

The feeling of being exposed. When a child is sexually abused, she feels ex-
posed both to herself and to anyone else present, and she wants to disappear.
As psychotherapist and author Gershen Kaufman, PhD, stated in *Shame: The
Power of Caring*:

> It is this sudden, unexpected feeling of exposure and accompanying self-
> consciousness that characterize the essential nature of the affect of shame.
> Contained in the experience of shame is the piercing awareness of ourselves as
> fundamentally deficient in some vital way as a human being. (1992, 9)

A sense of self-consciousness, inadequacy, and a deepening self-doubt. This follows quickly as a by-product of shame, causing the person to go deeper into
despair.

The feeling of being defective and "less than." Most victims of sexual abuse report feeling defective, damaged, or corrupted following the experience of being
abused.

The feeling of being alienated and isolated. Shame can cause us to feel isolated—set apart from the crowd. In fact, in primitive cultures people were "banished" from the tribe when they broke society's rules. Being shamed feels like being banished—unworthy to be around others. What follows the trauma of sexual abuse is the feeling of suddenly being different, less than, damaged, cast out. And although victims may long to talk to someone about their inner pain, they feel immobilized, trapped, and alone in their shame.

Self-blame. Victims almost always blame themselves for being abused, and this adds to their shame. Shame typically develops in childhood when the brain doesn't yet have the ability to comprehend the full picture or understand the reasoning behind someone else's words or actions. This is because the area of the brain known as the frontal lobe is still developing. This part of the brain helps us analyze data, solve complex problems, and make deliberate choices. It is key to us assessing situations, events, or behaviors that are initially confusing or even hurtful.

For children and teens, the ability to analyze and comprehend complicated situations remains especially challenging, as their frontal lobe is still developing and their limbic system (the automatic part of the brain that seeks to avoid what feels bad and pursue what feels good) is in the driver's seat. When children or teens are sexually abused, they don't yet have the ability to understand why something so painful would happen to them. For example, they aren't able to yet comprehend that the person who molested them had emotional or behavior issues or was re-enacting the same trauma that was done to them. Whatever the contributing factors, the person who abused them was entirely in the wrong and violated the boundaries of the child. However, given that the analytical, problem-solving area of the brain is still developing, children may not be able to recognize they carry no responsibility for the abuse. As children try to fill in the gaps on their own to understand why someone would abuse them, they may come up with reasons such as, "I did something wrong," or "I asked for this." And while none of these thoughts reflect reality, the accompanying shame can be powerful enough to convince former victims that they are true.

Rage. Rage almost always follows having been shamed—in fact, it is one of the most spontaneous, naturally occurring reactions to being shamed. Its presence serves a much-needed, self-protective function both by insulating the self against further exposure and by actively keeping others away.

Exercise: Your Feeling Experience of Shame

1. Although you may have experienced all the feelings and experiences listed above, you may resonate with some more than others. Think

about the abuse that you suffered and the various feelings that accompanied it. Ask yourself which items stand out to you the most for each of your abuse experiences.

2. If you feel like it, write about how the sexual abuse elicited feelings of humiliation, helplessness, alienation, and so forth.

HOW SHAME FROM CHILD SEXUAL ABUSE IS DIFFERENT THAN TYPICAL SHAME

Clinical literature makes a distinction between the experience of mild shame that everyone experiences from time to time in everyday human relationships and the shame that can result from disruptions and traumatic severance of relational bonds caused by violation, extreme degradation, betrayal, and defilement, all aspects of CSA. Variously named as extreme, catastrophic, chronic, traumatic, pathological, toxic, and abuse-related, the consensus among clinicians from diverse frameworks is that such shame can have a profound impact on a child's development and into later life.

With extreme shame, such as many victims of CSA have experienced, the victim can develop an internalized idea of self as defective, defiled, and fundamentally unworthy. The problem is not just the shaming experience per se but rather, when internalized, shame becomes part of the developing concept of self. Victims come to hide what they judge as the defective self, developing a fear of exposure and a fear of the cycle of self-disgust experienced when in a state of shame.

WHY DOES SEXUAL ABUSE CREATE SUCH SHAME IN THE VICTIM?

CSA creates intense shame in victims for many of the following reasons:

A reaction to being invaded. Shame is a natural reaction to being violated or abused. In fact, abuse, by its very nature, is humiliating and dehumanizing. This is especially true with sexual violations. The most private and vulnerable parts of the child's body are invaded, and this makes the child feel defiled.

A need for a sense of control. As human beings, we want to believe that we have control over what happens to us. When that personal power is challenged by a victimization of any kind, we feel humiliated and experience the indignity of being helpless and at the mercy of another person. We believe that we "should have" been able to defend ourselves. This is especially true for males.

And because we weren't able to do so, we feel helpless and powerless. This powerlessness causes us to feel humiliated—which leads to shame.

Self-blame. In addition to having an underdeveloped frontal lobe, as discussed above, children tend to blame themselves when something goes wrong in the family. This is partly due to the fact that children are very egocentric—meaning that they perceive everything being about them. Examples of this kind of thinking include, "If mom is upset it must be because I did something wrong," and "If my parents get a divorce, it is my fault." Also, one of the main reasons so many former abuse victims blame themselves is that the perpetrator blamed them. My client Crystal explained it this way:

> My father told me it was my fault, and I believed him. He told me I was too sexy, even as a little girl. He said I provoked him by wearing short dresses and shorts and that I deliberately showed him my panties. He said he couldn't help but become aroused.

Society's need to blame the victim. This tendency to blame oneself is reinforced by our culture's tendency to *blame the victim*, as we discussed earlier.

The shame caused by keeping a secret. Victims are often told that what is happening is a secret, and secrets induce shame. In addition, keeping a secret tends to isolate the person from others, preventing any possibility of them getting the support or the help they need.

The taboo against incest and sex with children. Victims have an internal "knowing" that what is happening is wrong based on the almost universal awareness of the taboo against incest and adult/child sex. This taboo was originally based on concerns about in-breeding in the case of incest, but today is mainly focused on the understanding that sex between children and adults is harmful to the child.

IDENTIFYING YOUR SHAME

It can be difficult, even with the descriptions of shame I've written about above, to figure out whether you are suffering from shame and if so, in what ways. The following section will help you to identify and connect with your shame in various ways: by noticing how shame feels in your body, by listening to the shaming words that you tell yourself, and by the beliefs about yourself that originate with shame.

How does shame feel? Shame can be a difficult emotion to identify because it manifests in different ways for different people. Often, we do not know we are experiencing shame until we notice physical indications of it in our body. Some people feel a hot burning sensation in the pit of their stomach, others feel a tight grip around their chest, and many feel an intense urge to disappear or hide. Shame is also experienced as a sinking or collapsing feeling. Other physical reactions can include your face flushing, a need to divert your eyes, and hunching your shoulders as if to protect your chest.

Exercise: How Your Body Reacts

Do you notice how your body reacts when you are feeling shame? Write about how you know when you are feeling shame. Here are some descriptions clients have shared with me:

- "I get this sinking feeling, like someone has pushed a button and sent me down to hell where I belong."
- "I just wish I could hide, so I end up getting away from the situation as fast as I can."
- "I feel like everyone is looking at me and laughing at me. My face turns red, and I start sweating, and this makes it even worse."
- "I feel like I become really small. I hunch my shoulders forward trying to make myself even smaller."

Here is a list of common reactions people have when they are feeling shame. Put a check mark next to the ones with which you identify:

- a need to avoid eye contact
- an intense urge to hide washes over you
- a strong desire to disappear
- a desire or tendency to cover your face
- putting your head down
- hiding your body with a pillow or coat
- your face flushing
- sweating or shaking
- shortness of breath
- a tight grip around your chest
- a hot burning sensation in the pit of your stomach
- nauseous/upset stomach
- your body collapsing

The more you become aware of how shame-based thoughts affect your body, the easier it will become to identify when physical sensations, such as the pain in your stomach or the tightness in your chest, indicate what you are experiencing internally.

THE VOICE OF SHAME

Shame can lead to thoughts that perpetuate a negative belief about ourselves. These thoughts are often referred to as "our shame voice." Some examples of what our shame voice might say include:

- "There's something wrong with me."
- "I'm not enough."
- "I don't matter."
- "I can't do anything right."
- "I'm useless."

These kinds of negative thoughts are common for former victims of child sexual abuse and may have been part of your self-talk for many years. They can commonly reoccur and can be easily triggered by everyday scenarios.

Exercise: Your Shame Voice

- Think about the most common negative things you say to yourself on a regular basis.
- Make a list of these statements and keep them close to you as a reference.

NOT JUST A FEELING—A BELIEF SYSTEM

Shame is not just a feeling the way anger, sadness, fear, joy, or guilt are feelings. Shame is the *experience* and the *belief* that one is fundamentally bad, defective, or unacceptable. Shame is caused by an intensely negative self-evaluation of who we are as a human being. Although we may experience shame regarding specific aspects of ourselves—such as our body characteristics, feelings, intelligence, skills, or behavior—this specific focus on one aspect of ourselves may be a smokescreen for a more general (and unconscious) perception of ourselves as being weak, flawed, or even defective. The overwhelming discomfort associated with shame makes it an intense threat to our sense of self and overall well-being.

Shame is the fuel for that harsh self-critical inner voice that tells you that you are "less than" when you compare yourself to others, which you probably do often. Unfortunately, the more you compare yourself with others, the more shame you feel, because in your eyes you never measure up. You are never as smart, as attractive, or accomplished as others.

Knowing what your experience with shame is and how it may be affecting you can help you better understand what's going on internally, name it, and challenge it.

THE DIFFERENCE BETWEEN GUILT AND SHAME

It is important to understand the difference between shame and guilt. Shame and guilt can feel very similar—with both experiences we feel bad about ourselves. Some have explained the difference between shame and guilt as follows: When we feel guilt, we feel bad about *something we did or neglected to do.* When we feel shame, we feel badly about *who we are.* Put another way: guilty people fear punishment, shamed people fear abandonment. When we feel guilty, we need to learn that it's OK to make mistakes. When we feel shame, we need to learn that it's OK to be who we are.

Another distinction between guilt and shame is that shame comes from public exposure of one's own vulnerability, whereas guilt is private, coming from a sense of failing to measure up to our own internal standards. When others discover or know we were once helpless, we tend to feel ashamed. We also feel exposed. But if we feel we caused our own problems, we cease to feel as vulnerable or exposed. This can explain why victims of abuse often blame themselves for the abuse. *It is easier—less painful—to feel guilt than to feel the shame of helplessness.*

Still another difference between guilt and shame is that we don't tend to feel bad about feeling guilty—in fact it's often viewed as a positive thing, especially in terms of how others perceive you. If you feel guilty about what you've done, others are more likely to forgive you. But shame is more taboo—so much so that we feel shame about feeling shame. This is partly due to the strong correlation between feeling shame and feeling inferior. We believe we should conceal feelings of shame, especially in a culture that so values achievement and success.

SHAME CREATES SHAMEFUL BEHAVIOR

In addition to the shame you feel because of the sexual abuse, many of you likely suffer from shame because of troubling behaviors you practice or because of the circumstances you find yourself in. Some of you have made the connection between your destructive behaviors and the sexual abuse, whereas others don't realize they are self-medicating or using these behaviors as coping mechanisms due to the trauma they experienced. Former victims of childhood sexual abuse often engage in behaviors such as alcohol or drug abuse, compulsive eating, shoplifting, compulsive gambling, promiscuity, and sexual addiction, and they often feel horribly ashamed because of it. As my client Rodney explained:

> I love my wife and kids so much, but I'm constantly putting my family at risk because of my sexual behavior. I have this compulsion to frequent prostitutes and to engage in kinky sex. I feel deeply ashamed every time I do it, but I can't seem to stop myself.

Another consequence of the shame surrounding child sexual abuse is that former victims often continue to be victimized in some way, such as getting involved with abusive partners, and yet many are unaware of the connection between this and their history of sexual abuse. And many women and men who are being physically or emotionally abused feel terribly ashamed because of the situation they find themselves in. They don't understand why they chose an abusive partner, and they feel horrible shame because they are unable to leave the abusive relationship.

Others have repeated the pattern of victimization by becoming the abuser in their relationships. Case in point, my client Alex:

> My wife recently left me. She said I've been emotionally abusing her for ten years. I realized I was critical of her, and sometimes I lost my temper and yelled at her, but I didn't think that would be considered 'abuse.' I agreed to go to therapy in order to get my wife back, and I'm coming to realize I did abuse her. I'm also discovering why I'm so angry and critical. I realize I'm carrying a lot of shame from my childhood—shame about things that happened to me that I've locked away for years.

Still others repeat the pattern of abuse by becoming abusive or neglectful of their children. This is how my client Lea explained it:

> I'm very critical of my children. I'm always worried about what other people think of them—and by extension—what they think of me as a parent. I'm coming to realize that I'm dumping some of my shame on them—shame that I need to begin to deal with concerning the sexual abuse I experienced. Because I feel so bad about myself, I end up seeing my children as bad.

SHAME TRIGGERS MORE SHAME

Kaufman, one of the first experts to write about shame, explains the phenomena of shame creating more shame this way:

> The main reason that shame begets shame is the phenomena of shame feelings and thoughts endlessly triggering each other. The precipitating event is relived internally over and over, causing the sense of shame to deepen, to absorb other neutral experiences that happened before as well as those that come later. (Kaufman, 573)

In other words, the shame you experienced surrounding the sexual abuse is constantly triggered by people, events, sights, sounds, and smells in your environment. For example, you stand next to a man in the elevator who is wearing the same aftershave as your abuser. Suddenly you are catapulted back to the past when you smelled this same aftershave as you were being abused. Not only are you triggered the way any PTSD victim can suddenly be when reminded of the trauma he or she went through, but you are showered with feelings of shame. In this way, shame can become paralyzing.

HIDDEN SHAME

To make matters worse, we tend to feel shame about feeling shame. This tendency only exacerbates it. It makes sense, therefore, that we may do our best to minimize, deny, or suppress shame. We do this by being compulsively perfectionistic, intensely fearful of being wrong, or compulsively driven to succeed or obtain power. Or, we may become consumed by a powerful need to gain the positive admiration of others—all in an effort to provide a counter-narrative to feeling shame.

Hidden shame—the kind of shame that masquerades as something else entirely—is very common among former victims of CSA. In fact, some of you reading this book may not be aware of how much you have been suffering from shame. This is because shame can be likened to a shapeshifter—it takes on various disguises to hide its true identity. Often, it disguises itself as arrogance or a feeling of super self-confidence. It is common for shame to be hidden behind a mask of bravado—fooling everyone around you, even fooling yourself. In essence you are "pretending" to feel good about yourself in order to make sure no one discovers your shame.

Those who are hiding their shame in this way may seem to have it all—success, charm, accolades from others. But if you look just under the surface, you'll see cracks in their armor. They can't take criticism; they dismiss any attempt on your part to correct them or point out the error of their ways. If you dare to correct them, they will quickly cut you down to size, sending a clear message that you better not try it again. This is because while they seem self-confident, they are so full of shame that they have built a wall to protect themselves from any further shame.

Having a wall up not only protects us from being further shamed, but it prevents us from truly connecting with others or having empathy for others. This is what my client Jan told me about her inability to connect with her children and husband:

> I'm very critical of my husband and children even though I don't mean to be. I seem to be more concerned with what other people think of them—and me by extension—than I care about their needs and feelings.

WHAT IF I DON'T FEEL ANY SHAME?

Some people ask, "Is it possible that I don't feel any shame even though I was sexually abused?" It is highly unlikely that you escaped being sexually abused without experiencing shame. In fact, it is far more likely that you may have numbed yourself to your shame. It is not uncommon for former victims to experience so much shame that they simply can't tolerate it. They need to shut it down, or dissociate themselves from it, just like victims often dissociate from their body when they are being abused. Although some people hide behind a defensive wall of bravado or arrogance to keep from taking in shame, you may have built up an internal wall to keep yourself from acknowledging the shame you already feel. In other words, shame may be so painful to you that you deny its existence. Signs that you may feel shame without realizing it include:

Perfectionism. As my client Juanita explained it:

> I don't allow myself to make excuses. I'm a perfectionist. If I make a mistake, I can berate myself for hours. So, I make sure I don't make any.

People-pleasing and "being good." Similar to perfectionism, focusing on always doing the right thing or never causing a problem can be an attempt to avoid ever being shamed.

Busyness. Always staying busy—never stopping to connect with your feelings or staying busy so you can avoid your feelings.

Blaming and gossiping. Staying focused on what other people are doing wrong so you can avoid any self-evaluation.

The following are still other signals of hidden shame:

- unwillingness to expose our vulnerabilities to others
- a tendency to over-apologize to others for minor transgressions
- an inability to accept help or compliments
- patterns of procrastination and underachievement
- slumped posture and avoidance of eye contact with others
- unexplained bouts of rage and blaming others
- an exaggerated split between one's public and private selves
- having an excuse for everything and denying personal responsibility
- a facility to convince others that everything is their fault and what is obvious is untrue (gaslighting)
- intolerance of being alone with oneself for extended periods of time
- sensations of heaviness and dread in our bodies
- unwillingness to forgive or a tendency to hold long-term grudges toward others

SHAME AND SEXUAL PROBLEMS

Not surprisingly, shame from childhood sexual abuse often shows up in the form of sexual problems. Here are some client examples:

- "I just don't have any sexual desire. I force myself to have sex with my husband, because I know it makes him feel unloved if we don't connect in that way, but I'm embarrassed to say that I seldom feel anything, and I'm often spaced out while it is happening."
- "I can't have orgasms. No matter what I try or who I am with, it just never happens for me. I come close, but then I shut down."
- "Often, when I'm having sex with my husband, I see my perpetrator's face. It really freaks me out. It's like I'm being sexually assaulted all over again."
- "I hate my vagina. I think it is ugly and dirty. I don't ever want to touch it or have anyone else touch it. This obviously interferes with my sex life, but touching my vagina is so repulsive to me that I instantly get turned off if someone tries."
- "I have these troubling fantasies of having sex with my father all the time. I'm so ashamed. I think I must be really, really sick."

- "I'm addicted to sex—any kind of sex. I constantly pressure my wife for sex, but even when she has sex with me, I crave it again a few hours later. I constantly masturbate to pornography, and I use phone sex and prostitutes every chance I get. It's like I'm a starving child constantly on the lookout for food."
- "Lots of men would love to last as long as I do sexually. But the truth is, I have a really difficult time ejaculating, and often it never happens."
- "When I'm around little girls who are around the age I was when I was molested, I suddenly get afraid I'll molest them. So, I get away from them as soon as I can."
- "I'm a whore. I have absolutely no self-respect. If a man wants me or I become attracted to a man, I have sex with him. It doesn't matter who the man is, it doesn't matter where I am. It doesn't even matter that I am married, or I might get caught. Nothing matters but the fact that I want sex, and I want it now."
- "I can't tolerate someone going down on me, because that's what my stepfather did, and I black out when I try."

If you have similar concerns, the good news is that you are not alone. Most former victims of child sexual abuse suffer from some kind of sexual concern or some form of sexual dysfunction. The other good news is that there is help and healing for these sexual concerns, many of which you will find in this book.

This was probably a difficult chapter to read and to absorb all the information. It was also probably difficult to stay in the present and in your body. If you notice that you feel spacey, overwhelmed, or numb, you may be reacting to some of the information you have read. Former victims of sexual abuse are often in the unconscious habit of dissociating whenever they feel threatened, triggered, or overwhelmed. For this reason, the following exercise can help you come back to the present and to your body.

BASIC GROUNDING TECHNIQUE

The following technique will help you remain grounded and in the present while reading this book. I recommend you use this "grounding" technique when you find yourself triggered by a past memory or when you find yourself "leaving your body" or *dissociating*, which is common for trauma victims (dissociating is a common defense mechanism those who are traumatized employ to numb themselves or otherwise separate themselves from the trauma).

1. Find a quiet place where you will not be disturbed or distracted.
2. Sit up in a chair or on the couch. Put your feet flat on the ground. If you are wearing shoes with heels, take off your shoes so that you can have your feet flat on the ground.
3. With your eyes open, take a few deep breaths. Turn your attention once again to feeling the ground under your feet. Continue your breathing and feeling your feet flat on the ground throughout the exercise.
4. Now, as you continue breathing, clear your eyes and take a look around the room. As you slowly scan the room, notice the colors, shapes, and textures of the objects in the room. If you'd like, scan the room moving your neck so you can see a wider view.
5. Bring your focus back to feeling the ground under your feet as you continue to breathe and to notice the different colors, textures, and shape of the objects in the room. This grounding exercise will serve several purposes:

   • It will bring your awareness back to your body, which in turn can stop you from being triggered or from dissociating.
   • It will bring you back to the present, to the here and now, again a good thing if you have been triggered and have been catapulted back into the past by a memory or a trigger.

   Deliberately focusing your attention outside yourself by being visually involved in the world breaks the shame spiral and allows those feelings and thoughts to subside.

No matter what your situation, whether you are aware of the reason for your negative self-image or self-destructive behavior, or you have yet to make the connection with the sexual abuse you suffered, it is important to know that you have hope. You don't need to continue to be plagued by the shame of child sexual abuse. This book will help you both to identify the shame you are suffering and help you to heal it.

You will never know what your life would have been like if you hadn't been sexually abused. The sad truth is that no matter how much healing you experience, you can't erase the trauma. It happened. What you can do is reduce or even eliminate the shame attached to the abuse. By focusing on the information and exercises this book offers, you have the power to do the following concerning your shame:

- You can stop blaming yourself for the abuse.
- You can stop feeling unworthy, "less than," and unlovable.
- You can give back the shame to its rightful owner—the abuser.
- You can stop feeling like you are tainted or damaged goods, that you are dirty or rotten inside.
- You can start accepting and even loving your body instead of hating it or being ashamed of it.
- You can stop blaming your body for "betraying you" by feeling some pleasure amid the humiliation and pain.
- You can stop blaming yourself for "going back," returning to the abuser after the first episode.

TWO

THE IMMEDIATE AND LONG-TERM EFFECTS OF SHAME

We can endure all kinds of pain. It's shame that eats man whole.

—Leigh Bardugo, *Crooked Kingdom*

THE EXTREME FORM OF SHAME that CSA causes can have multiple and far-reaching effects. Some of these effects are apparent and can emerge at the time of the abuse. Other effects are more gradual and less apparent but just as debilitating. It is important to learn about these effects for several reasons. First of all, if you come to recognize that your behavior or symptoms likely indicate that you were sexually abused, you will be less likely to remain in denial about the abuse or to minimize the damage the abuse has had on you. Second, if you become aware that the way you act is a direct result of the trauma you experienced, as well as the consequent shame, you will be more likely to understand and forgive yourself for inappropriate and unhealthy behaviors and less likely to shame yourself even more. Third, and perhaps most important, realizing how shame has affected you will motivate you to heal your shame instead of denying it, minimizing it, or turning your shame into abusiveness toward others.

In this chapter I will outline both the immediate, short-term consequences of the shame associated with CSA and the long-term effects.

THE IMMEDIATE CONSEQUENCES

Victims of CSA can face immediate psychological consequences such as shock, fear, anxiety, guilt, symptoms of post-traumatic stress disorder, denial, confusion, withdrawal, isolation, and grief. But the most common reaction and consequence of the assault is shame. The extreme shame of childhood sexual abuse can be experienced immediately: while the child is being abused, right after the abuse, or weeks and months after the abuse. Shame connects to the experience of CSA in several ways, including:

- Messages of shame related to the abuse are communicated to the child at the time of the abuse and afterward. These messages can become part of the child's self-image (Finkelhor & Browne, 1985).
- CSA may involve the experience of captivity and always involves power and control over the victim's body, either directly through sexual acts or indirectly through forced viewing of sexualized imagery such as pornography or witnessing sexual acts.
- CSA frequently includes social isolation and at times degradation.
- When extreme shame occurs in attachment relationships (i.e., incest) development of self-comfort strategies and emotion regulation is disrupted (Herman, 2011).

Here are examples of what former victims have shared regarding the shame they felt during and right after the abuse:

- "My father told me I'd asked for it because of the way I dressed. He told me that if I was going to dress like a whore, I deserved everything I got."
- "My molester told me it was a secret and that I couldn't tell anyone. But he didn't have to tell me that, because I already knew it. I already knew I wasn't going to tell anyone, because it was wrong, and people would stop liking me if they found out."
- "From the moment he first touched my penis, I knew it was wrong. I knew I should stop him. But I didn't know how. And this made me feel so weak and ashamed."
- "My abuser forced me, and this made me feel helpless. I was supposed to be big and strong and defend myself, but I couldn't. I was too weak, and that made me feel so much shame."
- "I didn't want him to be touching me in that way. It felt too private. But I wanted his attention, and I was afraid he would stop spending time with me if he didn't get his way. I sold myself out, and for that I felt horrible shame."
- "To be touched there—in my most private parts—felt degrading, humiliating. No one was supposed to touch me there."

Although many victims of CSA feel shame as the trauma is occurring, once each incident of abuse is over, victims can feel even more shame—an avalanche of shame. Once it sinks in that they have been physically violated or have been made to do things to the abuser they didn't want to do, victims are usually overwhelmed with shame.

My former client Greta described to me how the shame she felt due to the abuse affected her:

> I was a good kid before it happened. I felt friendly toward people, and they seemed to like me. I was innocent and sweet. But after the abuse started, I changed completely. I didn't feel friendly, and I sure didn't feel innocent. I felt like a bad person that no one should like. You can even see the change in me from photographs taken at the time. "Before" and "After." Before the abuse I was smiling, and you could still see the sweetness. After the abuse I was scowling, and there was a darkness to me.

Below are some of the immediate ways shame manifested in some of my other clients, along with the words they used to describe the feeling:

Feeling exposed. "I felt so ashamed because I thought everyone could tell from looking at me what I had done."

Feeling ugly, tainted, disgusting. "What happened to me made me feel so disgusting and creepy."

Feeling that no one would ever like or love them again. "I was sure no one would ever want to be my friend if they knew what I had done."

Feeling like they have "sinned"—that they are evil. "I was sure God was angry with me. I was even worried that he didn't love me anymore."

Feeling afraid others will find out what happened and blame them. "I knew it was my own fault. And I knew if my parents ever found out, they would blame me."

Becoming more secretive and withdrawn from others. "I just wanted to go away by myself and hide."

Becoming more distant from their parents. "From that time on, I was never close to my mother again."

Feeling self-hatred and self-loathing. "I absolutely hated myself for what I did."

Becoming self-abusive. "I began to hate myself so much that I started punishing myself. I put lighted cigarettes on my arms and legs."

Becoming reckless and self-destructive. "I didn't care what happened to me after that. I started getting into cars with strange boys and letting them do whatever they wanted to me. It's a miracle I wasn't raped or killed."

Growing to hate their body. "I absolutely hated my vagina. I feel like it was a traitor. I didn't want that man to touch me, and I didn't want to feel any pleasure when he did, but my vagina betrayed me."

Experiencing tremendous rage. "After the abuse I took all my anger out on my younger sister and brother. I wanted to hurt them the way I was being hurt."

Becoming passive, victim-like. "Before the abuse I was pretty confident. I spoke up when I needed to. I didn't let anyone boss me around. But afterward it was like I'd had the air sucked out of me. I was too afraid to speak up—too afraid of what would happen to me if I tried to defend myself."

When did you first experience shame as a result of the sexual abuse you experienced? Do you remember feeling shame while the abuse was happening or immediately afterward? Did you feel shame the first time you encountered someone you cared about—like your mother or father? Or whenever you were around your peers? Did you feel shame whenever you were naked or when taking a bath or shower? Were you overwhelmed with shame when you got into bed that first night?

Exercise: Your First Memories

Write about your first memories of feeling shame during or right after you were sexually abused. Try to remember how you felt before the abuse versus how you felt afterwards. Don't worry if you can't remember feeling shame; not everyone felt it overtly, but if you did, describe how you felt—your emotions and your feelings in your body.

THE LONG-TERM EFFECTS OF SHAME

The shame that CSA causes creates long-term damage in a multitude of ways. I have divided these long-term effects into separate categories: (1) self-esteem and self-image issues; (2) body-image issues; (3) emotional health; (4) physical health; (5) self-blame and self-criticism; (6) self-sabotage; (7) self-destructive behavior; (8) addictions; (9) rage and antisocial behavior; (10) victim mentality; (11) abusive behavior; (12) isolating behaviors; (13) relationship issues, including inability to trust and to be intimate; (14) sexual concerns and problems, including unhealthy sexual fantasies and obsessions; (15) reenacting the abuse. Let's take a closer look at each of these.

Self-esteem and self-image. Shame has a strong influence on one's sense of self. People who were sexually abused often see themselves as fundamentally bad even though they were not responsible for what happened. The shame from CSA causes tremendous ongoing damage to a victim's self-esteem and self-image. Victims can feel "marked" because they imagine that everyone knows what they have done. The sexual abuse they suffered causes them to feel broken, unworthy, dirty, ugly, and sinful, and these feelings cause them to believe that they are damaged goods and that no one will ever love them. In time, the shame former victims feel slowly whittles away at their self-esteem, often causing them to hate themselves. Sadly, the self-esteem issues that shame brings on can create a cycle: a person's feelings of inferiority can lead to negative experiences that reinforce those feelings.

Body image and body hatred. Many former victims are extremely uncomfortable exposing their body to others. They can especially be fearful of attracting attention or being seen as a sexual object. Because of their fear, they frequently hide their body by wearing clothes that are too large. Former victims also tend to have body image issues. Many suffer from anorexia or body dysmorphia (a disorder in which the person can't stop thinking about one or more perceived defects or flaws in their appearance—a flaw that appears minor or can't be seen by others). Some feel disgust with their body, and others hate their body because they feel that it betrayed them when it responded by feeling pleasure. They will often neglect their body by not keeping it clean, not giving it adequate nutrition, not wearing a coat even when it is freezing outside, and so forth.

And they often punish their body by smoking, overeating, eating unhealthy food, abusing alcohol and drugs. They can become self-destructive by cutting or burning themselves, driving recklessly, putting themselves in dangerous situations. They tend to especially hate their genitals or whatever parts of their body were involved in the abuse. They view their body and their genitals as dirty, ugly, repulsive, and shameful. Some former victims want nothing to do with their sexual organs to the point that they refuse to wash them, and others mutilate their genitals by cutting, burning, piercings, putting foreign objects into orifices to the point of pain or damage.

Emotional health. CSA has often been associated with a higher risk of mental health problems in adulthood. A study of sexually abused children followed over forty years found that women who were sexually abused in childhood were more than seven times more likely to have received a diagnosis of post-traumatic stress disorder, nearly nine times more likely to have a substance abuse problem; and nearly 8.5 times more likely to have received a diagnosis of borderline personality disorder than non-abused women. Survivors of sexual abuse often struggle with their emotional health, and shame can make that struggle more difficult. Shame contributes to the development of many post-traumatic stress symptoms. Specifically, shame can lead to anxiety, depression, suicide ideation, and dissociation. It may also lead to survivors wanting to disconnect from their emotions altogether. Those who conceal information due to shame can experience worse psychological symptoms than the symptoms that result from the abuse itself.

Physical health. Shame can manifest itself through psychosomatic symptoms, which are the "expression of emotional pain through bodily symptoms." Researchers have found that CSA is strongly associated with physical symptoms that don't have a clear medical explanation, and shame plays a role in many of these symptoms (e.g., chronic pelvic pain, irritable bowel syndrome, and fibromyalgia in the neck, shoulders, and back). Shame has also been associated with a weakened immune system. Perhaps most significantly, female victims tend to suffer from frequent gynecologic problems, including chronic pelvic pain, dyspareunia, vaginismus, nonspecific vaginitis. Former victims are less likely to have regular Pap exams and may seek little or no prenatal care.

Self-blame and self-criticism. Many former victims become extremely self-critical, chastising themselves constantly for their mistakes and imperfections, and many blame themselves when anything goes wrong.

Self-sabotage. Many former victims feel so bad about themselves and carry so much shame that they don't believe they deserve to be happy. This can cause them to sabotage their relationships, their careers, and their success.

Self-destructiveness. Many former victims have so much shame and hatred toward themselves that they become self-destructive. This includes thoughts of self-harm or actual self-harm or self-mutilation such as cutting, burning, stabbing. It also includes thoughts of suicide or actual suicide attempts. In a general sense, victims are often self-destructive in other ways as well, such as engaging in dangerous activities such as unprotected sex, reckless driving, driving while intoxicated or under the influence of drugs, extreme sports, associating with dangerous people, engaging in criminal behavior.

Addictions. It is common for former victims to self-medicate with alcohol or drugs. Others develop addictions such as compulsive shopping, compulsive gambling, or other compulsive behaviors as a way to distract themselves from their shame and the memories of the abuse. Finally, sexual addiction is very common among former victims. This can include compulsive masturbation and porn addiction as a way to deal with sexual anxiety, and frequenting prostitutes and other illicit sexual activities as a way to reenact the sexual abuse they experienced. (There are two chapters dedicated to reenactments and sexual acting out later in the book.)

Rage and antisocial behavior. Shame and rage are inextricably connected. You can't be violated without feeling both rage and shame—rage at being violated, shame for being humiliated or for not being able to fight off your attacker. Rage is often manifested in bitterness and hostility toward others if projected outward—being easily angered, yelling, frequent fighting (both physical and verbal), abuse of children or partners, road rage. If rage is held in and directed at oneself, it can lead to depression, self-hatred, self-harm, self-punishment. Many former victims act out their rage and shame by getting involved in anti-social behaviors such as breaking the law. These activities can be both a reflection of feeling like they no longer fit into society and acting out against what they feel is society letting them down: "No one was there to stop my abuser, so why should I obey society's rules?"

Victim mentality. Childhood sexual abuse can cause victims to feel helpless and hopeless. The victims couldn't find a way to stop the abuser, and no one came to rescue them. These feelings of helplessness and hopelessness can come to characterize some former victims. They didn't have the ability to escape or fight back, so they continue to be unable to defend themselves as an adult whenever they are treated inappropriately or attacked again.

Abusive behavior. Some former victims create a wall of defensiveness to protect themselves from further victimization or further shaming. Although this starts out as a protective measure, soon this wall prevents them from connecting with others and from having empathy for others, which sets the stage for abusive behavior. In addition, many former victims reenact the abuse they experienced by becoming abusers themselves.

Isolating behaviors. The shame that survivors of childhood abuse experienced can cause them to remain isolated from others. The unconscious or even conscious rationale is, "If I'm not around other people, I don't risk being further shamed." Isolating behaviors include feeling extremely anxious when socializing with others, being unable/unwilling to socialize with others, remaining withdrawn and being unable to strike up conversations or being unable to respond to overtures from others when they are in social situations, remaining closed up in one's home and seldom going out.

Relationship issues. Not surprisingly, many victims of CSA have difficulty when it comes to creating and maintaining healthy relationships. Their shame has caused them to have low self-esteem, so they are often exquisitely sensitive and can often get their feelings hurt. And former victims also tend to have trust issues, which is understandable, because their trust was betrayed if their perpetrator was someone they cared about or trusted. Last, but not least, being able to become emotionally intimate with a partner can be especially difficult, because emotional intimacy can feel smothering.

Sexual issues and problems. It is no surprise that the shame that former victims feel often affects their ability to function in a healthy way sexually. Common sexual problems include a lack of sexual desire; difficulty becoming aroused or feeling physical sensations; feeling emotionally distant or not present during sex; approaching sex as an obligation; experiencing negative feelings

such as disgust, anger, fear, shame, or guilt when touched; an inability to orgasm; painful intercourse; difficulty being able to engage in any sexual activity
that reminds them of the abuse; sexual dysfunction such as vaginismus for
women (an involuntary contraction of the vaginal muscle that prevents penetration); and erectile dysfunction and delayed ejaculation in men. Former victims are often plagued by flashbacks or intrusive or disturbing sexual thoughts
while they are engaged in sex, and some experience shame during sexual arousal
even when arousal is occurring in healthy situations.

Reenacting the abuse. In an attempt to avoid feeling the overwhelming
shame they are experiencing, some former victims identify with their abuser
by taking on his or her mannerisms, speech, and behavior and passing on the
abuse to others by becoming emotionally, physically, or sexually abusive toward
their romantic partners and their children. It also includes developing a pattern
of allowing others to abuse them (emotionally, physically, sexually) or allowing
others to take advantage of them. They may also reenact the abuse by becoming
involved with partners or friends who are replicas of their abusers.

MODERATE EFFECTS OF SHAME

The shame that former victims of CSA experience also has many less serious
consequences. Although these milder effects of shame do not generally bring
as much devastation into the lives of victims of child sexual abuse, they can
nevertheless be painful and quite troublesome and can affect former victims'
lives in significant ways.

- sensitivity to correction or criticism; easily shamed
- defensiveness: creating a wall between yourself and others in an attempt
  to block out criticism
- tendency to be self-critical, harsh, and/or unforgiving of oneself
- perfectionism as an attempt to avoid further shaming (if you don't make
  a mistake, you won't be criticized or shamed)
- people-pleasing behavior in an attempt to avoid further shaming, abuse
- an inability to speak up for oneself, to say what you really mean out of
  fear of offending or hurting someone and thus risking further shaming
- lack of motivation (unable to follow through on set goals, plans), confusion (unable to discover what career path to follow, unable to commit
  to a partner)
- unreasonably high expectations of self and others
- drive to be successful and/or powerful for the purposes of gaining control over others

Now that you understand more about how shame can affect victims of childhood sexual abuse in general, it is important to consider the specific ways it has affected you. You've probably recognized some of your own behavior and ways of thinking as you've read the lists above, but now please take the time to complete the following exercise.

Exercise: How Has Shame Affected You?

1. Look over the list of severe and moderate effects and decide which items apply to you. Put a check mark next to these items. This is not an either/or situation; you may experience several or many of these effects.
2. Be aware of how you feel as you do this assessment. Some of you may already be aware of the ways shame has affected you, so this might feel like a validating experience (it can feel good to have someone confirm what you already know to be true). Many of you, however, may not have realized that shame caused you to experience these feelings and behaviors. It can feel liberating to finally make sense of what in the past seemed to you (and others) to be unexplainable behavior. It can also feel good to realize that you are not alone and that other victims experience the same feelings. On the other hand, this exercise can bring up feelings of sadness and anger as you realize, in this concrete way, the extent to which the abuse and the accompanying shame have affected your life.

Understanding the various ways that shame may have affected you can be a giant step toward healing your shame. Perhaps you can now imagine how talking to an individual counselor or joining a group of other survivors can be a very freeing experience. And knowing that it was inevitable that you would be affected in these ways by the sexual abuse can help you begin to forgive yourself for ways that you have harmed yourself and others.

WHO SUFFERS THE MOST SHAME, AND WHY?

Although most victims of childhood sexual abuse experience shame, some suffer from it more than others. In addition to the typical shame victims experience, there is debilitating shame—a more all-encompassing, destructive form of shame. Debilitating shame can hinder victims' ability to function normally, often weakening them to the point that it causes them to be emotionally incapacitated. Those who experience this more debilitating form of shame include:

Males

In general, males tend to experience more shame from the abuse than females. This is true for several reasons, the primary being that males are raised to be tough and strong and to defend themselves from those who attack them. If a young boy is overpowered by a sexual aggressor, he feels tremendous shame because he was not able to defend himself and thus sees himself as "weak." In addition, male victims tend almost always to blame themselves and often don't even identify their experience as abuse, thus preventing them from seeking help. This is especially true if their perpetrator was close to their age or was female.

Those Sexually Abused by a Member of the Same Sex

Being sexually abused by someone of the same sex can be particularly shaming, because usually additional shame surrounds the idea of homosexuality, which is taboo in many people's minds. Sexual abuse between those of the same sex often brings up troubling questions such as "Why would this person approach me?" "Is there something about me that made him think I was gay?" "I enjoyed it, does this mean I am gay?" "Does this make me gay now?"

Victims of Multiple Instances or Chronic Abuse

Some victims suffered child sexual abuse one time or a few times over a short period of time. This experience is, of course, damaging enough. But others endured the ongoing shame-inducing trauma of sexual abuse throughout their childhood and/or by multiple abusers. These victims suffer from what has been called complex trauma.

Complex trauma is a relatively new term to describe the damage that occurs from repeated/chronic exposure to traumatic stressors from which one cannot escape, including childhood abuse. As a consequence of this kind of ongoing shaming, children suffer from extremely low self-esteem, feelings of worthlessness, and self-hatred. They feel inferior, "bad," unacceptable, and different from others—much like anyone who has been abused and shamed but to a more intense degree.

When this happens, these victims' lives become characterized by shame. They live in a constant state of self-criticism and self-blame, or they become exquisitely sensitive to criticism from others and defend against it at every turn. They set unreasonable expectations for themselves and are never satisfied with their performance or achievements. They find it impossible to take in positive expressions of love or admiration from others, or even compliments. Some withdraw into depression and passivity. These people have truly been "broken" by debilitating shame.

In addition, victims who are abused by more than one perpetrator tend to question themselves: "Why does this continue to happen to me?" "What am I doing to attract abusers?" They become convinced that they are to blame for the abuse, otherwise why would it keep happening to them?

Victims of Incest

Incest is considered to be the most common—and the most damaging form of child sexual abuse. It is defined as any sexual contact between a child or adolescent and a person who is closely related (parent, sibling, grandparent, aunt, uncle, cousin) or perceived to be related (stepparents and live-in partners of parents). While most victims are female and most perpetrators are male, incest can include female perpetrators and male victims. In the majority of cases, it is a father or stepfather who abuses a child. Incest can include a wide range of sexual activities, including fondling, intercourse, and sodomy. While incest can occur only one time, it most often takes place repeatedly over time.

More than any type of child abuse, incest is associated with secrecy, betrayal, powerlessness, guilt, conflicted loyalty, fear of reprisal, and self-blame/shame. Incest is almost universally regarded as harmful and wrong and is considered a deviant type of sexual behavior that is against the law. Therefore, when incest does occur, both the perpetrator and the victim are bound to secrecy, which creates tremendous shame for the victim. Victims may realize, on an unconscious level, that important boundaries have been crossed and that this has created a breakdown of trust within the family. Secrecy, which can create shame, is at an intense level. Most cases of incest involve an imbalance of power, due to a significant discrepancy in age, power, and/or experience. The perpetrator often uses coercion, threats, or manipulation to get the victim to go along with the sexual acts imposed on him or her. In addition, the perpetrator often has substantially more personal power due to his or her role as a parent, grandparent, and so forth, or is an older sibling left in charge.

Some forms of incest are particularly shaming—such as parent/child incest. The child is likely to feel like he or she is betraying the other parent, or even taking away the other parent's partner. It is important to note that incest victims rarely experience a single incident of sexual abuse. The abuse is usually repeated over time, sometimes for many years. It is also more likely that they experience chronic, multiple types of abuse, including sexual, physical, emotional, and psychological, within the family or caregiving system by adults who are expected to provide security and nurturance. Thus, in addition to all the other damage incest can cause a child, it also creates the same type of damage that victims of multiple or chronic abuse can experience—complex trauma.

In this chapter I have provided an overview of the many ways that the shame associated with childhood sexual abuse damages victims. My primary purpose in providing this overview was certainly to educate you, but in addition it was to help you overcome any denial you may have. It is harder to believe that you managed to escape the abuse unscathed when you read in black and white how very damaging it likely was to you. In particular, it is difficult to ignore the damage that the shame related to CSA has had on you personally.

You can now see that the negative effects of shame can be overwhelming and debilitating. But this doesn't mean that the situation is hopeless. It is possible to heal your shame. And you don't have to face your shame alone. This book will guide you step by step through the process of healing your shame. And my hope is that you begin to feel—by reading my words and feeling my support—that I am with you on your journey.

THREE

WHY YOU MUST HEAL YOUR SHAME TO HEAL FROM CHILD SEXUAL ABUSE

Trauma is perhaps the most avoided, ignored, belittled, denied, misunderstood, and untreated cause of human suffering.

—Peter Levine

I FIRMLY BELIEVE that unless you heal the shame attached to child sexual abuse, you cannot heal from the trauma itself for several important reasons. First, the shame experienced due to the trauma of CSA can haunt victims in a powerful and often unrecognized manner. This shame can impair the healing and recovery process by causing victims to stay stuck, unable to forgive themselves for being abused or for what they consider their part in the abuse.

In addition, shame is an emotion that piggybacks on top of trauma. It complicates the healing and recovery process on many levels, including psychologically (victims blame themselves for being vulnerable or for not stopping the abuse from happening) and spiritually (the experience often changes their relationship with a higher power). Therefore, recovering from shame is an integral part of healing from childhood abuse.

Finally, shame is at the core of nearly every symptom that victims experience—from low self-esteem and body image issues to sexual issues.

This is why I believe that shame must be addressed if there is any real hope for recovery from child sexual abuse. Although healing from CSA certainly involves other important aspects, none is more important than ridding yourself of shame. In fact, once you have healed from your shame, you will feel so much better about yourself that you will have more motivation and courage to face other aspects of healing. You'll have more strength and energy to tackle other issues because you won't be weighed down under the heavy cloak of shame.

These are the words past clients expressed once they were successful at facing and then eliminating their shame:

"Before I addressed my shame and figured out why I hated myself so much, my life was miserable. Now I know that I'm basically a good person, and I deserve to be happy."

"I always blamed myself for the abuse, but now I know it wasn't my fault. Now I can feel angry at my abuser instead of taking it out on myself."

"I used to compare myself with other people—and I always came up short. I wasn't as smart as they were, I wasn't as pretty. I wasn't as popular. I always felt 'less than.' Now I've stopped obsessively comparing myself with everyone. I feel so much better about myself since I've gotten rid of some of my shame."

"I used to feel like people were always looking at me and criticizing me. Now I realize the only one who was judging me was me."

"I used to sabotage every good relationship, every positive thing that happened to me because I was so full of shame. Now I recognize it and I spend time telling myself I deserve love and success. I don't completely believe it yet—but at least I don't push good things away as much."

When you free yourself from the clutches of shame, it is like a veil has been lifted, and you suddenly see the world much clearer—and more accurately. You realize that people aren't looking at you and judging you. You realize that you don't have a sign on your head that says "sexual abuse victim" and that no one can know this about you unless you tell them. Instead of feeling isolated and "less than," you can begin to feel more like a part of life. You feel more comfortable reaching out to others, opening up to others.

SHAME CAN HAMPER RECOVERY

Not only does shame from CSA cause a multitude of problems, as we have discussed, but this very same shame affects and often stands in the way of a victim's ability to recover and heal. A review of twenty-eight studies exploring the relationship between shame and the psychological sequelae (a condition that is the consequence of a previous disease or injury) of CSA provided evidence that shame can hinder psychological adjustment following CSA. These studies found that the presence of shame mediated a range of psychological outcomes, including: (1) sexual revictimization in adulthood, (2) body surveillance and alexithymia, (3) shame and suicide ideation, (4) self-harming behaviors, (5) dissociation, (6) body related trauma, (7) anxiety and depressive symptoms, and (8) the effectiveness of group psychotherapy on reducing PTSD symptoms.

Here are some specific ways in which shame from CSA can hamper a victim's ability to recover:

Correlation with dissociation. Dissociation can be a major problem for victims of CSA. Although it was meant to be a protective mechanism at the time of the trauma (helping children to avoid feeling the full brunt of the trauma as well as the assault on their body) victims can be easily triggered and dissociate as a reaction, causing them to be disconnected from themselves and others. This removal from the present can become dangerous. Several studies indicate a correlation between shame and dissociation. For example, in a clinical sample of ninety-nine women with and without a history of CSA found that higher levels of shame proneness are associated with higher levels of dissociation, especially among women who experienced CSA. (CSA alone is not strongly related to dissociation, but it was strongly suggested that shame can influence the emergence of dissociation).

Correlation with PTSD. Recent theory and research to explain persistent PTSD suggests that trauma memories that are poorly elaborated and integrated into autobiographical memories may engender persistent reexperiencing of the trauma. Post-traumatic stress disorder symptoms, especially reexperiencing symptoms, occur when individuals fail to process the trauma memories emotionally and cognitively, leaving them more vulnerable to being triggered by sensory cues resulting in a sense of current threat. Abuse-related shame constitutes a current internal inability to feel like one is good and lovable. In the short run, shame motivates the child to push memories and thoughts about the abuse out of mind. With time, persistently high levels of shame may be part of a dynamic, whereby shame-motivated suppression of traumatic events is unsuccessful and contributes to high levels of intrusive recollections and memories. In this way, shame could disrupt an individual's ability to integrate memories and thoughts about the abuse in a meaningful resolution to the trauma.

Relationships and social connection. It has been found that victims of CSA can heal in safe, supportive relationships with others. But shame presents obstacles to building relationships and reconnection. Findings from ten studies emphasize the multifaceted influence of shame on relationships, including (1) experience of being disconnected from the world, (2) disruptions to peer friendships, (3) disruptions in relationships with nonoffending mothers, (4) difficulties with and avoidance of sex and intimate relationships, (5) sexual revictimization in adulthood, (6) conflict in close relationships, (7) difficulties with sexual identification and orientation (in males), and (8) difficulties with aggression (males).

Barrier to disclosure. For many survivors, disclosure represents the beginning of healing and recovery. Shame may act as a barrier to disclosure, thus limiting or distorting seeking help. Findings show shame is a major influence on the decision to disclose as well as the impact of disclosure and that responses by others following disclosure can illicit shame. For example, in my practice clients report that shame is the primary reason why they are unable to disclose their abuse to family or to partners. This is borne out in a 2013 qualitative study of women conducted by Taylor and Norma in which 76 percent of participants reported that shame was the most frequently mentioned reason for not disclosing CSA and seeking help. Males tend to disclose CSA at significantly lower rates than women primarily due to shame around the issues of homophobia, ideals of masculinity, and pressure to protect family members.

A negative effect on sense of self. Several studies found a strong influence of shame on a victim's sense of self referred to as *self-as-shame* or the *affected self* versus the *recovering self.* Specifically, shame following CSA can disrupt development, resulting in a chronically shame-based self with at times an enduring impact on emotions, relationships, and behaviors. Some survivors experience the self as forged together with the experience of shame.

HOW SHAME AFFECTS YOUR MENTAL STATE
AND YOUR EFFORTS TOWARD RECOVERY

In addition to the effects of shame on recovery listed above, there is still one more troubling consequence. Studies show that shame is not only an effect of CSA but has an influence on other effects. In particular, CSA-related shame may have an adverse influence on adult survivors' mental health, exacerbating other psychological effects, relationships, disclosure, self-concept, and recovery.

Specifically, research findings suggest that CSA significantly influences psychological effects and trauma symptoms. Collectively the studies provide evidence that shame *can hinder psychological adjustment* following CSA. In summary, the presence of shame causes a range of psychological outcomes, including:

- sexual revictimization in adulthood
- body surveillance and alexithymia
- suicidal ideation
- self-harming behaviors
- anxiety and depressive symptoms
- effectiveness of group psychotherapy on reducing PTSD symptoms

OTHER EFFECTS RELATED TO UNHEALED SHAME

It is important to heal the shame caused by childhood sexual abuse for many obvious reasons. One need only look over the list of all the after-effects of shame from the previous chapter to recognize this importance. But some risks related to unhealed shame are not necessarily apparent.

PTSD

Specifically, one quantitative study highlighted successful interventions for victims of child sexual abuse. Ginzburg et al. (2009) found that reductions in guilt were not associated with reductions in PTSD, but reductions in shame are associated with reductions in PTSD. This finding gives support to a new, though insufficiently tested therapeutic maxim: *work on shame, and you work on PTSD.*

Reenactment

Reenactment is a common ongoing problem for former victims. Many continue to be abused either emotionally, physically, or sexually. Others identify with the aggressor and abuse or fantasize about abusing others, including children and those with less power. They frequently cross boundaries with children or whenever they are in a power position: boss/employee, teacher/student, doctor/patient relationships. Becoming addicted to sex or pornography, entering careers such as prostitution or stripping are also examples of reenactment.

The sad truth is that no one escapes childhood sexual abuse unscathed. An even sadder truth is that most former victims don't escape without perpetuating the cycle of violence in some way. In many cases, those who were sexually abused become both abusers and victims throughout their lifetimes. Research clearly shows that those who have been abused either absorb abuse or pass it on. Individuals with a history of childhood abuse are four times more likely to assault family members or sexual partners than are individuals without such a history. Females who have a history of being abused in childhood are far more likely to continue being victimized as adults.

In general, trauma appears to amplify the common gender stereotypes: men with histories of childhood abuse are more likely to take out their aggression on others, whereas women are more likely to be victimized by others or to injure themselves. Although most victims of sexual abuse don't go on to abuse children, many do. All too often a sexually abused male (less often, a female) will feel compelled to sexually abuse children. This includes sexually abusing their own children. If he marries a woman who was also sexually abused (which happens more times than not), she often will become a silent partner—someone who is in such denial about her own abuse that she stands by while her own children are being molested. Not all victims of childhood sexual abuse molest their own or other people's children, but sometimes they are so afraid of repeating the cycle that they cannot be physically affectionate toward their own children.

Sexual Revictimization

Self-blame is a particularly damaging aspect of child sexual abuse. Self-blame and shame cause victims of CSA to be especially vulnerable to later sexual re-victimization. Research over the past decade has consistently shown strong evidence that those who were sexually victimized as a child or adolescent are far more likely to be sexually assaulted as an adult. In one recent study, it was found that former victims of CSA stand a *thirty-five times greater chance of sexual assault* than non-victims. The following information primarily applies to female victims, but it can apply to male victims, especially homosexual men.

Shame and self-blame increase the likelihood of revictimization among former victims of CSA, partly because they develop behavioral problems that lead to revictimization. For example, former victims tend to have alcohol and drug problems. Reexperiencing symptoms are often numbed by alcohol and drug use, which can serve to impair judgment and defensive strategies. According to research, former victims of child sexual abuse are about four times more likely to develop symptoms of drug abuse. Adolescents who had been sexually abused were two to three times more likely to have alcohol use/dependence problems than non-victims. Oshri, Tubman, and Burnette (2012) found that CSA was a significant precursor to alcohol abuse, as well as to co-occurring alcohol use.

Former victims tend to denigrate themselves and often feel worthless. Victimized women, in particular, believe that they have brought the abuse on themselves and that they do not deserve to be treated with respect or loved unconditionally (Filipas & Ullman, 2006).

Shame is related to an avoidant coping style because the person who is shame-prone will be motivated to avoid thoughts and situations that elicit this painful emotional state. A victim who is experiencing avoidant symptoms may be prone to making inaccurate or uninformed decisions regarding potential danger because of the fact that the trauma has been denied, minimized, or otherwise not fully integrated (Noll et al., 2003). The reexperiencing symptoms can lead to a repetition compulsion where the failure to accommodate to a traumatic experience may lead to a subconscious drive to reenact the experience to achieve a sense of mastery over the original trauma (van der Kolk, 1989).

Certain kinds of abusive men target women whom they perceive as vulnerable. Many abusive men unconsciously, and sometimes consciously, look for women who appear to be weak and vulnerable. They can intuitively sense or have learned from experience that they can more easily manipulate and control this type of woman.

The severity of childhood abuse increases the likelihood of revictimization. Factors such as the use of force and threats, and whether there is penetration and longer duration of the abuse and closeness of the relationship between victim and offender are associated with higher risk of revictimization (Classen, 2005).

Female victims tend to have sexual behavior problems and oversexualized behavior. Children who have been sexually abused have more than three times as many sexual behavior problems as children who have not been abused (Darkness to Light).

Female victims tend to have low self-esteem and poor body image. Obesity and eating disorders are more common in women who have a history of child sexual abuse (Darkness to Light). Girls and women who have a poor body image are more likely to feel complimented by male attention and are more vulnerable to males taking advantage of their need for attention.

Female victims may feel powerless because the abuser has repeatedly violated their body and acted against their will through coercion and manipulation. When someone attempts to sexually violate them as an adult, they may feel helpless and powerless to defend themselves.

Female victims don't tend to respect their bodies. They may feel stigmatized and may feel like "damaged goods," so they don't feel like there is any point in protecting their reputation or their body.

Female victims don't tend to be attuned to warning signs that a person may be a sexual perpetrator. They may be accustomed to being treated poorly, or they may be dissociated or otherwise "checked out" to the point that they are not aware of their environment. If a woman is not "in her body," she doesn't know when she is in a dangerous situation.

Female victims don't tend to have good boundaries. Child sexual abuse is a breaking of normal, healthy, agreed-upon boundaries. Because of this, the line between involuntary and voluntary participation is blurred for many former victims. Many don't know how to say no to unwanted sexual advances, don't know how to defend their boundaries, or even to identify what their particular sexual boundaries are.

HOW SHAME CAN SHAPE ONE'S PERSONALITY

Most victims of child sexual abuse are changed by the trauma, primarily because of the amount of shame they carry from that day forward. Sexual abuse can cause a victim to become so overwhelmed with shame that the trauma can define them and prevent them from reaching their full potential. It can cause someone to remain fixated at the age she was at the time of the victimization, and it can motivate a person to repeat the abuse over and over in her lifetime.

Not only does shame create multiple problems for former victims, but it can literally shape their personality, character, and body structure. For example, when most people think of a person who has been deeply shamed, they think of someone who is reticent, insecure, withdrawn. Their posture may reflect the intense amount of shame they feel—they tend to keep their head down and their shoulders slumped. They may have difficulty looking other people in the eye, and they may shy away from relationships. They seldom offer an opinion, and they tend to go along with what others want. In other words, their entire system may be bent on avoiding contact with others for fear of being called out and humiliated further.

On the other hand, shame can cause a person to develop in the exact opposite manner. When this occurs, we have someone who is far more rigid and less malleable. Instead of the slouched shoulders and caved-in chest of the first type, this person's chest is puffed out and their posture can be almost military-like. Instead of avoiding others' gaze, they can have a very direct, almost confrontational gaze. And far from withholding their opinion, they tend to impose their opinions on others and dare others to disagree with them. They can be controlling and often arrogant.

BECOMING SHAME-BOUND

Sometimes children have been so severely shamed or experienced so many shame-inducing experiences that they become "shame-bound" or "shame-based," meaning that shame has become a dominant factor in the formation of their personality. Shame-based people suffer from extremely low self-esteem, feelings of worthlessness, and self-hatred. They feel inferior, "bad," unacceptable, and different from others.

In addition to the shame-inducing trauma of child sexual abuse, shame-based people are also commonly survivors of severe physical discipline, emotional abuse, neglect, and abandonment—which all send the message that the child is worthless, unacceptable, and bad. These acts also convey the message that adults will treat you any way they want to because you are a worthless commodity. Many shame-based people were also humiliated for their behavior (i.e., chastised or beaten in front of others, being told, "What's wrong with you?" or "What would your precious teacher think of you if she knew who you *really* are?").

Many people react with anger whenever they are made to feel humiliated, devalued, or demeaned. But shame-based or shame-bound people often defend against any feeling of shame with rage. They tend to be extremely sensitive and defensive, and they rage when they feel criticized or attacked—which is often. Because they are so critical of themselves, they believe everyone else is critical of them. And because they despise themselves, they assume everyone else dislikes them. If you are shame-bound, one teasing comment or one well-intentioned criticism can send you into a rage that lasts for hours. Because you feel shamed by the other person's comment, you may spend hours making the person feel horrible about himself, in essence, dumping shame back on him.

Because shame-based people feel very vulnerable underneath all their defensiveness, they tend to attack others before they have a chance to be attacked. In essence they are saying, "Don't get any closer to me. I don't want you to know who I really am." This kind of raging works—it drives people away or keeps people from approaching in the first place.

Those who defend against shame build a protective wall with the goal of keeping out any hint of criticism from others. Strategies used for this purpose can include being critical of others before they have a chance to criticize you, refusing to talk about any of your shortcomings, turning criticism back on the other person, accusing the other person of lying or exaggerating their complaints about you, and projecting your shame onto others.

IDENTIFYING WITH THE AGGRESSOR

A related way that some victims suppress their feelings of helplessness is by "identifying with the aggressor." We find that phenomenon to be particularly common with male victims. In most societies it is not acceptable for males to be perceived as victims, so they tend to blame themselves and even convince themselves that they caused the behavior in the abusive person. Because of this a boy may also come to identify with the aggressor—that is, become like his abuser. The only way left for him to discharge his shame and aggression is to do to others what was done to him.

A TENDENCY TO USE DISTRESS REDUCTION BEHAVIORS

If you don't allow yourself to face your shame and work on healing it, you will continue to suffer from many of the effects of shame we have been discussing. Specifically, as a reaction to the trauma of being sexually abused, former victims are at significant risk of self-injury, suicidal behavior, risky sexual activities, bingeing and purging, and a host of other seemingly impulsive, compulsive, and/or addictive activities. Most of these negative behaviors are brought on because of the amount of shame the former victim is experiencing (whether or not they are aware of it).

Why would a person intentionally engage in self-defeating, even life-threatening activities, especially when they lead to additional emotional pain and social alienation? The answer is that advances in trauma and attachment psychology suggest that many seemingly dysfunctional behaviors serve adaptive functions, especially for those exposed to adversity in childhood.

Based on this growing body of research, John Briere developed a model that addresses activities ranging from self-injury to compulsive gambling. This model, which he calls *reactive avoidance* (RA), frames these behaviors not as manifestations of psychological illness but, rather, attempts to *distract, numb, block, or otherwise avoid distress associated with triggered, or highly painful memories*. From a reactive avoidance perspective, such behaviors are referred to as distress reduction behaviors (DRBs) as opposed to terms such as acting out, dysfunctional, self-defeating, or impulsive behaviors.

The RA model suggests that the goal of many so-called maladaptive behaviors is not self-destructiveness but, instead, pain relief; and, from the person's perspective, emotional survival. These seemingly impulsive behaviors are acts of desperation—the need to quickly reduce emotional pain before it can overwhelm limited emotional regulation skills and produce greater suffering. Add to this sense of desperation the fact that when sexual abuse occurs during a child's development, it can have adverse effects on certain developmental processes, such as emotional regulation, cognitive style, and coping mechanisms.

FUNCTIONS OF DISTRESS REDUCTION BEHAVIORS

According to Briere, distress reduction behaviors (DRBs) typically distract or pull attention or awareness away from emotional pain and distress. The avoidance behaviors associated with RA are typically side effects of unprocessed trauma and early attachment problems. Those who have childhood histories of abuse, neglect, and/or insecure attachment tend to develop a number of seemingly dysfunctional or self-defeating behavior patterns. They include:

- intentional self-injury
- triggered suicidal behavior
- risky or compulsive sexual behavior
- problematic substance use
- food bingeing and purging
- compulsive gambling
- compulsive shoplifting
- compulsive shopping
- setting fires
- extensive preoccupation with internet activities
- thrill or sensation-seeking behavior
- compulsive skin picking and hair pulling
- problematic internet use

Instead of needing to use any of the distress reduction behaviors listed above, it is far better to face your shame and actively work on alleviating it. These side effects of unprocessed trauma can be avoided or alleviated by allowing yourself to face your trauma and your shame head-on, as you can learn to do by reading this book and following the suggestions offered. There will be much more help for how to avoid or discontinue these negative behaviors in chapters 12 and 13.

Admitting your shame, bringing it out of the shadows, out of the darkness, is one of the first and most powerful things you can do to heal it. Shame tends to increase and become more problematic when hidden. But when brought out into the light of day, the things you are ashamed of don't seem so heavy, so dark, so negative. Like a secret you've been carrying for years, as soon as you reveal it, it becomes lighter, less of a burden.

PART II

FREEING YOURSELF OF THE SHAME
OF CHILD SEXUAL ABUSE

FOUR

FACING THE TRUTH

Every person must choose how much truth he can stand.
—Irvin D. Yalom, *When Nietzche Wept*

IN ORDER TO HEAL from the shame of childhood sexual abuse you need to admit to yourself what really happened to you. This may sound simple, but it is far from it. Child sexual abuse is such an assault on body, mind, and spirit that the natural reaction is to protect yourself from the brutal reality of what occurred.

Former victims use several defense mechanisms to protect themselves from remembering and facing the truth about the sexual abuse they suffered: *denial, repression, suppression, minimization, rationalization,* and *projection*. In most cases, these psychological responses operate outside a person's conscious awareness and control. In this chapter and chapter 5, we will discuss these defense mechanisms as well as the issue of memory—or in the case of child sexual abuse—lack of memory. Finally, we will discuss the confusion former victims often experience based on the multiple misconceptions about what constitutes child sexual abuse.

DENIAL

As humans, we will do almost anything to avoid feeling shame. One of the best ways to avoid feeling the shame of having been sexually abused is to deny that it happened. Even if you can admit to yourself that you were abused, you may still be in denial about various aspects of the abuse. For example, you may have admitted to yourself that you were sexually abused but at the same time convinced yourself that "it wasn't all that bad" (minimization), or that your perpetrator didn't mean to harm you (rationalization). Or you may have even convinced yourself that it wasn't abuse because you enjoyed it, or you were the one who initiated it (denial).

Denial is a powerful, *unconscious* defense mechanism intended to protect us from having to face intense pain and trauma. It can even allow us to block out or "forget" intense pain caused by emotional or physical trauma such as childhood sexual abuse. The denial process is designed to prevent us from facing things that are too painful to face at the time. But it also defends us against the truth and can continue way past the time it served a positive function.

Victims of child sexual abuse often deny that they were abused, deny that it caused them harm, and deny that they need help. What follows are the most common reasons why victims of CSA tend to deny what happened to them and/or minimize the damage it caused them:

- They don't want to feel the shame, pain, fear, and betrayal that acknowledging the abuse would cause. The abuse is either walled off from conscious awareness and memory, so that it did not really happen, or it is minimized, rationalized, and excused, so that whatever did happen was not really abuse. Unable to escape or alter the unbearable reality that they were sexually abused, some children alter it in their mind.
- They don't want to admit that they were helpless victims. As we have discussed, it is humiliating and degrading to acknowledge that another person can overpower you or manipulate you into doing things you did not want to do. Instead of admitting either of these two things, victims often prefer to take responsibility for the abuse.
- They don't want to admit that someone they cared about could manipulate them and cause them such damage. For those who were sexually abused by a family member, a close friend of the family, or an authority figure they respected such as a priest, a teacher, or a coach, to face the fact that they were abused is to experience the pain, sometimes unbearable, of admitting that someone they respected or loved could treat them in such horrendous ways. The most common way that children explain behavior on an abuser's part, especially by someone they respect or love, is to blame themselves.
- They repeated the cycle of abuse by abusing other children. In this situation, they may have an investment in believing that children are never really "forced or manipulated" into sex with an adult or older child, but they do so willingly and get pleasure from doing it. This kind of denial often keeps former victims from admitting that they themselves were abused.

My client Jack refused to admit he had been sexually abused because by doing so he would be confronted with the fact that he had abused another child. Jack had done what so many male victims do—he "identified with the aggressor"—meaning that he took on aspects of the abuser's identity. This was an unconscious way for him to deny that he had been victimized. Unfortunately, this denial contributed to his becoming an abuser himself.

Jack was abused by his older brother starting when he was nine years old and his brother was fifteen. Jack adored his brother and longed for his acceptance and for him to include him when he went out with his friends. His brother manipulated Jack into performing oral sex on him by sometimes including him in his social activities. When Jack hesitated, his brother blatantly ignored him.

By the time Jack was eleven, he began touching his younger sister who was approximately the same age he was when his brother began abusing him. He was often left in charge of her—something he resented—so he had easy access to her. And because she adored him, she readily agreed to everything he asked her to do.

When Jack finally told me about abusing his sister, this is how he described it: "It was just like what happened with me and my brother. At first, she resisted a little, but then she liked it. Sure, I started it, but it didn't hurt her. I figured I just gave her a head start just like my brother did with me."

When I tried to explain to him that what his brother did to him was considered child sexual abuse because his brother was so much older than he, because his brother had a great deal of power and influence over him, and because he had used this power and influence to manipulate Jack into doing his bidding, this is how he responded:

> The only part of what happened with my brother that bothered me is that he was a guy. I worried at first that it made me gay—but then I proved to myself that I could get it on with a girl when I got involved with my sister. In fact, by the time I reached adolescence, my brother and I had stopped, but my sister and I continued until she left home.

Jack was clearly in denial about the fact that he had been sexually abused by his older brother and that he had reenacted this abuse with his sister.

Healing Jack's Shame

Jack needed to learn that repeating what was done to him by molesting his sister was a typical reaction to having been abused. As I explained to him, this is true for several reasons. First of all, children tend to reenact important events in their life—especially traumatic events—in their play and with other children. Thus, we see a young girl who was molested taking off her doll's clothes and having another doll touch her genital area or get on top of her.

Children and adolescents sometimes do the same kind of reenactment with their playmates—encouraging other children to take off their clothes, playing sexual games, and touching each other. This is "typical" behavior on the part of former victims in that it helps them to process what happened to them. But unfortunately, they can essentially pass on to another child what was done to them—exposing other children to sex before they are emotionally and physically equipped to cope with their sexuality and sexual feelings.

Often reenactments go beyond repeating what was done to you in an innocent way. Sometimes they are a way for victims to take out their anger on someone smaller or weaker than themselves, as was the case with Jack and his brother. There is a difference between showing other children what was done to you as an innocent way of processing your own abuse and the act of identifying with the aggressor, as in Jack's case. Even though it began innocently enough— he wanted to show his sister what he had learned from his brother and prove to himself that he wasn't homosexual—the act had an element of power and control. Jack had an investment in denying that his brother had taken advantage of him because he loved his brother and wanted his love and attention, but he was also (unconsciously) angry with his brother. Because he was afraid of his brother, he took out his anger on someone weaker than himself—his sister. In other words, Jack wanted to exert power over his sister the way his brother had with him.

REPRESSION VERSUS SUPPRESSION

Repression (unconsciously blocking out traumatic events) and suppression (consciously choosing to "forget" traumatic events) are survival skills that help former victims to move on with their lives instead of being so completely overwhelmed with feelings of fear, shame, or guilt that they can't function. Unfortunately, these defense mechanisms can make it difficult to face the truth about having been sexually abused.

Painful feelings and memories can be very upsetting. Instead of facing them, we often unconsciously hide them from ourselves (repress) in hopes of forgetting them entirely. That does not mean that the memories disappear. They can influence behaviors and can impact our relationships without us realizing it.

It can be especially painful to admit that someone you loved and you believed loved you could traumatize you in this way. Sometimes, instead of facing the truth, we consciously suppress the memories of what happened. This was the case with my client Ginger:

> I knew for a long time before admitting it in here that I was abused by my grandfather, but I just couldn't face it. It was just too painful to admit to myself that someone I loved so much and someone who had been so kind to me could also do such vile things to me. It just didn't compute; you know what I mean? And so, I pretended. I pretended that it never happened. After each episode, I just went right back to my life without missing a beat. I continued playing, or doing my homework, or whatever it was I was doing before he came into my room.

As I continued to work with Ginger, we discovered that because her grandfather was the only one who had been kind to her when she was growing up, in order to cope with the abuse, she starting thinking of him as two separate people—the kind, loving grandfather and the one who did bad things to her. As we worked to help her admit to herself that they were, in fact, the same person, Ginger experienced a tremendous amount of pain. For weeks after that she would sometimes cry for our entire session. "No wonder I couldn't face the truth before," she told me after several weeks. "I wasn't strong enough, and I had no one to be with me with my pain. It's hard enough now as an adult to face it, even with your support. No wonder I 'pretended' it didn't happen."

CONFUSION

Many people are confused as to whether they were, in fact, sexually abused, for many reasons: Some make the assumption that if they were not penetrated, they were not sexually abused. Those who were abused by a female don't tend to consider it sexual abuse. And many believe that if they experienced any pleasure, it meant that they were a willing participant. Still others were told by the perpetrator that he was "teaching them" about sex and they believed him.

Child sexual abuse can also be very confusing to a child or an adolescent while it is occurring. And it can be equally confusing to adults grappling with the reality of what happened to them as a child. Questions such as, "Do certain things have to happen in order to make it 'sexual abuse'?" Or "Was I really abused, or was I a willing participant?" are quite common for victims.

Confusion about What Child Sexual Abuse Is

Many former victims do not believe that what happened to them would be considered abuse. Why? Because they are misinformed as to what child sexual abuse is. Many people think of childhood sexual abuse as an adult having intercourse with a child—penetration of a penis inside a vagina; or, in the case of male-on-male sexual abuse, a male penetrating the child's anus with his penis. But childhood sexual abuse is not limited to intercourse. In fact, most sexual abuse of a child does not involve intercourse.

You also may not think that you have been sexually abused if you were an adolescent who was older than thirteen years old when the act or acts occurred. But sexual abuse includes an adult having sexual contact with an adolescent as well as an older adolescent having sexual contact with a younger child or adolescent. In general, we need to follow the two-year rule. That means that if you were thirteen and someone sixteen years old had sexual contact with you, this would be considered abuse. If you were fifteen and your abuser was eighteen or older, depending upon the laws where you live, this might be called *statutory rape* and is punishable by law.

In the United States, the "age of consent" is the legal age at which an individual is considered mature enough to consent to sex. The age of consent varies from state to state, country to country, but it is typically between the ages of sixteen and eighteen. In some states, the law is even more stringent. For example, California Penal Code 261.5 makes it a crime for anyone, regardless of age, to have sex with a minor under the age of eighteen. It is considered statutory rape even if the minor willingly participated, as the law deems minors to be legally incapable of consenting to have sex.

Although this may be the law, current research has shown that, in fact, adolescents' brains are not really developed enough for them to give informed consent until they are in their early twenties. In addition to the physical and psychological imbalance that exists between an adult and a child younger than sixteen years of age, when we add to this the more obvious imbalance between the power and resources of an adult compared with a child, it becomes abundantly clear that the relationship is not one of equals.

WHAT CONSTITUTES CHILD SEXUAL ABUSE?

Below is a comprehensive list of the various forms of childhood sexual abuse that exist, including more subtle forms of abuse. Child sexual abuse includes any contact between an adult and a child or an older child and a younger child *for the purposes of sexual stimulation of either the child or the adult or older child* and that *results in sexual gratification for the older person*. This can range from non-touching offenses, such as exhibitionism and child pornography, to fondling, penetration, incest, and child prostitution. A child does not have to be touched to be molested.

Many people think of childhood sexual abuse as being an adult molesting a child. But childhood sexual abuse also includes an older child molesting a younger child. By definition an older child is usually two years or older than the younger child but even an age difference of one year can have tremendous power implications. For example, an older brother is almost always seen as an authority figure, especially if he is left "in charge" when their parents are away. The younger sibling tends to go along with what the older sibling wants to do out of fear or out of a need to please. In some cases, the older sister is the aggressor, although this does not happen as often. In cases of sibling incest, the greater the age difference, the greater the betrayal of trust, and the more violent the incest tends to be.

Child sexual abuse can include any of the following:

Genital exposure. The adult or older child exposes his or her genitals to the child.

Kissing. The adult or older child kisses the child in a lingering or intimate way.

Fondling. The adult or older child fondles the child's breasts, abdomen, genital area, inner thighs, or buttocks. The child may also be asked to touch the older person's body in these places.

Masturbation. The adult or older child masturbates while the child observes; the adult observes the child masturbating; the adult and child masturbate each other (mutual masturbation).

Fellatio. The adult or older child has the child fellate (orally stimulate the penis) him or her, or the adult fellates the child.

Cunnilingus. This type of oral-genital contact requires either the child to place mouth and tongue on the vulva or in the vaginal area of an adult female (or older female child) or the adult to place his or her mouth on the vulva or in the vaginal area of the female child.

Digital (finger) penetration of the anus or rectal opening. Perpetrators may also thrust inanimate objects such as crayons or pencils inside.

Penile penetration of the anus or rectal opening.

Digital (finger) penetration of the vagina. Inanimate objects may also be inserted.

"Dry intercourse." A slang term describing an interaction in which the adult rubs his penis against the child's genital-rectal area or inner thighs or buttocks.

Penile penetration of the vagina.

Showing pornography. Showing the child or adolescent pornography, usually for the purpose of initiating the child into sexual contact or to sexually stimulate the child.

Creating pornography. Photographing a child or adolescent in the nude or in costume for the purposes of sexual arousal or sale to others.

More Subtle Forms of Childhood Sexual Abuse

Most of you are reading this book because you already know that you were abused in childhood and that you suffer from shame because of it. But in addition to the abuse that you have already identified, I venture to say that you may have also been abused in other, less obvious ways. Below is a description of the lesser known, more hidden forms of sexual abuse. These forms of abuse can be just as shaming as the more obvious, overt forms.

Subtle forms of sexual abuse can include any of the following. Keep in mind that it is the intention of the adult or older child while engaging in these activities that determines whether the act is sexually abusive.

Nudity. The adult or older child parades around the house in front of the child.

Disrobing. The adult or older child disrobes in front of the child, generally when the child and the older person are alone.

Observation of the child. The adult or older child surreptitiously or overtly watches the child undress, bathe, excrete, or urinate.

Inappropriate comments. The adult or older child makes inappropriate comments about the child's body. This can include making comments about the child's developing body (e.g., comments about the size of a boy's penis or the size of a girl's breasts). It can also include asking a teenager to share intimate details about her or his dating life.

Back rubs and tickling. These can have a sexual aspect to them if the person doing it has a sexual agenda.

Emotional incest. Emotionally incestuous parents turn to their child to satisfy needs that should be satisfied by other adults—namely: intimacy, companionship, romantic stimulation, advice, problem solving, ego fulfillment, and/or emotional release. Parents who have been divorced or widowed often attempt to replace the lost spouse with their own child. Emotional incest also occurs when a parent "romanticizes" the relationship between herself and her child, treats the child as if he or she were her intimate partner, or when a parent is seductive with a child. This can also include a parent "confiding" in a child about his or her adult sexual relationships and sharing intimate sexual details with a child or adolescent.

Approach behavior. Any indirect or direct sexual suggestion made by an adult or older child toward a child. This can include sexual looks, innuendos, or suggestive gestures. Even if the older person never engaged in touching or took any overt sexual action, the sexual feelings that are projected are picked up by the child.

Hopefully, these lists have helped further educate you as to what constitutes sexual child abuse. Although you may be aware of many forms of abuse, you may be surprised to discover that behaviors you thought were normal are considered abusive and can cause considerable damage to a child's psyche, in addition to causing great shame in a child.

This is what one client shared with me after reading this list:

> I knew I had been molested by my grandfather, but I didn't realize that what my uncle and my cousins did to me was also considered sexual abuse. It's actually shocking to realize that I was such a target for sexual abuse in my family—that there was no safe place. I always thought there was something wrong with me—that I attracted it in my life. Now I realize it ran in my family, like a disease.

Questionnaire: Were You Sexually Abused?

Did a family member, a caretaker, a sibling or other older child, an authority figure, or any other adult or older child:

1. lie or sit around nude in a sexually provocative way?
2. walk around the house in a sexually provocative way (nude, half dressed)?
3. frequently walk in on you while you were getting dressed, while taking a bath, or while using the toilet?
4. flirt with you or engage in provocative behavior such as making comments about the way your body was developing?
5. show you pornographic pictures or movies?
6. kiss, hold, or touch you inappropriately?
7. touch, bite, or fondle your sexual parts?
8. make you engage in forced or mutual masturbation?
9. give you enemas or douches for no medical reason?
10. wash or scrub your genitals well after you were capable of doing so on your own?
11. become preoccupied with the cleanliness of your genitals, scrub your genitals until they were raw, tell you that your genitals were dirty, shameful, or evil?
12. force you to observe or participate in adult bathing, undressing, toilet, or sexual activities?
13. force you to be nude in front of others? force you to attend parties where adults were nude?

14. peek at you when you were in the shower or on the toilet, insist on an "open-door" policy so they could walk in on you at any time in the bathroom or in your bedroom?

15. make you share your parents' bed when you were old enough to have your own bed (assuming other beds were available)?

16. have sex in front of you after you were old enough to be upset, confused, or aroused by it?

17. tell you details about their sexual behavior or about their sexual parts?

18. take photographs of you nude or engaged in sexual activities (once again, after you were old enough to be embarrassed by it)?

19. after you reached adolescence or older, ask you to tell them about inappropriate details about your sexual life?

20. allow you to be sexually molested without trying to stop it?

21. deliver you to other people so that they could molest or rape you, or bring people over to the house who would molest or rape you?

22. make you into a child prostitute?

23. continue to make sexually inappropriate comments or to touch you in sexually provocative ways even after you reached adulthood?

If you answered yes to even one of the above questions, it means that you were sexually abused. It is also likely that if you answered in the affirmative to one question, you may have answered yes to several, because perpetrators of child sexual abuse usually subject their victims to various types of abuse.

It can be painful and disorienting to come to the realization that you were, in fact, sexually abused, but please believe me, it is better to know than to remain in the dark. When we are unaware of what has happened to us, we are extremely vulnerable to being manipulated or revictimized and to being surprised and even damaged by our own behavior.

FURTHER CONFUSION

Many former victims do not realize that what happened to them as a child or adolescent was considered abuse because their image of child sexual abuse is limited to an older man abusing a child of the opposite sex. This is particularly true for males victimized by another male, those who were abused by a female, victims of sibling abuse, and victims of clergy abuse.

The Special Problem of Males Abusing Males

It can be especially difficult for males who have been sexually abused by another male to identify their experience as abuse, especially if the two were close in age. Although male on male abuse certainly can include sadistic or violent aggression, most often the perpetrator employs various subterfuges, gradually leading the child to participate in sexual acts. This can make it difficult for the child to realize he is being abused. The victim must come to realize that even though he may believe he participated willingly, his participation was obtained by ruse, lies, force, or fear (whatever the degree of physical, moral, or psychological constraint used).

As Michel Dorais, the author of *Don't Tell: The Sexual Abuse of Boys*, explained in his book, some boys were particularly vulnerable because they were interested in exploring a situation that presented itself to them, whether it was getting closer to someone they were fond of, satisfying their sexual curiosity, or simply not displeasing their aggressor. What characterizes the abuse in such cases in that the experience goes far beyond what the child anticipated, *and more important, beyond what he was ready to agree to or go through.*

When the situation involves two boys of different ages—the elder taking advantage of the younger—it can be even more difficult for someone to realize that he has been abused. The relationship between strength and power is often less evident in such cases than it is when the abuser is an adult. It can be difficult to distinguish between *sexual exploration* between peers and *sexual exploitation*. Again, the answer lies in the balance or imbalance of power. An abuse has occurred between peers when the younger has been coerced into sexual activities demanded of him. Sometimes, as in the case of abuse that an older brother perpetrated, only years later—when time has provided perspective, and the younger child has had time to develop more emotionally—what was once considered an exchange of friendly services comes to be recognized as being abusive.

Abuse by Females

You may not consider yourself a victim of childhood sexual abuse if the person who molested you was a female. This is true for several reasons. First of all, we typically don't think of females as sexual offenders. We think of women as nurturers and caretakers, not someone who would deliberately hurt or use a child in this way. In fact, some females play on this perception by masking their inappropriate behavior as caretaking such as bathing, dressing, or comforting behavior toward the child. This can make it very difficult for a child to understand that he or she is being sexually abused.

This was what my client Andrew shared with me about how the sexual abuse by his mother, under the guise of caretaking, affected him:

> My mother used to insist on washing my genitals even after I was old enough to do it myself. She said it was because she needed to make sure that I was clean underneath my foreskin. I almost always got an erection and would feel horribly humiliated. For years I assumed there was something wrong with me, because I was sexually attracted to my own mother. It wasn't until years later that a therapist told me that it was natural for my penis to become erect when someone touched it—it didn't matter who touched it. The therapist also told me that I was too old for my mother to be washing me like that (she continued washing me until I became a teenager). I realize now that there were other inappropriate ways my mother acted around me—such as walking around in front of me naked, wanting me to hug her when she was naked, and wanting to take a nap with me with both of our clothes off. It has taken me a long time, but thanks to therapy, I can finally admit that my mother was being seductive toward me and that she actually molested me by touching my penis like that.

Females who sexually abuse children include relatives such as mothers, sisters, aunts, and grandmothers. They also include teachers, babysitters, childcare workers, coaches, camp counselors, and scout leaders. Female perpetrators molest both male and female children, as well as adolescents. One research study showed that a majority of female offenders were family members who tended to abuse within their role as caretakers; 25 percent were babysitters, teachers, or day-care workers (Ruden et al., 1995, p. 969).

Compared to males, female offenders are more likely to sexually assault with another person. Those who are coerced into sexual offending are motivated by fear and dependence upon the co-offender, and they tend to report a history of childhood sexual and physical abuse.

Self-initiated female offenders who sexually assault prepubescent children have been shown to display significant psychopathologies, and they are likely to display symptoms of post-traumatic stress disorder and depression. These female offenders report extensive physical and sexual abuse by caregivers.

Many cases of child sexual abuse involve women in a position of power over children, such as teachers. In the past fifteen years, we have witnessed an increase in the number of teachers who have been charged or convicted for sexual abuse of a student (the Mary Kay Le Tourneau case being the most widely publicized). One typology, the teacher lover/heterosexual nurturer, describes female offenders who sexually abuse adolescent boys within the context of an acquaintance or position-of-trust relationship. These females are less likely to report severe child maltreatment; instead, their sexual abuse behaviors often result from a dysfunctional adult relationship and attachment deficits.

Often sexual abuse by a female goes unreported by boys because they consider sex with an older female as a "rite of passage." For example, male adolescents who are sexually abused by a female teacher often feel as if they weren't abused at all, but that they willingly got involved sexually with the teacher. When the abuse is finally discovered, many of these former victims insist that, in fact, they felt they were the instigator of the sexual relationship. But whether or not the youth felt like he was abused, the truth is that sexual involvement with adults is harmful to children and adolescents. At their age they are simply not capable of making a free choice when it comes to sex with an adult.

Even when male victims do report the offense, they are frequently met with a response that assumes no real harm was done. But the truth is, many young men who became involved with an older female later suffer from significant problems, including hypersexuality, aggression against females, and difficulty trusting others.

Victimization by female offenders can have results just as devastating as victimization by male offenders, including (1) self-blame, (2) shame and guilt, (3) low self-esteem, (4) problems with sexual functioning, (5) avoidance of sex, (6) sexual compulsivity, and (7) substance abuse.

Sibling Sexual Abuse

Sibling sexual abuse is an insidiously destructive form of child abuse characterized by secrecy, shame, and concealment. Many researchers believe sibling incest to be the most underreported form of sexual abuse. It is not uncommon for victims to *minimize* the importance of the incestuous behaviors as an embarrassing part of childhood and be reluctant to disclose this shameful and seemingly irrelevant aspect of their childhood. Further, they seldom are able to connect the incestuous behavior with their current problems.

Sibling sexual abuse involves forcing or enticing a child or young person to take part in sexual activities, whether or not the child is aware of what is happening. The activities may involve physical contact, including assault by penetration (e.g., rape, oral sex, penetration of fingers or objects) or nonpenetrative acts such as masturbation, kissing, rubbing, and touching outside of clothing. It may also include noncontact activities, such as involving children in looking at or the production of sexual images or pornography, watching sexual activities, encouraging children to behave in sexually inappropriate ways, or grooming a child in preparation for abuse. Sexual abuse can take place online, and technology such as smart phones can be used to facilitate offline abuse.

Sibling sexual abuse is a particularly confusing form of incest due to the fact that victims often don't realize that they are being abused or that the abuser is causing them any damage, even though it is considered by most experts to be one of most damaging forms of incest.

Although sexual behavior between siblings is often considered to be "child sex play" or exploration that is mutual and consensual, in fact, it is often the case that sibling sexual abuse involves coercion, force, or an abuse of power and control. Typically, the abuse occurs when an older sibling coerces or forces a younger sibling to engage in sexual activities. An age difference can certainly be a factor, but the power imbalance can also be influenced by other factors such as cognitive ability. Gender may also present considerable power differences, particularly where family, culture, or religion portrays women and girls as being of lesser status than men and boys. Disabled children may be particularly vulnerable to sibling abuse.

The most common reported pattern of sibling sexual abuse involves an older brother abusing a younger sister. But a significant number of females have abused younger male siblings. In addition, younger siblings have been known to abuse older siblings, and same-sex abuse also occurs. Sexual behavior between siblings of the same age, or where the perpetrator was younger than the victim, can also take place, and with no coercion evident, and may still be abusive. The factor that primarily characterizes sibling sexual abuse is the exploitation of power. Dependency and power imbalances may be significant even when age differences are small.

Males are far less likely to report abuse than female victims because of how males are socialized. Males have a difficult time admitting that: (1) they have been victimized; (2) a female had control over them; (3) many males feel that engaging in sexual activity with an older female is an "initiation" into manhood; (4) they were sexually abused by a male. Males who were victimized by an older brother—especially if they found it physically pleasurable—may experience confusion about their sexual orientation.

Researchers Bank and Kahn found that most sibling incest falls into two categories: "nurturance-oriented incest" and "power-oriented incest." The former is characterized by expressions of affection and love, whereas the latter is characterized by force and domination.

Research has also demonstrated that sibling-perpetrated sexual abuse is typically accompanied by physical and emotional abuse and is considered to be the most violent form of child sexual abuse, according to some experts. According to Wiehe, "Violence between siblings is far more frequent than between adults or between parents and children." Sibling abuse is also characterized by, on the average, a greater number of sexual acts over a longer period of time, may start at an earlier age, and is more likely to involve sexual intercourse (as opposed to those who engaged in sexually abusive behaviors in a community setting).

It is uncertain whether the aftereffects of sibling sexual abuse differ from those of other forms of sexual abuse (guilt, shame, substance abuse, revictimization, diminished self-esteem, depression, difficulty maintaining relationships, and/or dissociative disorders). Wiehe suspects that sibling abuse "probably impacts greatest on self-esteem" and may, when the perpetrator is close in age to the victim, result in "difficulties in peer relationships, even from childhood." Survivors of sibling sexual abuse often speak about their inability to establish and maintain friendships and intimate relationships, specifically an inability to trust.

Clergy-Perpetrated Sexual Abuse (CPSA)

Indications are strong that sexual abuse by clergy (CPSA) has particularly devastating effects. According to research (Fogler et al., 2008) clergy-perpetrated sexual abuse can catastrophically alter the trajectory of the psychosocial, sexual, and spiritual development of a victim. Fogler et al. drew together the literature and provided some theoretical foundations presented in a special issue of the *Journal of Child Sexual Abuse*, attributing the damaging impact of sexual abuse by clergy to the way in which it undermines the victims' trust, sense of self, sexual identity, and social and cognitive development.

Brady (2008) drew strong parallels between clergy-perpetrated sexual abuse (CPSA) and abuse within the family, finding that they are both particularly damaging and difficult for children to deal with. These include the fact that:

- the families of many victims were closely allied with the life of their church—a "spiritual family," so to speak
- the abuse tended to occur over an extended period of time, similar to many cases of incest
- adults frequently did not believe reports of abuse when alerted to it, which often occurs in cases of incest
- church leaders tried to silence victims to avoid scandal, also a repeated theme in incest

Many victims did not disclose the abuse until adulthood, again similar to many cases of incest. A number of recent studies on CPSA shows that boys may be particularly susceptible to abuse of this type. A large-scale study on abuse allegations in the Catholic Church in the United States and a smaller study in Australia on allegations against Anglican clergy found that the majority of these allegations involved male victims.

Like many survivors of CSA, survivors of clergy abuse can experience numerous challenges throughout their lives, such as depression, suicidal ideation, suicide attempts, substance use disorders, and difficulties forming adult relationships. Although some controversy surrounds this, it is also believed by many experts that clergy abuse can damage the faith lives of its victims (many survivors interviewed described their experiences as "soul murder").

To understand this concept, it's important to consider how religious leaders are viewed in many congregations. These leaders are spiritual role models and, in some cases, are considered people through whom the divine acts. For some survivors, their perception of the abuse as children was that they were being directly assaulted by God.

In addition, perpetrators often carry out abuse in ways that entangle the abuse with children's faith lives. Many interviewed were abused in religious places such as sacristies or confessionals and/or were asked to engage in religious activities such as reciting prayers while they were being abused. In some cases, religious objects such as crucifies or holy water were used as part of the abuse.

Determining the prevalence of child sexual abuse within faith-based environments is difficult because these environments vary from small, independent congregations to massive organizations such as the Roman Catholic Church. The well-known John-Jay study found that 4,392 Catholic priests in the United States faced allegations of abuse between 1950 and 2002, about 4 percent of the total number of priests who served during that period. A study examining news reports of arrests for child sexual abuse in Protestant settings nationwide found 326 cases between 1999 and 2014.

Hopefully, the information on denial, minimization, repression, and suppression; the clarification of exactly what constitutes child sexual abuse; and the descriptions of lesser-known types of CSA have all helped you to take a closer look at whether you were a victim of child sexual abuse. If you are still confused, especially if you are filled with self-doubt because you have only a few memories or no memories, the following chapter will help you gain still more clarity.

You deserve to know the truth. It truly will set you free. It will help you to rid yourself of your debilitating shame and help you to break the cycle so that you will not be continually revictimized or treat those you love in the same ways you were treated.

It is incredibly painful to continue to face the truth, and you will likely go in and out of denial. It takes time and courage to face the truth about the fact that the people you love most and who are supposed to love you are also capable of abusing you. It takes time to let your mind comprehend the fact that the same people who were good to you at times could also be so cruel. It takes strength and time to process the pain you felt as a child due to the sexual abuse you suffered as a child and still feel today. You'll need to give yourself the time you need to become strong enough to face what you will need to face. And you'll need to be patient with yourself when you waffle between what is and isn't true.

Even though I encourage you to come out of denial and face the truth about what happened to you, you are the only one who will know when it is time to do so. Don't allow anyone to push you into facing the truth until you are ready. What happened to you may be beyond your ability to face right now. You may need to begin counseling or spend more time in counseling if you are already working with someone to become strong enough to face the truth. If this is true for you, don't add to your shame by being critical of yourself. There is no shame in taking the time you need to uncover and face the truth.

FIVE

OTHER REASONS FOR CONFUSION: SELF DOUBT, FUZZY MEMORIES

There are many who don't wish to sleep for fear of nightmares. Sadly, there are many who don't wish to wake for the same fear.
—Richelle Goodrich, *Dandelions: The Disappearance of Annabelle Fancher*

OVER THE YEARS I have had many people come to me because they suspected they had been sexually abused as a child. They often begin our first session the way my client Alyson did:

I have some vague feelings that I was sexually abused by my father, but what if I'm wrong? What if I'm just making it up?

I asked Alyson why she felt she might have been abused and she explained:

Well, I have a lot of the symptoms that I've learned are common for victims of sexual abuse. And lately I've felt really strange around my father. I don't know why, but I'm no longer comfortable in his presence, especially when we are alone. And I don't want him to touch me—even to hug me or give me a peck on the cheek.

I told Alyson, as I do all my clients who come to me with similar concerns, that it is good that she came into therapy and that I would be happy to work with her so she could determine the truth for herself.

Aside from denial, minimization, repression, and suppression, other reasons for confusion and self-doubt when it comes to child sexual abuse are *fuzzy memories or no memories* and *believing the lies that were told to you by the abuser or your family*. Let's address these reasons for self-doubt one by one.

PROBLEMS WITH MEMORY: FUZZY MEMORIES OR NO MEMORIES

Like Alyson, a major reason why you may question whether you were abused or hesitate to talk to someone about your experiences with sexual abuse is that you may not have a clear memory of what happened. You may have only vague memories or no memories at all—only a strong suspicion based on your feelings and perhaps your symptoms. It's difficult to believe your feelings when you have no or very few actual memories. And some people doubt the memories they do have, fearing that "I'm just imagining" or "I'm making this up."

Dissociation

One reason why you may have no memories or only vague memories is the common practice of victims to *dissociate*. Some victims *dissociated* (disconnected from themselves in the moment, taking their mind somewhere else), whereas others were traumatized so severely that they lost all memory of the attack—much like car accident victims often experience amnesia after the crash (repression).

According to the *Diagnostic and Statistical Manual of Mental Disorders 5th edition*, dissociation is a "disruption of and/or discontinuity in the normal integration of consciousness, memory, identity, perception, body representation, motor control and behavior." It is a normal phenomenon that everyone has experienced. Examples of mild dissociation include daydreaming, "highway hypnosis," or "getting lost" in a book or movie, all of which involve "losing touch" with an awareness of one's immediate surroundings.

During traumatic experience such as crime victimization, abuse, accidents, or other disasters, dissociation can help a person tolerate what might otherwise be too difficult to bear. In situations such as these, the person may dissociate (detach or disconnect) from the memory of the place, circumstances, and feelings surrounding the overwhelming event, thus mentally escaping from the fear, pain, shame, and horror.

When faced with an overwhelming situation from which there is no physical escape, children may learn to "go away" in their head. Children typically use this ability as a defense against physical and emotional pain or fear of that pain. By the process of dissociation, thoughts, feelings, memories, and perceptions of the trauma can be separated off in the mind. This allows the child to function normally.

For example, when a child is being sexually abused, to protect herself from the repeated invasion of her deepest inner self she may turn off the connection between her mind and her body, creating the sensation of "leaving one's body." This common defense mechanism helps the victim to survive the assault by numbing herself or otherwise separating herself from the trauma occurring to the body. In this way, although the child's body is being violated, the child does not have to "feel" what is happening to her. Many victims have described this situation as "being up on the ceiling, looking down on my own body" as the abuse occurred. It is as though the abuse is not happening to them but just to their body.

Dissociation helps the victim to survive the violation, but it can make it difficult to remember the details of the experience later. And it can create problems when it comes to victims coming to terms with whether they were actually abused. If you were not in your body when the abuse occurred, it will naturally affect your memory. If you don't "remember" the physical sensations of what the abuser did to your body or what you were made to do to the abuser's body, it can cause you to doubt your memory and add to your tendency to deny what occurred.

Tragically, ongoing traumatic events such as abuse are often not one-time events. For those who are repeatedly exposed to abuse, especially in childhood, dissociation is an extremely effective coping mechanism or skill. However, it can become a double-edged sword. It can protect the victim from awareness of pain in the short run, but a person who dissociates often may find that in the long run his sense of personal history and identity is affected.

Dissociative Amnesia

Dissociative amnesia is the inability to recall autobiographical information. For example, betrayal trauma theory holds that for incest survivors, dissociative amnesia serves to maintain connection with an attachment figure by excluding knowledge of the abuse (betrayal blindness). This, in turn, reduces or eliminates anxiety about the abuse, at least in the short run.

Betrayal trauma theory is based on attachment theory and is consistent with the view that it is adaptive to block from awareness most or all information about abuse (particularly incest) that a caregiver commits. Otherwise, total awareness of the abuse would acknowledge betrayal information that could endanger the attachment relationship. *Betrayal blindness* can be viewed as an adaptive reaction to a threat to the attachment relationship with the abuser and thus explains the underlying dissociative amnesia in survivors of incest. Under these circumstances, survivors often are unaware that they were abused, or will justify or even blame themselves for the abuse. In severe cases, victims often have little or no memory of the abuse or complete betrayal blindness. Under such conditions, dissociation is functional for the victim, at least for a time.

Due to dissociation, dissociative amnesia, or betrayal blindness, you may have to trust the fact that you wouldn't have the symptoms that you have and you wouldn't have the deep sense that "something happened" unless you had been sexually abused.

The Role of Alcohol and Drugs

Sometimes the reason victims don't have clear memories of the abuse but only vague feelings or emotional or physical symptoms is that the abuser drugged or plied then with alcohol. It is rather common for perpetrators to sedate their victims with alcohol or drugs to gain control of them and ensure that they will not tell anyone about the abuse. Victims who were sedated often describe their memories as "fuzzy" or have only short "snapshots" of memories that they may have a difficult time making sense of.

This was my client Kim's experience:

When I was a kid around nine years old, I would have the weirdest sensation just before I went to sleep at night. The room would start spinning around, and then I would feel like I had become very small and the room seemed huge. These sensations only lasted a few minutes, and then I would sink into sleep, but I remember them very clearly, and they were very disturbing. I don't remember when these sensations stopped, but they went on for years.

I first started drinking alcohol when I was a teenager; I think it was my senior year. All my friends were drinking, and I joined in. The drink that was most popular at that time was a screwdriver. Someone would get their hands on a bottle of vodka and everyone would fill their glasses with orange juice and vodka. But I hated the taste of vodka, and the orange juice didn't make the taste any better for me, so I drank beer instead. Somehow, I remembered the taste of vodka, although to my knowledge I hadn't had it before that first night with my friends.

I would try to drink all night like my friends, but I hated the feeling of being drunk. One night I managed to keep up with my friends and ended up feeling like I was spinning when I went to bed. It felt just like I'd felt before going to sleep when I was a kid.

The next day I started having flashes of memory about one of my babysitters being on top of me. The flashes didn't make any sense, so I just pushed them out of my head. After that the flashes often came when I smelled vodka or was around someone who drank it. This went on for years.

It wasn't until I began therapy in my early twenties that things started coming together. I had started having panic attacks whenever I was alone at night. Up until that time I'd always lived with someone—my parents, and then college roommates. But I had recently gotten a job in the city and an apartment of my own. The problem was, I couldn't sleep when I was alone, and just the thought of going to bed if no one else was in the house made me panic. I'd start hyperventilating, and this would make me dizzy, which just added to my panic.

I worked with the therapist for several months and got my panic attacks under control, but I couldn't figure out why I was having them or why I was afraid to be alone. My therapist asked me all kinds of questions: 'Did someone ever come into my room at night and scare me? Had I ever been sexually abused? Had I been date-raped at college? Was it possible that I had been given a date-rape drug at a party?' But I had no memory of anything like that happening to me.

It took us six more months of therapy for my memories to come back. It turned out that when I was about eight years old, my parents, who were both teachers, went on a trip to Africa for the purposes of research. We had no relatives close by, and they didn't want me to miss school, so they left me with a student of my father's—a young man who had been working as his intern. The young man had been very responsible, and my father was quite fond of him, so he assumed he would take good care of me. Unfortunately, the young man turned out to be a child molester. Each night he gave me enough vodka for me to pass out and then he molested me.

I had no actual memories of the abuse because I was unconscious from alcohol when he abused me. But I was able to piece the puzzle pieces together with the therapist and my parents. Most important, my father found out the young man had been arrested several times for child molestation by the time he was in his thirties, and we found out that it was part of his modus operandi to give kids alcohol.

YOUR SYMPTOMS AND TRIGGERS CAN BE YOUR "PROOF"

Let's compare your lack of specific memories with what often happens when someone has been in a traumatic car accident. Let's say that you wake up to find yourself in the hospital. You notice that one of your arms is in a sling and that one of your legs is in a cast and that you have cuts and bruises all over your body. There's no one around, and you feel panicked, thinking, *What happened to me?*

Then someone you know comes into your hospital room and tells you that you were in a horrible car accident. You feel shocked because you have absolutely no memory of it. Not only that, but you can't remember anything just before the accident.

Just because you have no memory of the accident doesn't mean that it didn't happen, right? You have the broken bones and the bruises to prove it.

The same is true of child sexual abuse. You may not have any memories, but you have the results of the abuse as proof that it did happen. You have your nightmares, your flashbacks, the unexplained pain in your vagina or anus, your negative reactions to being touched on certain parts of your body, your powerful reactions when you see a movie about someone being raped or about a child being molested. You have the fact that certain types of sexual acts or positions or certain kinds of touches turn you off, the fact that you dissociate when you are around certain people, places, and things. These are, in essence, your "memories."

The bottom line is that you may never have actual "memories" in the sense of being able to "remember" or "recall" actual events. But that doesn't mean you weren't abused. Many of the clients I have worked with who do not have tangible memories have other indicators that they were abused. Some have flashbacks—involuntary recurrent memories in which an individual has a sudden, usually powerful, reexperiencing of part of a trauma or elements of a past trauma. These experiences are often frightening, catapulting the person back in time. Others have what are called "body memories" such as pain in their genitals, anus, or breasts for no apparent (or medical) reasons and vaginismus (involuntary contractions of the vaginal muscles preventing penetration or making penetration extremely painful). Still others have such telltale symptoms as being repulsed by thoughts of sex, a fear of sex, an inability or repulsion to being touched, obsessive rape fantasies (either of someone forcing sex on you or you forcing yourself on someone else) or sexual addictions.

IMPLICIT MEMORIES

Trauma "memories" often manifest in intense physical, perceptual, and emotional reactions to everyday occurrences and objects (triggers). These emotional and physical responses, called "implicit memories," keep bringing the trauma alive in a former victim's body and emotions again and again, often many times a day. Their bodies tense, their hearts pound, they see horrifying images, and they feel fear, pain, or rage. They freeze in fear or feel a sudden wave of painful shame and lose the capacity to speak. They feel an intense impulse to run away and hide from others. Because child sexual abuse usually occurs in the context of family, neighborhood, and close attachment relationships, these arenas can become land mines full of potential triggers, tripped by the simplest daily routines.

As Janina Fisher, PhD, explains in her book *Transforming the Living Legacy of Trauma*, decades of research on the effects of trauma confirm that overwhelming experiences are less likely to be recalled as a series of images that we can describe in a clear coherent narrative. Instead, trauma is more likely to be remembered in the form of sensory elements without words—body sensations, emotions, changes in breathing or heart rate, bracing, tensing, or just feeling overwhelmed. When *implicit* memories are evoked by triggers, we re-experience the sense of danger, threat, humiliation, or impulses to flee that we experienced at the moment of threat—even if we have no conscious verbal memory of what happened.

When many former victims say "I don't remember anything," they don't realize that they *are*, in fact, remembering when they suddenly feel startled or afraid, when they feel shame or self-hatred, or when they start to tremble or shake. Because trauma is remembered emotionally and somatically more than in a narrative form that can be expressed verbally, former victims often feel confused or crazy. Without a memory of words or pictures, they simply do not recognize that what they are feeling *is* memory.

Most people also do not realize that we remember in different ways. With the *thinking brain* we can remember the story of what happened but without a lot of emotion connected to it. With our *sensory systems* we might "see" the images or "hear" the sounds connected to the event. Our emotions may allow us to remember how something felt. Our *bodies* might remember the impulses and movements and the physical sensations (sinking, tightening, trembling, feelings) experienced at the time.

Many former victims feel uncomfortable stating that they were sexually abused because they do not remember whole events, when their memories are fragmented, or unclear, or consist of a few images, rather than an entire mental video of the events. They doubt themselves and think, *It can't be true because I don't remember exactly what happened* or *I must be making this up or I would remember more clearly*. But it is important to realize that trauma cannot be remembered the same way other events are recalled because of the effects trauma has on the brain. When you feel the impulse to doubt your memory or intuition that something happened to you, remind yourself that recalling events as a story or narrative is not the only way to remember. You may be remembering a lot more than you think.

TRIGGERS

You may be surprised to learn how much you do remember when you include the feelings, thoughts, and physical reactions you experience when you are triggered. Generally, a *trigger* can be defined as any stimulus that is sufficiently reminiscent of a past event or process that it activates *implicit* (feelings, sensations, and nonverbal thoughts) or *explicit* (the what, when, and where of remembered events) memories in the present.

You may also be surprised to learn that your seeming "overreaction" to certain things has an explanation. For example, maybe you aren't a coward after all but just experiencing a lot of fear memories. You may not be an "angry person" but are simply experiencing feeling memories of anger that have been triggered when someone is selfish, controlling, or domineering.

Exercise: Discovering Your Triggers

- Start by noticing what events, sensory experiences, or people tend to trigger you (catapult you into the past, remind you of a sexual abuse experience or some aspect of an abuse experience).
- Begin making a list of these triggers.
- As time goes by, notice if you see patterns regarding what triggers you.

The most common triggers for those who experienced child sexual abuse are:

- sounds, smells, or tastes that remind you of the abuser or the environment where the abuse took place
- the smell of alcohol; someone being drunk
- being in the dark
- someone reminding you of your abuser
- someone coming too close to you physically
- someone wanting to be emotionally close to you before you are ready
- being alone with someone
- being alone with a stranger in a small room
- being around pornography or someone who is watching pornography
- family get-togethers (especially for those who were abused by a family member)
- being touched
- someone flirting with you or making sexual comments
- being seduced
- being manipulated (if you do this, I'll do that)
- being pressured (oh, come on, I know you'll like it if you just try)
- secrets/clandestine activities
- feelings of betrayal
- lies and cover-ups

- blackmail, threats
- being "bought"
- cameras and video cameras

Exercise: Identifying Your Triggers

- Take a close look at that list of triggers and decide which of them applies to you. Put a check mark next to each one that you believe might be a trigger for you.
- Now work on figuring out why a particular trigger reminds you of the abuse. It usually helps if you write your ideas on paper. Feel free to "free associate," meaning just let your ideas flow freely without censoring them. You can always go back later and cross out an idea if you no longer think it applies. The idea is to begin the process of labeling and understanding your triggers.

Remember: your symptoms and triggers *are* your memories. We will go into far more detail about triggers in chapters 12 and 13, including information on how to cope with triggers. In the meantime, continue to create your triggers list.

OTHER INDICATIONS THAT YOU WERE ABUSED

In addition to all the symptoms we have discussed, other indications that you were sexually abused may include:

- Knowledge that other children in the family were sexually abused. For example, if your sister has told you that your father, grandfather, uncle, or sibling sexually abused her, it is likely that he abused you as well, especially if you suffer from many of the symptoms listed earlier. Familial child molesters seldom abuse only one family member. In fact, it is a common occurrence for incestuous fathers to start with one child of a certain age and then move on to the next child as the first one gets older.
- Discovering that a family member or another person that you spent time with growing up has been arrested for child sexual abuse. If this person had access to you as a child, the chances are high that he or she abused you, especially if you have some of the symptoms common to child sexual abuse victims.

- Being afraid or repulsed every time you are around a person (especially if this is accompanied by unexplained pain in your vagina, breast, testicles, anus, or penis).
- The fact that you wake up at the same time every night for no apparent reason. This is a rather common occurrence for many victims because many abusers, especially family members, often wait until everyone is asleep to go into the child's room to molest her or him. Clients whose fathers went to bars at night typically wake up each night around 2 a.m. when their drunken father would come home.
- Being overly fearful and/or overly cautious about allowing your children to go to their friend's home or for anyone to babysit your children for fear that they will be molested. It is understandable that parents need to be cautious nowadays, but former victims of sexual abuse can go to extremes when it comes to worrying about their children being abused, which can be a sign that they themselves were abused.

My client Lucy had no memory of being sexually abused, but she had many other indicators that she had been. These included:

- frequently waking up at night with the sense that someone was standing over her in her bed
- painful intercourse in spite of the fact that she had been checked out medically and nothing was found to be wrong with her physically
- being unable to let anyone touch her breasts—even her husband
- being unable to allow her children to spend the night at a friend's house, and having an almost paranoid fear that her husband (or any man) would molest her children if they were left alone with them
- an inability to allow anyone else to change her babies' diapers for fear that they would molest the baby

It wasn't just one or two of these indicators, but the indicators in their entirety that finally led Lucy to believe that, in fact, she had been sexually abused in spite of the fact that she had no actual memories. If you find that you have many of the symptoms listed in this chapter, it may indicate that you were sexually abused in spite of not having memories of being abused. Although some of the symptoms you have can be explained by other trauma or other experiences, it is important to look at all your symptoms as a unit to see if they could point in the direction of childhood sexual abuse.

LIES YOU WERE TOLD

Still another reason why victims are often confused about whether they were sexually abused is that they were lied to so often that they no longer know what the truth is. Children who are sexually abused are told all kinds of lies. The perpetrator lies to them by telling them that it is OK for adults to have sex with children, that it is a good way for the child to learn about sex, or that it is the way adults show love toward one another. The perpetrator may tell his victim that his wife doesn't give him enough sex, and so he needs it from the child, or he may tell the child that she or he owes him because he has been so affectionate, or kind, or generous (gifts, money).

Most perpetrators can be extremely manipulative and convincing, capable of covering up their activities and charming parents as well as children. An abuser will seldom, if ever, admit to having molested a child. Even if he is caught in the act, he will blame someone else—usually the child. I had the experience of working with the father of a client who told me, "I wouldn't have touched her if she hadn't kept getting in my lap and wiggling all around until I got an erection. She acted like she wanted it."

Victims are also lied to by their families who tell them that they are making it up, that the perpetrator didn't mean any harm, or that he or she was just trying to be "friendly." Partners of sexual abusers often don't want to face the truth about the man or woman they love, so they lie to themselves when they see any sign of abuse or accuse their child of lying if she or he tells.

And finally, victims are lied to by society, which tells them they should come forward and tell if anyone tries to touch them "in their private places" but then doesn't believe them when they do come forward.

When it comes to childhood sexual abuse, people resist dealing with the truth on many levels. They deny that childhood sexual abuse occurs as frequently as it does; they deny that anyone *they* know is involved in it, either as victim or abuser; and they deny that it *really* harms the child. Some convince themselves that the child will not remember it, and thus they ease their own conscience. And, of course, some deny that they were ever sexually abused themselves, or that they themselves abused a child.

So, perpetrators lie about it, silent partners and family members ignore it, and victims repress it. With all these lies and all this denial going on, it makes sense that a child who is sexually abused will be confused about it and doubt their own reality. Moreover, a great deal of misinformation surrounds childhood sexual abuse.

In order to clear up some of the confusion, let's examine some common myths about childhood sexual abuse and counter them with facts—facts that have been validated by research, hundreds of clients' reports, and my own clinical work.

> MYTH: Adults need to teach children about sex so they will grow up to be good lovers.
> FACT: The opposite is true. Children who were sexually abused grow up to be adults who suffer from numerous sexual problems.

Victims of child sexual abuse report the following after-effects of having been abused: feeling stigmatized and confused about sexual and nonsexual encounters, wanting to avoid sexual contact, or an aversion to be touched in certain ways or on certain parts of their bodies, and involvement with compulsive sexual activity (sexual addiction, compulsive masturbation, addiction to pornography). In addition, in several research studies, a high percentage of prostitutes have reported histories of child sexual abuse.

Children need their developmental years in which to play and grow freely, unencumbered by sex. They need their time of innocence to mature and develop emotionally and sexually at their own pace. Then, as young adults ready to learn about sex, they can embark on that adventure with age-appropriate sex partners of their own choice.

> MYTH: Being sexual with a child doesn't really damage them as long as it doesn't include violence or pain.
> FACT: It always includes harm and pain, even if it is emotional rather than physical.

Evidence reveals that childhood sexual abuse of any kind results in emotional and psychological damage often lasting a lifetime. As mentioned, children need time to be children before they are capable of handling a sexual relationship. Sexuality foisted upon them too early amounts to abuse, and it is still abuse even in the complete absence of physical pain.

> MYTH: Most child molesters are strangers.
> FACT: The majority of abusers are relatives, most notably stepfathers, fathers, uncles, brothers, and grandfathers.

When asked to describe a sexual abuser, many people still think in terms of a stranger. Few realize that the majority of abusers are, in fact, relatives. *Eighty-five percent of childhood sexual abuse occurs in the home.*

According to David Finkelhor, a noted expert in child sexual abuse, having a stepfather constitutes one of the strongest risk factors, more than doubling a girl's chance of being sexually molested. Moreover, a stepfather is five times more likely than a natural father to sexually victimize a daughter.

Offenders are likely to be young and middle-aged adults; more than 90 percent of them are men, according to Finkelhor. However, not all incestuous abuse is necessarily perpetrated by adults. In a 2009 study by Finkelhor for the U.S. Justice Department, 35.8 percent of all sex crimes reported to the police were underage offenders. He also discovered that one in eight juvenile sex offenders was under the age of twelve.

LACK OF VALIDATION

Still another reason why you may doubt yourself is that when you were being abused, those around you may have acted as if it wasn't happening. No one acknowledged the abuse, so even when it was in their presence, you probably felt that it wasn't real, or that it wasn't that bad. This can add to your confusion now. (I've had clients whose mother walked in on their father abusing them but denied having seen this.) Because no one validated your experience, you couldn't trust your own experience and perceptions. And other people's denial probably led you to slip into denial yourself.

But it is important to trust your feelings and intuition, especially if you have many symptoms of sexual abuse. No one wants to "make up" having been sexually abused, so you wouldn't have these feelings if there wasn't truth to them.

Begin by making a commitment to tell yourself the truth about the experiences you do remember. You may have been trying to fool yourself by minimizing or whitewashing the things that happened to you, such as telling yourself it wasn't so bad. Admit to yourself that it was bad—bad enough to have affected you even today. Call the trauma by its real name: sexual abuse, sexual assault, rape, incest, molestation. You weren't "having an affair" or "having sex" with the abuser, and he was not "caressing you" or "making love to you."

Exercise: The Truth Book

Encourage yourself to tell the truth by starting a "truth book" in which you make a commitment to yourself to write only the truth—not the way you wish things were, but the way things actually were and the way you really feel about it. Getting your story down in black and white is a permanent testament to your feelings of shame, pain, fear, anger, and betrayal and eventually to your survival and recovery. Write in as much detail as possible the things you do remember, including what led up to the abuse, the abuse itself, and what happened after the abuse.

- Start by writing all the symptoms and other indicators that point to the strong possibility that you were abused.
- Now write all the details of the abuse that you can remember: what led up to the abuse, when it happened, where it happened, who did it, exactly how it was done, how many times it was done, how it felt, what happened afterward, including how you felt then and how you feel about it now. Write about how it has affected your life. If you had more than one abuser, write the details of each abuse experience separately.

By continuing to deny to yourself what happened to you, you are doing to yourself exactly what others have done to you in the past: You are negating and denying yourself. Allowing yourself to remember is a way of confirming in your own mind that you didn't just imagine it. It is also a powerful way for you to begin to realize that the abuse was not your fault. You can add to your truth book as time goes by and you have more memories or become more certain about the memories you have.

GIVE YOURSELF PERMISSION TO REMEMBER

Most victims of sexual abuse would just like to take a giant eraser and "make it all go away." Unfortunately, it will not go away, no matter what you try, and your efforts to deny it or forget it can cause other problems (e.g., alcohol or drug addiction) or prolong the pain (sexual acting out). Instead of continuing to deny the truth to yourself, make a commitment to tell yourself the truth.

My client Eva did just that. She determined that she would remember no matter how painful it was or how long it took. It started with her having flashbacks of someone coming into her room at night and sitting on her bed. She assumed it was her father but she couldn't make out his face. She didn't want it to be her father, she loved him and couldn't imagine he would do anything to hurt her. And yet she noticed that when she was in his presence, she felt odd, as if she was out of her body. She also noticed that sometimes if she used the bathroom after her father had, she smelled a scent that made her feel nauseous.

As time went by, she continued to write in her truth book and be open to exploring feelings that were coming up. She also made a point of observing how her interactions with her father made her feel. For example, she noticed that she often felt uncomfortable in his presence, so she made sure to never sit or stand next to him, and she managed to elude his attempts to hug her. Then she started noticing that her father often made off-color comments around her, such as making jokes about her breasts and her behind. She also noticed that he often looked her up and down, that he had a look on his face that was seductive and even sinister at times. And that smell in the bathroom—that turned out to be a sensory memory. She had a flashback one day of her father ejaculating on her stomach, and during the flashback she "remembered" the smell of his ejaculate. That was the same smell she sometimes smelled after her father had been in the bathroom. As painful as it was to admit to herself, the puzzle pieces were coming together, and Eva was having to admit to herself that her father had sexually abused her.

As we have been discussing in this and the previous chapter, it is very common for former victims of childhood sexual abuse to have no or little memory of the actual abuse. If you suspect you were abused, it can be helpful to talk to a therapist about your suspicions. A good therapist will not decide *for you* whether you were abused but will work with you, as I did with Eva, to explore your feelings and support you in your efforts to discover the truth for yourself.

Many misconceptions surround childhood sexual abuse, including *what constitutes abuse, who the abusers are, and how they operate.* The goal of this and the previous chapter was to help you gain more clarity about these issues. For some of you, these two chapters may have answered all your questions, and you may now feel very clear that you were sexually abused. Others may still feel confused and still have unanswered questions. My sense is that the upcoming chapters will likely help bring you more clarity and answer your questions. The more you learn about child sexual abuse, the less confused you will be as to whether you are, in fact, a victim.

SIX

STOP BLAMING YOURSELF

I will never understand why it is more shameful to be raped than to be a rapist.

—Sara Erdmann

EVEN IF YOU ARE now willing and able to acknowledge the abuse, there may still be something in the way of you fully recognizing that you were, in fact, a victim; you may still blame yourself for what happened. Coming to understand that the abuse was not your fault can continue to be difficult because of troubling beliefs that former victims tend to harbor.

Below are common reasons why you may hold fast to the idea that the abuse was your fault, along with explanations why these beliefs are absolutely untrue.

I WAS A WILLING PARTICIPANT

A common reason why many former victims blame themselves for the abuse is that they believe they were willing participants. Perpetrators of sexual abuse are master manipulators and can fool a child into thinking that he or she wanted the touching, enjoyed the touching, or actually initiated the sexual activities, when in reality this is not the case.

Sex abusers often engage in what is called "grooming," a process by which an offender draws a victim into a sexual relationship and maintains that relationship in secrecy. It is a gradual, calculated process that ensnares a child into a world in which he or she begins to feel like a willing participant in the sexual abuse. The perpetrator works to separate the child or adolescent from peers, typically fostering in the child a sense that he or she is special to the offender and giving a kind of attention or love to the child that he or she needs.

Typically, grooming includes six stages:

Stage 1—Targeting the victim. The offender targets the victim by sizing up the child's vulnerability, which includes his or her unmet needs, sense of isolation, and sense of low self-esteem. Children with less parental oversight are the most desirable prey.

Stage 2—Gaining the victim's trust. The offender gains the victim's trust by gathering information about the child, getting to know his or her needs and how to fill them.

Stage 3—Filling a need. Once the offender begins to fill the child's needs (extra attention, gifts), that adult may assume more noticeable importance in the child's life, and the child may begin to idealize the offender.

Stage 4—Developing a special relationship. The offender uses this special relationship with the child to create situations in which they are alone together (e.g., babysitting, tutoring, coaching, special trips). This isolation further reinforces a special connection. A special relationship can be even more reinforced when an offender cultivates a sense in the child that he or she is loved or appreciated in a way that others, not even parents, do not provide. Offenders are also good at creating a wedge between the child victim and his or her parents. This affords them more ability to manipulate the child.

Stage 5—Sexualizing the relationship. Once the offender has created a sufficient emotional dependence and trust, he or she progressively sexualizes the relationship. *Desensitization* occurs through talking, showing pictures or videos, or creating situations (like going swimming or taking a shower together) in which both offender and victim are naked. At this point, the adult exploits a child's natural curiosity and physical sensations when stimulated to advance the sexuality of the relationship.

Stage 6—Maintaining control. Once sexual abuse begins, the offender commonly uses secrecy, threats, and blaming the victim to maintain the child's continued participation and silence, especially because the sexual activity may cause the child to want to withdraw from the relationship. For example, it is common for offenders to threaten to hurt children if they tell, or to end the relationship or to take away the positive things they associate with the relationship such as gifts or outings. Blaming the child is another way the offender can maintain control.

Sometimes the initial relationship of trust between a child and an adult or older child transforms so gradually into one of sexual exploitation that the child barely notices it. Between the time when the attention a child is receiving seems to be something positive in the child's life and the moment when the sexual abuse begins, something significant has occurred. But the child may not be sure what it was and often remains confused about the person who has been significant to him but has now begun to abuse him.

In my client Elaine's case, the sexual abuse between her and her stepfather happened so gradually that for years she was confused as to whether she had been sexually abused or had willingly participated in the sexual relationship. In fact, she first came to see me because she was overwhelmed with guilt and shame about what she called "the affair" she had with her stepfather and her feeling that she had betrayed her mother by taking her husband from her.

Elaine's mother remarried when Elaine was nine years old. This made Elaine very happy because she liked her mother's new husband, Jacob, very much. Her own father had abandoned Elaine and her mother when she was two years old, and she missed having a father. Jacob treated her like she was his own daughter, taking her to the park, playing board games with her, and taking an interest in her schoolwork. He even included her in their marriage ceremony and took her with them on their honeymoon.

Because Elaine's mother worked at night, this often meant that Elaine and Jacob were left alone in the evening with him helping her with her homework and then watching TV together. Jacob tended to sit close to Elaine when he was helping her with her homework, and Elaine found comfort in this. Sometimes he put his arm around her or put his hand on her leg. When they watched TV at night, they got in the habit of snuggling up together under a quilt, especially in the winter. Over time, Elaine grew used to having Jacob be very physically close to her.

As she explained to me in our therapy sessions, Elaine couldn't remember exactly when things changed or how. She does remember that she and her stepfather got into the habit of scratching each other's backs while they watched TV. Then this changed to them rubbing each other on the chest and stomach as well. She told me she felt a little squeamish about this at first, but the feeling soon passed, and it began to feel as normal and natural as scratching each other's backs. Then it was just a matter of time before Jacob started touching her vagina. She knew this was wrong, but by that time she said it felt so good that she just let it happen.

Jacob's slow but progressive seduction of Elaine never felt to her like she was being used or misused. In fact, it felt to her like the sexual relationship that eventually developed was just as much her choice as his. She had no idea that he had been slowly, methodically grooming her for sex, just as surely as any other sex offender grooms his prey. And because she loved Jacob, just as much as any girl loves her father, Elaine was unwilling to admit that he had done anything wrong. Even years later, when Elaine discovered that Jacob was indeed a pedophile who had married once before to have access to another woman's child, she refused to believe that he might have married her mother for the same reason. It took months of therapy before Elaine stopped blaming herself for betraying her mother and began to realize that she had been cleverly manipulated into doing Jacob's bidding, that she was a victim of sexual abuse as surely as if a stranger had done this to her.

(It is a rather common practice for pedophiles to befriend and even marry a woman who has a child who is the abuser's preferred age in order to have access to the child. Some pedophiles even marry a woman with the specific goal of her having a child that he can molest.)

I AGREED TO IT

Many victims continue to feel shame and to blame themselves because they believe they "consented" to the sexual abuse. But it is very important for you to understand, once and for all, that you cannot be held responsible for so-called choices you made concerning the sexual abuse. This is because as a child you could not make a *free choice*. A free choice is made when you understand the consequences of your actions and when you are not coerced, bribed, intimidated, or threatened into satisfying someone else. You were only a child and, therefore, incapable of making such a decision. Even if you were a teenager when the abuse occurred, you could not give consent. As we now understand, teenagers' brains are not developed fully enough for them to be able to make free, conscious choices.

You were an innocent child when you were abused. Even if you were an experienced teenager, you were not emotionally and mentally equipped to deal with the ramifications of sexual abuse.

I DIDN'T STOP IT

Many of my clients have blamed themselves for not stopping the abuse. Typical comments include, "What was wrong with me, why did I just lie there?," "Why didn't I just run away?," and "Why didn't I try to push him away?" To fully understand why a sexual abuse victim didn't try to stop the abuse, we need to understand how the body is programmed to deal with trauma.

The human body typically reacts to an aggressive threat much the same way an animal does. We've all heard of the "fight or flight" reaction, but in reality, it is the Four F's—fight, flight, freeze, and fawn.

1. *Fight:* This response is activated when someone reacts aggressively to a threat. Humans do this by punching, hitting, kicking, scratching, or yelling in order to defend themselves.

2. *Flight:* This response is activated by fleeing or running away.
3. *Freeze:* When you know you can't fight back (because you will be over-powered) or try to run away, this response is activated. You may go numb or you may dissociate.
4. *Fawn:* This response has only recently been added to the list. It is activated when you try to appease or subdue your attacker in order to get away without being physically hurt, further injured, or killed.

Most former victims are extremely hard on themselves for not having done something different before, during, or after the assault. Learning a little about the autonomic nervous system will help you to gain more understanding and compassion for why you reacted the way you did to the abuse. Your body's nervous system is always assessing and responding to cues of safety, danger, or life threat in the environment. This is called "neuroception" and occurs automatically. It originates from the most primitive part of the brain, the brain stem. An aspect of polyvagal theory, neuroception stipulates that our actions are automatic and adaptive in the service of survival. In essence, before your brain can make meaning of an experience, your autonomic nervous system has already assessed the environment and begun to respond.

It is especially important to understand that if you froze, your inability to act was not your fault. It was your nervous system doing what it has biologically been programmed to do. It shut down as the last resort to keeping you alive. Although this may seem counterintuitive, if we look to the animal kingdom, we see that this is the way animals have learned to survive.

A smaller, physically weaker animal will not try to fight off a larger, more powerful attacker. Instead, instincts tell them to flee. If this doesn't work, they will freeze. Usually, this freeze mode is interpreted as the prey being dead, so the would-be attacker loses interest. We as humans react in similar ways. We don't try to fight off someone who is obviously much more powerful than we are. We know it is useless, and we fear that if we do try to fight him off, we risk being hurt even more.

Fawning behavior can be even more difficult to understand than freezing. Pete Walker coined this term in his book *Complex PTSD: From Surviving to Thriving.* Not only do you have to try to understand why you didn't fight off your perpetrator, but you have to try to justify the fact that you ended up being nice about it. This sense of being too compliant can be difficult to accept unless you realize that it was a very smart thing to do. In essence, your body and mind were telling you, "Do whatever you have to do to survive."

I ENJOYED IT

Another issue that may add to your tendency to blame yourself for the abuse is the question of receiving pleasure. Children are not equipped to deal with the complicated emotions surrounding sexuality; in fact, adults sometimes have a difficult time understanding the complex feelings that can come with sexual experiences. To make matters more confusing, although often emotional and physical pain are involved with child sexual abuse, there can be pleasure as well. Victims have often reported experiencing some physical pleasure, even with the most violent and sadistic types of sexual abuse. This confuses victims, causing them to believe that perhaps they gave consent or may even have instigated the sexual involvement. The reasoning goes like this: "If my body responded (a pleasurable sensation, an orgasm, an erection), it must mean that I wanted it."

It is very important to understand that experiencing physical pleasure does not signify consent. Our bodies are created to respond to physical touch—no matter who is doing the touching. And many victims of abuse were so deprived of affection that they spontaneously accept any physical attention, no matter what the source.

Often receiving some physical pleasure while being exploited and abused can create a split between body and mind—the body experiences pleasure while the mind feels disgusted by it. For this reason, it is important to understand that pain and pleasure are not necessarily contradictory. In fact, sexuality is one area where they can coexist. Many victims have described experiencing erotic feelings while at the same time experiencing severe pain.

What can complicate things even more is that in addition to experiencing physical pleasure in the midst of pain or humiliation, many victims report feeling important, recognized, or even loved by their abuser when he or she was molesting them. And so, although confusion and ambivalence about whether they were suffering or receiving pleasure is understandable, it doesn't have to be one or the other exclusively. It is possible to feel both, in different parts of oneself.

It is especially confusing for male victims who experience erections and/ or ejaculations during sexual abuse. Many people wrongly believe that if a boy or man is in a state of fear or anxiety, he will not be able to have an erection or to ejaculate, but this is simply not true. In fact, aggressors make a concerted effort to have their young male victims experience sexual excitation or orgasm for several reasons: when a victim interprets his sexual excitement as consensual participation, he feels all the more guilty or confused, which will discourage him from telling someone or making a complaint. He is also afraid that his disclosure will be discredited if he received physical pleasure, because popular reasoning would be, if it was really abuse, how could the boy have felt gratification? Moreover, to some offenders, ejaculation by his victim signifies that he has complete control over the child's body, and this apparent pleasure confirms the abuser's fantasy that the boy provoked what has happened, wished for it, or at the very least derived pleasure from it—thus making his actions less abusive.

In my client Daniel's case, his abuser, an older boy in the neighborhood, began innocently enough by telling Daniel he would teach him how big boys masturbated (the neighbor boy was sixteen; Daniel, thirteen). It became a game at first, with the two boys masturbating in front of each other to see who would ejaculate first. But then the older boy told Daniel he wanted to show him how to have "real sex" with girls when he got older. He convinced Daniel to take down his pants and before he knew it, the older boy was holding him down and sodomizing him. Daniel described the pain as excruciating. "I thought I was going to die, it hurt so bad."

When the older boy was finished, Daniel got angry with him and told him he never wanted to see him again. But the older boy told him, "You'll be back, you liked it. You got a hard on, didn't you?" All of a sudden Daniel was overwhelmed with shame because he remembered that, in fact, he had gotten an erection during the attack. This confused him, and he remembered telling himself that he must have enjoyed it or he wouldn't have gotten an erection. He did stay away from the older boy from that time forward, but it began a lifetime of self-doubt and concern that he might be homosexual or that he must be masochistic.

Boys who do end up being homosexual after being sexually abused by a male will often be confused as to whether they, in fact, "seduced' the abuser, or whether the abuser played a role in "initiating" them into homosexual sex. Dorais found that the stronger the boy's impression that he participated actively in the sexual experiences, the stronger his belief that he revealed himself to be homosexual, the more he will tend to internalize the burden of the abuse. The more he felt physical gratification, the more the abuse will seem to him to be an initiation into homosexuality.

I KEPT GOING BACK

Even after you have finally come to realize that you were an innocent child who did not *cause* the abuse or *choose* to be abused, you may still blame yourself for other aspects of the abuse, such as the fact that you kept going back to the abuser. If this is your situation, I ask you to think about the circumstances at the time of the abuse. For example, did you go back to the abuser because you were lonely, and this person paid a lot of attention to you? Or did he give you candy and let you play video games? Did he provide you with alcohol or drugs? Most important, I encourage you to remember that you were just a child and you can't really be held responsible for things you did as a child, because you simply were not old enough to think clearly or to always do the right thing— even in terms of taking care of yourself. To children, getting attention or getting candy can far outweigh the fact that they are putting themselves in danger by being around the molester. And you had no way of knowing just how damaging the abuse was to your self-esteem and your psyche.

This was my client Lenny's experience:

> My mother and father blame me for continuing to go over to my uncle's house, and they are right. I did go over there even after my uncle started abusing me. He was so nice to me, and he took me places, like the park, the circus, and the zoo. And my aunt was nice to me, too. She held me when I cried because my mother didn't seem to want me or because my father had yelled at me. I felt special when I was with them, but at home I was just ignored or yelled at.
>
> My mother says my uncle paid me for my silence. After she found out about it, she constantly yelled at me, 'Why did you go there? You must have known what was going to happen?' And the problem was, she was right. I did know what would happen. But it was either go there and put up with the abuse for a short time but be loved the rest of the time, or stay home where I would be ignored or yelled at all the time. I guess I made my choice.

THE TRUTH ABOUT CHILD SEXUAL ABUSERS

Because many victims continue to blame themselves for the abuse and/or have such a powerful need to protect their perpetrator, it is important to become educated about just who sexual perpetrators are and what their motives are. There is generally a lack of information about child molesters as well as a tremendous amount of misinformation. Earlier in the book I presented information about sexual abuse in general, in the form of "myths and truths." I will do the same thing here regarding perpetrators.

> MYTH: A father who "loses control" and molests his daughter is not as bad as the child molester who goes around stalking children.
> FACT: The incest offender is often just a child molester who stays home.

Many victims of child sexual abuse don't want to admit to themselves that their father, their abuser, should ever be seen as a typical "child molester." They want to believe, instead, that their father has a "special" relationship with them—that he loved them so much that he couldn't control his urges and ended up crossing the line, or that their mother didn't give him enough affection or sex and so their father had to seek it elsewhere. I even had a client who defended her father by saying:

> We were Catholic, and it is a sin for a man to go outside the home to get sex, even when his wife refuses him. So instead of sinning by having an affair, he stayed home and had sex with me, which is better.

The truth is, father-daughter incest is considered by most experts to be the most traumatic form of incestuous abuse, and incestuous abuse is considered the most traumatic form of childhood sexual abuse. General agreement is that the roots of incestuous assault are to be found in feelings of anger, insecurity, and isolation harbored by the aggressor. A father who molests his daughter may blame it on the victim or his wife, stress at work or alcohol abuse, unemployment, or myriad other "causes," but the truth is that the problem resides in himself as a result of deviant arousal and will travel with him wherever he goes. If you put him in another family, the molestations will still take place. In this sense, he is no different from any other child molester.

MYTH: A man sexually abuses children because his wife is not satisfying his sexual and emotional needs.

FACT: In many cases, childhood sexual abuse, like rape, is typically an act of violence and anger, not of sex.

Aggressors rarely commit childhood sexual abuse to satisfy purely sexual needs. Instead, they do it to meet a number of needs: to exercise power over someone; to seek revenge against a wife or mother for what he considers neglectful or abusive treatment; to seek from the child what he lacks so desperately in himself. Many child molesters are, in fact, unable to maintain a sexual relationship with an adult woman because of overriding feelings of inadequacy and insecurity.

MYTH: Child molesters, many of whom were themselves abused as children, are emotionally disturbed—therefore, they are not responsible for their behavior.

FACT: Some professionals do consider child molesters to be emotionally disturbed, but at no time are they rendered incapable of assuming responsibility for their actions.

It is true that many perpetrators were sexually abused as children. Many were exposed to sexual behavior in the home or to pornography. Current research has found that even more were physically abused as children. Such victimization is believed to underlie the attraction to and victimization of children. Remember, child sexual abuse, like adult rape, usually has more to do with violence and needing to have power over someone than it does with sex. Those who were abused as children, whether sexually, emotionally, or physically, often repeat the cycle of violence both as a way of gaining a sense of power over someone smaller and weaker than themselves and as a compulsion to repeat the abuse, this time with a different conclusion (they are now the one in power). But victimizing helpless children does not undo the childhood trauma they experienced. And there is no excuse for continuing the cycle of abuse and doing to another innocent child what was done to you.

My father was sexually abused by several people when he was growing up. I know that's why he molested me—he just couldn't help himself. How can I be angry with him when I know he was just out of control? And how can I tell anyone about what he did to me, and probably get him into trouble, when he was a victim, too?

Comments like this one that my client Sadie made are quite common.

Having been abused oneself does not guarantee that one will become an abuser. In fact, a majority of people who were abused do not go on to become abusers. Consider, for example, the fact that women seldom molest children, even though more girls are molested than boys. Many victims, such as you, seek help in order *not* to continue the cycle.

Many child molesters suffer from a disorder called *pedophilia*, a specific combination of "deviant arousal" and "character disorder." In lay terms, this means that the molester is both sexually excited by children and sees nothing wrong with gratifying himself at their expense. Although the consensus among the experts is that pedophiles do not consciously choose to be attracted to children, they do choose to *act* on their urges. No matter how much he may have been deprived or victimized, the child molester is still responsible for his actions. People who are sexually attracted to children do not have to act on it. They have several other options: to make certain they are never alone with a child, to seek professional help, or to warn other family members of the attraction.

Some argue that the child molester is out of control and that he has a compulsion to sexually abuse children, just as some people have a compulsion to drink or overeat. Child molesters are out of control, and they do need help. But we must not fall into the trap of excusing their behavior on these grounds, any more than we excuse a drunk driver who gets in a car accident and severely maims or kills the other driver. Yes, we can encourage him to seek help and even provide such help, but we hold him responsible for his choice to drive while intoxicated.

One thing brought up over and over when talking to perpetrators is that they do know right from wrong, they did know they needed help, but they chose not to get it. And they are generally more bent on denying responsibility for their actions and finding ways of continuing their behavior than they are on seeking help.

> MYTH: Just because a man makes a mistake and molests one child doesn't mean he will do it again with other children.
> FACT: It is rare that an offender molests one child and then stops.

Like an addict, when a sex offender molests one child, he quickly becomes hooked. In fact, the typical molester's sexual activity accelerates rather than dissipates after the first incident. His attempts often become more overt, the abuses occur more frequently, and the acts become more intrusive. The compulsion to repeat the sexual abuse is so great that the behavior is likely to continue even after he has been caught. Child molesters go to great lengths and put a vast amount of energy, time, and effort into maintaining their behavior, much like any addict. Many seek jobs, hobbies, and volunteer activities that involve youngsters. Some men have even been known to marry a woman in order to gain access to her children, in addition to molesting other children he has access to.

THE TRAITS OF CHILD SEX OFFENDERS

An effective way to help you understand once and for all that you were not to blame for the abuse is to learn more about the traits of child molesters. The reason this is important is it will help you to recognize that *you didn't cause the person who sexually abused you to become abusive*. He or she was already abusive before they met you. The fact is: *You didn't have to do anything to cause a molester to become abusive*. He abused you because it was inevitable due to his emotional makeup, his background, and his choices. In other words, this person was a ticking time bomb, just waiting to go off. You just happened to be in the vicinity when he did.

Sex offenders are classified according to victim, preference, and behavior. Several typologies of sex offenders have been proposed over the years, starting with Groth et al. in 1982—the fixated-regressed dichotomy of sex offending— which is still widely used today.

The most important distinction between child sexual abusers is whether or not they are pedophiles. Pedophiles' primary sexual attraction is to children, typically prepubescent children. With Groth's typology, pedophiles are referred to as "fixated offenders," whereas non-pedophiles are commonly referred to as "regressed offenders."

Please read the following information about these two types of abusers carefully. Notice what stands out to you, what you recognize in terms of possibly describing your abuser and his or her behavior.

The Fixated Offender

According to Groth et al., this offender is characterized as having a persistent, continual, and compulsive attraction to children. These individuals are usually diagnosed with pedophilia if they have recurrent, intense, sexually arousing fantasies of at least six months in duration involving prepubescent children. The fixated offender's actions are typically premeditated in nature and do not result from any perceived stress. In addition, this type of offender has had little to no age-appropriate sexual relationships. The fixated offender is more likely to choose victims who are male and not related to him. Pedophilia is a strong predictor of sexual recidivism.

The Regressed Offender

The regressed offender's behavior usually emerges in adulthood and tends to be precipitated by external stressors, as well as disordered childhood relationships and childhood abuse. Although not all sexual offenders report being sexually victimized during childhood, negative developmental experiences figure prominently in many types of sexual offending behavior. Recent research suggests that there may not be only one type of abuse that serves as a developmental risk factor for sexual offending. Instead, multiple types of abusive experiences, or a pathological family environment, may precede offending behaviors. In addition, studies have found that child sexual abusers have often experienced heightened sexuality in childhood, and juveniles who commit sexual offenses are more likely than non-sex offenders to report exposure to sexual violence, sexual abuse, emotional abuse, and neglect.

Stressors can be situational, such as unemployment, marital problems, and substance abuse, or can related to negative affective states such as loneliness, stress, isolation, or anxiety. This offender is not primarily attracted to children for sexual gratification and often engages with adult sex partners. He is more likely to choose victims who are females. He tends to victimize children to whom he has easy access—often his own children.

THE FBI TYPOLOGIES

The FBI expanded on the typologies of Groth et al. to include seven subgroups of offenders. I will not include this information here in the interest of space, but I encourage you to read about these subgroups in order to further understand child molesters.

WHY THE INFORMATION ON ABUSERS IS IMPORTANT

The information in this chapter, if absorbed and taken seriously, explains exactly what happens when a child or adolescent is sexually abused and explains exactly why it is that it is never the child's fault. Whenever you begin to doubt this truth, remind yourself:

- You did not consent to the abuse; you did not want to be abused but were manipulated by a master manipulator (groomed).
- If you were abused by a pedophile, you can be absolutely certain that you did nothing to attract him or her. The reason a pedophile was attracted to you is the same reason a heterosexual man is attracted to a woman. It is his *sexual orientation*. The same is true for pedophiles. Their sexual orientation is to children, plain and simple. *The reason a pedophile was drawn to you was because you were a child.*
- If you were abused by someone you love (your father, your grandfather, an uncle) who tried to convince you that this is what people who love each other do, or that he was trying to teach you about sex, remember: what he did to you was not only deviant behavior that is against the law, but behavior that was harmful to you. If he loved you, he wouldn't do things to you that harmed you.

- It is also important to recognize that your abuser has a deviant mind-set that colors and shapes the way he perceives things. In other words, you can't trust your abuser's version of the truth. So, if your abuser blamed you for the abuse by saying that you were seductive—that you dressed in seductive ways, and so on—and that is why he abused you, you now know that this isn't true. In his need to protect himself from the truth he will likely perceive things from an extremely distorted perspective.
- If your molester is an abusive person (i.e., he physically or emotionally abuses your mother or siblings), hopefully you can now begin to recognize that sexually abusing you is another example of his abusive nature and yet another way for him to dominate and control someone.
- If a teacher, coach, or another person of authority told you he was in love with you and this made you feel special remember: this same person may have told the same things to other students or teammates. Pedophiles often have a history of abusing several children at a time.
- If you were neglected or abused in your family, if you had no father in the house, or for any other reason you were particularly vulnerable, you were easy prey to a sex abuser. This means you were absolutely blameless.
- If your mother's boyfriend or new husband hit on you, and you were seduced by him, hopefully now you realize that a common tactic of pedophiles is to become involved with women who have children in order to gain easy access to a child.

SITUATIONS THAT MAKE IT ESPECIALLY DIFFICULT TO STOP BLAMING YOURSELF

Incest

It is especially difficult for children to avoid blaming themselves when it is a parent who sexually abused them. Children want to feel loved and accepted by their parents, and because of this they will make up all kinds of excuses for a parent's behavior—even abusive behavior.

Incest often leads to *traumatic bonding*, a form of relatedness in which one person mistreats the other with abuse, threats, intimidation, beatings, humiliation, and harassment but also provides attention, some form of affection, and connectedness. Traumatic bonding is particularly damaging because victims tend to take on the aberrant (abnormal or deviant) views of their abusers about the incestuous relationship. For example, molesters often believe that incest is not harmful to children and that it is a normal expression of love between a parent and child. As a result, victims frequently associate the abuse with a distorted form of caring and affection that later negatively influences their choice of romantic relationships. This can often lead to them entering into a series of abusive relationships. This traumatic bonding also discourages the victim from disclosing. In fact, many incest victims will go several rounds of psychological or psychiatric treatment as an adult before they risk revealing that incest occurred.

In addition to traumatic bonding, victims of incest often suffer from both *relational trauma* and *betrayal trauma*. Relational trauma leads to significant loss of trust in others and increased anger, hurt, and confusion about their family relationships, changes in beliefs about the safety of close relationships in general, and negative views of the self in relation to others.

Betrayal trauma encompasses the unique hurt associated with violation by those who have a basic obligation and duty to protect and nurture and extends to those who refuse to believe or help the victim, adding to the victim's traumatization. The threat to attachment needs is so profound that the victim may be impelled to disavow the betrayal that he or she experienced.

Psychologist Jennifer Freyd introduced the concept to explain the effects of trauma perpetrated by someone on whom a child depends. Freyd holds that betrayal trauma is more psychologically harmful than trauma committed or caused by a non-caregiver.

In addition to feeling betrayed when the perpetrator is your father or stepfather, some victims also feel betrayed by their mother. For example, in cases in which a mother chooses the abuser over her daughter, the abandonment by the mother may have a greater negative impact on her daughter than did the abuse itself. This rejection not only reinforces the victim's sense of worthlessness and shame, but also suggests to her that she somehow "deserved" the abuse. As a result, revictimization often becomes the rule rather than the exception, a self-fulfilling prophecy that validates the victim's sense of core unworthiness.

According to Christine Courtois and Richard Kluft, many effects that incest victims suffer are due to the following shame-related circumstances. These same circumstances often explain why incest victims persist in blaming themselves for the abuse:

- feeling like a passive or willing participant
- having an erotic response
- self-blame and shame
- observed or reported incest that continues

- parental blame and negative judgment
- failed institutional responses
- shaming and blaming from others
- ineffectual effort to stop the abuse

Sibling Abuse

Victims also tend to blame themselves when it comes to sibling abuse in particular because the younger sibling often believes that he or she was an equal participant. Although he may carry around a lot of guilt for breaking the incest taboo, often the younger sibling—who was being manipulated or dominated by his older sibling—seldom recognizes that he was a victim. Often, only years later, when time has provided perspective, what was considered a mutual arrangement comes to be recognized as being abusive.

This is what occurred with my client Jeffrey, starting when he was eight years old. His sister Barbara was four years older than he and was often left in charge of him while their parents worked. One afternoon, while he was taking a nap, Barbara came into his bed and began touching his penis. Although this alarmed him and he felt it as an intrusion, Jeffrey was afraid to push his sister away. She tended to get really angry when he refused to obey her and sometimes hit him to make him do so.

After a while it began to felt good, so Jeffrey went along with what his sister was doing. Eventually, Barbara began performing oral sex on him and insisted on him doing the same to her. This went on for several years, and Jeffrey suffered from a great deal of guilt and shame because of it, especially as he got older and realized that what was happening was wrong. But Jeffrey never thought of what happened to him as "molestation." He felt he and his sister were both guilty of incest. It wasn't until many years later, when Jeffrey started therapy with me, that he learned he had been victimized by his sister.

What needs to be stressed here is that victims of sibling abuse, perhaps more than any other victims of sexual abuse, either blame themselves for the abuse or believe they participated willingly. Many victims of sibling sexual abuse do not even identify themselves as victims. Older brothers and sisters may take advantage of the sexual naïveté of younger siblings to initially trick them into incestuous behaviors. Sexual behaviors are frequently couched in the context of play, and young victims are likely to find these activities pleasurable.

Consistent with other forms of child sexual abuse, sibling abuse can include a grooming aspect. In early stages, the sexual nature of the behaviors is less apparent, hidden in special hugs and games and play wrestling. A naive, young victim is unlikely to recognize these seemingly benign behaviors as inappropriate. Often a progression of the behaviors is involved, evolving over time to increasingly explicit, invasive, and even coercive sexual activities. These behaviors are more likely to be experienced by the victim negatively or as "wrong." However, a victim's participation in the activities to that point too often leads to the victim's confusion about responsibility for the behaviors.

As the abuse progresses, and a victim becomes aware of the meaning of the behaviors, he or she may become a more reluctant participant and attempt to resist. However, the offender's secret is protected due to threats of physical violence or threats of exposure and subsequent punishment. This particular threat is especially powerful if both parties are aware that their parents favor and will likely take the side of the offender. Victims who feel guilt and shame and who have an unsupportive family are unlikely to feel safe enough to report behavior for which they feel responsible.

Many victims carry the secret into adulthood, remaining confused about issues of mutuality and consequently feeling ridden with guilt, shame, and low self-esteem. The secret can be so deeply buried that adult survivors fail to connect the incestuous behaviors of their childhood with current life problems such as depression, anxiety, poor job performance, and interpersonal difficulties.

Abuse by Clergy

In the case of clergy abuse, victims often blame themselves because they hold the perpetrator in such high esteem that they can't imagine the person would do such a thing unless provoked. This was the situation with my client Gary who came from a devout Catholic family. Gary became an altar boy as soon as he was old enough to do so. He, like all the rest of the parishioners, adored the priest, a kind, gentle man. That is why it was so shocking to Gary when one day the priest asked him to stay after mass and then proceeded to molest him.

Gary just couldn't wrap his mind around what the priest had done. He knew it was a sin, and he knew that priests weren't supposed to be sexual. And so, in order to make sense of what had happened, he blamed himself. He decided he must have seduced the priest in some way. He even thought that because he had begun to masturbate a few months earlier, the priest must have known about it and was perhaps trying to punish him or teach him a lesson. He immediately stopped masturbating, and he tried never to look at the priest or stand too close to him, but nothing seemed to work. The only conclusion Gary could make was that he was a terrible sinner who had brought this on himself. Unfortunately, Gary's reaction—to blame himself—is a common one when it comes to clergy abuse.

Grooming by Religious Leaders

The grooming performed by religious leaders (priests, ministers) is even more effective and powerful than the typical grooming that occurs in most sexual abuse scenarios. Within the religious community, a predator may spend weeks, months, even years grooming a child in order to violate them sexually.

Susan Raine and Stephen Kent created a theoretical framework for analyzing and discussing religiously based child and teen sexual grooming, the first of its kind. They examined the research on abuse in a number of religious denominations around the world to show how some religious institutions and leadership figures in them can slowly cultivate children and their caregivers into harmful and illegal sexual activity.

Religious grooming frequently takes place in a context of unquestioned faith placed in sex offenders by children, parents, and staff. Perpetrators—who may include religious and spiritual leaders, volunteers, camp counselors in religious-based camps, and staff in religious schools—prepare the child and significant adults and create the environment for the abuse. Often, by the time the abuse actually happens, the child feels that he has given consent.

Abusers draw not only on their positions of power and authority as adults, which is potent in and of itself, but also on the assertions about God's will—the ultimate unquestionable authority for religious adherents—and a figure that can inspire fear as much as awe and love.

When abuse is disclosed, it is often met with skepticism or denial, even by the child's family. Because devotion to the institution shaped social identity, especially for more devout individuals, members of a religious community may be entirely suspicious of the victim's claims, favoring instead the religious figure and his or her status and perceived credibility. In some cases, an entire society may be groomed. For example, Ireland is an entire nation that exhibited a "culture of disbelief" toward abuse claims after widespread revelations of abuse in the 1990s. Members seems to have a greater loyalty to the institution than to the abused victims.

UNDERSTANDING THE LIMITATIONS OF BEING A CHILD

It will help you to stop blaming yourself for the abuse if you continue to remind yourself of the fact that you were just a child when it occurred. This is because victims of abuse often feel older than they were at the time, sometimes because they were given adult responsibilities when they were a child; sometimes because they had stepped in to take an adult role with siblings when their parents were absent or intoxicated; sometimes because their parents treated them like adults when it came to their expectations of how they should behave; sometimes because they had already experienced so much pain. But make no mistake about it: no matter how much you may have felt like an adult, you were really only a child, with a child's mind and a child's body.

More important, remember that you did not have the power of an adult. Because you were a child, you were limited in terms of what you could do to save yourself. If you tried to fight back, what chance did you have of overpowering your abuser? If you tried to run away, especially if your abuser was a family member, where would you go? If you tried to tell, who would believe you? The following exercise hopefully will help get this point across.

Exercise: Remind Yourself of How Powerless a Child Really Is

- The next time you are around children who are the age you were when you were first abused, take a close look at them. Pick a child who is the age that you were then and observe him or her closely.
- Notice how small the child is compared to the adults around her or him.
- Notice how easy it would be for an adult or older child to physically pin down the child or otherwise prevent her or him from leaving.
- Notice how dependent the child is on the adults around him or her. For example, the child may appear to be independent but she needs parents or adults to feed her, cloth her, drive her places.

This is what my client Ryan noticed during the exercise:

I was watching a little boy who was about nine years old. He was acting really tough, playing with some older kids while his mother talked to another woman at the mall. He was yelling and rough-housing with them, and I heard him brag about how strong he was, how he had taken karate lessons. All of a sudden, one of the bigger boys grabbed one of his arms and pinned it behind him. The younger boy struggled and tried his best to get free, but to no avail. He suddenly seemed very small and helpless.

The experience of watching this kid was really a wake-up call for me. When I was ten, I also felt really tough—like nothing or no one could hurt me. But that was just an illusion. I wasn't that tough at all. I couldn't fight off my molester. I was too small and too weak. All this time I had been fooling myself into thinking I could have fought him off if I'd wanted to. But I didn't have a chance in hell.

REALIZE THAT YOU WERE POWERLESS IN THE SITUATION

In order to accomplish this step, you must admit to yourself that you were *victimized* and that you had no control over the situation. For some of you, this will be very difficult, especially those of you who have defended against your suffering by convincing yourself that you could have changed things ("If only I'd"), those who need to operate under the delusion that you are always in control, and those who identified with the aggressor rather than admit you were a powerless victim.

If you were molested by a pedophile, the truth is that you were the victim of a mastermind, an expert manipulator—someone who was capable of outsmarting you. Although this might hurt your ego, it is absolutely the truth.

If you were molested by a family member, remind yourself of how powerful the incest taboo is and how realizing that you were breaking that taboo may have motivated you to keep the secret. Remind yourself of your role in the family and your powerful attachment to the family member who abused you, as well as the power your abuser likely had over you.

My hope is that the information in this chapter has finally convinced you that the abuse was not your fault. The following exercise will be helpful in cementing this reality into your mind and body.

Exercise: Letter to Your Inner Child

- If you can, find a photo of yourself as a child. If you find one of you taken at the time of the abuse, or when the abuse first began, this is ideal. Take a long look at the photo and try to connect emotionally with the child in the photo. Imagine how she or he was feeling, especially about the abuse.
- Now write a letter to (or talk to) the child in that photo (your inner child). Tell her all of what follows that applies to your situation:
  - Tell her that the abuse was not her fault.
  - Tell her that she was an innocent child who did not understand what was happening.
  - Tell him that he was outsmarted by a manipulative adult who had far more power and control than he did.
  - Tell him that it didn't matter that he went back—this didn't mean he wanted it.
  - Tell her that no matter what the abuser told her, she did not entice him with the way she dressed, the way she moved, or the way she looked at him.

- o Tell him that even if he felt some pleasure, it didn't mean he was a willing participant.
- o Tell her that it was normal for her body to respond.
- o Tell her that her body did not betray her.
- o Tell her that she is still lovable, still worthy of good things.

SEVEN

ACKNOWLEDGE YOUR PAIN
AND GRIEVE YOUR LOSSES

Emotional pain cannot kill you, but running from it can. Allow. Embrace.
Let yourself feel. Let yourself heal.

—Vironika Tugaleva

IF YOU ARE NOW WILLING to acknowledge that you were indeed a victim of child sexual abuse, congratulations. It is not an easy thing to admit, even to yourself. You've managed to get past your denial, your resistance to seeing yourself as a victim, and any other obstacle in your way of facing the truth. In doing so, you've taken a giant step forward.

On the other hand, some of you may continue to find reasons for not acknowledging that you were a victim of child sexual abuse, as well as reasons why you believe the abuse was your fault. If this is where you are, it's OK. But realize that these reasons are likely your way of avoiding the truth and avoiding your feelings about what happened. As long as you can tell yourself it didn't really happen, or that it was your fault, you don't have to face your feelings of shame, betrayal, pain, loss, fear, and anger. Please read this chapter anyway. It may help you to face your feelings even while you are still in denial.

For those of you who have managed to admit the truth to yourself, you need to take one more step in admitting what happened to you. You need to allow yourself to acknowledge how much you have suffered because of the sexual abuse. The trauma you endured caused you great shame, great pain, great fear, and great harm. You need to acknowledge this to yourself, identify this shame, pain, fear, and harm, and allow yourself to express your pent-up emotions because of them.

What happened to you was horrible. It was something no human being should have to suffer. But *ignoring* your pain, trying to put it behind you, or pretending that it wasn't as terrible as it was will not help the situation. *Denying* your shame and other emotions attached to the abuse simply doesn't work.

Trying to *avoid* being shamed again by becoming a perfectionist or by building a defensive wall between you and others doesn't work. *Isolating* yourself and avoiding others does not work. *Projecting* your shame onto others doesn't work.

What does work is to address your pain and other emotions head-on. This involves *allowing yourself to feel your emotions surrounding the abuse and providing yourself with compassion for your suffering*. All this will be difficult, more difficult for some than for others. But you don't have to do it alone or blindly, with no guidance. I will be with you all along the way, guiding you, encouraging you, offering you compassion and understanding.

The sexual abuse you endured not only caused you to feel shame, but other feelings as well, such as sadness, fear, and anger. You need to bring these feelings to the surface and find ways to release them in safe, nonthreatening ways. Unless you do this, your feelings of deep sadness about what happened to you will permeate your being, causing depression, lack of motivation, and emotional paralysis. Your feelings of fear and sense of betrayal will get in your way of being able to trust others and allowing yourself to be vulnerable with others. Your feelings of anger will cause you to act out—either against yourself or others.

THE CONSEQUENCES OF SHUTTING OFF FROM YOUR EMOTIONS

As humans we have an innate tendency to move away from pain and, instead, shut ourselves off from our emotions. We also tend to despise weakness and are taught, beginning in childhood, to "suck it up" when we are hurt—to be strong instead of allowing ourselves to cry or feel our pain. This is especially true for male children and children involved with sports. This belief system shows up in the numbers of children who are bullied because they are perceived as weak. And it shows up in the way we respond to the victims of bullies. We tell children, "Don't let them see you cry" instead of acknowledging to them how frightening, humiliating, and damaging it is to be taunted, pushed, or beaten by those who are bigger or stronger than they are. But the truth is, unless we face and process our emotions, we tend to either become a slave to them when they erupt out of us unannounced, or we become walking zombies, completely disconnected from our emotions.

Other consequences of avoiding your emotions can include:

- You end up not really knowing yourself. This is one of the most important consequences, because it includes not understanding why you react to situations the way you do and not knowing the difference between what you think you want and what you really need.

- You lose the good along with the bad. When you shut down the so-called negative feelings such as anger, fear, and sadness, you also shut down your ability to experience positive feelings such as joy and love.
- Your emotions become distorted or displaced. People who attempt to avoid their feelings often end up *projecting* onto other people (accusing others of being angry, sad, afraid when you are the one experiencing these emotions) or *displacing* their anger (taking their anger out on innocent people).
- It damages your relationships. The more you distance yourself from your feelings, the more distant you become from others, as well as yourself.

In this chapter I will guide you through the process of identifying and releasing your emotions connected with the abuse. At times it will be difficult, but it will be worth it. You'll feel more connected to yourself and to others.

Exercise: Connecting with Your Emotions

Many former victims are so disconnected from their emotions that they don't know what they are feeling at any given time. The following exercise will help you begin to identify and connect with your emotions.

- For this exercise, you will focus only on these four emotions—anger, sadness, fear, and shame/guilt—in that order.
- Begin by asking yourself, "Am I feeling angry?" Try to "go inside" to connect with this feeling or pay attention to whether you notice anger in your body (tense shoulders, tight jaw, clenched fists). If so, using the following sentence stem, complete the following several times (either out loud or in writing):
  - "I'm feeling angry because _____."
  - "I'm feeling angry because _____."
  - "I'm feeling angry because _____."
- Next, ask yourself, "Am I feeling sad?" Once again, complete the sentence stem:
  - "I'm feeling sad because _____."
  - "I'm feeling sad because _____."
  - "I'm feeling sad because _____."

- Now ask yourself, "Am I feeling afraid?" Complete the sentence stem:
  - "I'm feeling afraid because _____."
  - "I'm feeling afraid because _____."
  - "I'm feeling afraid because _____."
- Last but not least, ask yourself, "Am I feeling shame and/or guilt?"
  - "I'm feeling shame because _____."
  - "I'm feeling shame because _____."

Try to "check in" with yourself at least once a day to find out what you are feeling. This simple exercise will accomplish several things. First of all, it will help remind you to connect with yourself and your emotions instead of constantly "tuning out" or "going away" as might have become your habit from childhood. Second, it will get you in the habit of identifying what emotion (or emotions) you are feeling at any given time. Third, after you have made it a habit to identify what you are feeling, you can begin to address the question, "What do I need?" So, if you discover that you are angry, you can move on to discovering and then naming what you need in order to address the emotion of anger.

CONNECTING TO YOUR FEELINGS ABOUT THE ABUSE

Many former victims of sexual abuse have spent so much time holding themselves together, protecting themselves, and trying to "move on" that they never really had a chance to process the trauma they experienced and the pain they suffered. And shame can keep people from acknowledging just how horrible their abuse experiences were. On top of everything else, many former victims have a strong belief that to stop and acknowledge their pain and suffering is to "feel sorry for themselves" or "have a pity party."

"I simply don't believe in dredging up the past. I can't do anything to change it, so why put myself through the pain and agony of remembering it and having to feel it all over again. Better to keep the past where it belongs, I say—in the past."

My client Bill's attitude is very common among former victims. They not only see no advantage to expressing their emotions connected to the abuse, but they see an advantage in keeping all those feelings buried.

But the truth is, we can't heal what we don't feel. We can't heal what we continue to deny, minimize, repress, or suppress. Instead of staying in denial or pretending that you weren't hurt by the abuse, you need to admit to yourself how truly devastating being sexually abused was for you. Instead of dismissing your wounds in order to appear strong, begin to identify and attend to your wounds the way you would a physical wound. If you had a large cut on your body, you wouldn't just ignore it, hoping it would just go away. You would know that you needed to cleanse the wound and put medicine on it to help it to heal.

The First Step: Connect with Your Suffering

When you think about the sexual abuse that you suffered, what do you feel? Do you feel sad for the girl or boy that you were? Do you feel sad that you had to handle the trauma all by yourself? Sad that no one was there to help you? Feeling sad for the child or adolescent that you were is completely appropriate. In fact, it is necessary if you are to heal your shame. This is due to the fact that in order to heal your shame, you must have self-compassion.

Self-compassion is the antidote to shame. Therefore, it is crucial that you learn how to provide it for yourself—that you begin to view yourself from a more compassionate perspective instead of being as critical of yourself as former victims tend to be. As it is with most poisons, the toxicity of shame needs to be neutralized by another substance if we are truly going to save the patient. Compassion is the only thing that can neutralize shame.

Kristin Neff, professor of psychology at the University of Texas at Austin, is the leading researcher in the growing field of self-compassion. In her ground-breaking book *Self-Compassion* (2011), she defines self-compassion as

> being open to and moved by one's own suffering, experiencing feelings of caring and kindness toward oneself, taking an understanding, nonjudgmental attitude toward one's inadequacies and failures, and recognizing that one's experience is part of the common human experience. (p. 224)

Whereas compassion is the ability to feel and connect with the suffering of another human being, self-compassion is the ability to feel and connect with *one's own suffering*. More specifically for our purposes, self-compassion is the act of extending compassion to one's self in instances of perceived inadequacy, failure, or general suffering.

Self-compassion encourages you to begin to treat yourself and talk to yourself with the same kindness, caring, and compassion you would show a good friend or a beloved child. Just as connecting with the suffering of others has been shown to comfort and even help heal others' ailments or problems, connecting with your own suffering will do the same for you.

You have, within your power, the ability to heal your shame through self-compassion. You can learn specific compassionate attitudes and skills that can reverse your tendency to view yourself in a blaming, condemning, and self-critical way. This will help those of you who continue to blame yourself for the abuse to begin to understand that you did nothing to deserve the abuse, but that you do deserve to be treated with respect by others. And it will help those who have built up a defensive wall to protect yourself from further shaming by making it safe for you to face the shaming events of your childhood and, therefore, no longer need to defend yourself against them.

Exercise: How to Connect with Your Suffering

You can't truly experience self-compassion if you can't connect with your suffering and the emotions surrounding the abuse. The following exercise may help:

- Find a quiet place where you can be alone, let down your guard, and think about the abuse.
- Either in your head or on paper, complete the following sentence: "When I think about the abuse I suffered, I feel _____."
- Complete this sentence several times until you have no more responses.

You may feel surprised to discover all the emotions you feel due of the abuse—sad, betrayed, afraid, angry, guilty, or ashamed.

- Now, for each emotion that you identified, complete the following sentence, "I feel sad because _____."
- Complete each sentence several times. For example:
  "I feel sad because I was so all alone."
  "I feel sad because I was just a little girl, and he was a huge man, and there was no one to protect me."
  "I feel sad because there was no one to comfort me afterward."
  "I feel sad because from that day forward I felt like a terrible person."
- Continue the same process with every feeling you uncover:
  "I feel afraid because _____."
  "I feel ashamed because _____."
  "I feel angry that _____."

Instead of feeling sad or afraid or angry or ashamed, some people feel self-critical when they think about the sexual abuse. Do you still blame yourself for putting yourself in the situation? Do you still blame yourself for not telling someone, or for going back to the abuser? Or do you just not connect at all to the child or adolescent you were? The following exercise may help if you are feeling any of the above.

Exercise: Seeing Your Experience from a Different Perspective

- Write an accounting of one of your experiences with child sexual abuse from the perspective of a stranger or a storyteller. For example, your story might begin something like this: "There was once a little girl who had a mean stepfather who sexually abused her . . ."
- This technique can help you view your childhood abuse experience from a different perspective entirely. In fact, this way of telling your story has helped some victims to recognize their suffering for the very first time.

Here is what my client Hope wrote:

There was once a little girl who had a mean stepfather who sexually abused her. She was afraid to tell her mother, because she always defended her stepfather, no matter how mean he was. She knew her mother would take her stepfather's side and not believe her. And because her stepfather threated to kill her if she ever told, she silently endured this horrible abuse for years. Eventually, she felt so desperate and hopeless that she tried to commit suicide. She took a handful of her mother's pills and became unconscious. She was admitted to the hospital still unconscious and remained that way for several days. Her mother cried and cried because she was afraid that she had lost her daughter. Eventually, the little girl woke up, but she was never the same. For years she walked around as if she were just half awake, not feeling much of anything.

- Once you have written your story, take a close look at it. Does your story help you to feel more compassion for yourself? Does it provide you with a different perspective about what happened to you? Does it help you remove any denial or minimization you have felt about your abuse? Does it help you connect with your emotions about the abuse? If so, write about any insights and feelings that your story elicits in you.

Here is Hope's experience from doing the writing:

Writing a story about what happened to me was a bit strange at first, but then I really got into it. It helped me see my experience differently than I have ever seen it before. First of all, I'm not that in touch with myself or my feelings, so it helped me to really experience what happened to me, and I realized how bad it was. I already knew most of the story, but I was shocked when I found myself writing about the suicide attempt. I had forgotten all about that. Seeing it written down made me face what really happened. In that moment I really did feel more compassion for that little girl—me. If someone else had gone to that extreme, I would know for sure that she was suffering unbearable pain.

ACKNOWLEDGE YOUR PAIN AND GRIEVE YOUR LOSSES

Grief is a deep anguish in response to a significant loss. Just as you need to grieve when someone you love dies—whether it is a beloved pet, a close and loyal friend, or a relative—you need to grieve the loss of your innocence, your sense of safety, the loss of the love and respect you once had for your abuser, the loss of your connection with others or with your own body. But unfortunately, we tend to resist expressing our feelings of grief and sadness—and for good reasons.

Some people fear that if they begin to grieve, they will never stop. Others are afraid they will become depressed if they allow themselves to feel their pain. And others sense that they don't have the emotional strength to endure the pain. Still others fear that allowing themselves to grieve will transport them back in time to childhood, and they will be unable to come back to the present. These are all valid fears, so let's address them one by one:

- *The fear of becoming overwhelmed with the pain and grief.* Many former victims resist feeling the pain surrounding the abuse because they sense that there is so much pain that they could easily become overwhelmed by it once they allow themselves to feel it. They sense that because they have held in the pain for so long that once unleashed it will create a flood of emotions that they will not be able to contain again. There can be some truth to this in the beginning.

  I had been working with my client Angela for more than a year. She suspected that her father had sexually abused her, but she struggled with whether she could trust her memories. Periodically she would see images of her father forcing her to touch his penis. She would wake up from dreams where he was standing over her with a menacing look on his face, and she frequently experienced pain in her vagina and anus.

  For months she vacillated back and forth between believing that her father had sexually abused her and thinking she was making it up.

"Why don't I have clear memories? Why only these dreams and vague memories?" she complained.

In time, Angela became clear that, in fact, her father had sexually abused her for years, starting when she was about six years old and continuing until she was around eleven.

> Facing the truth about what my father did to me has broken my heart. I loved him so much, and I looked up to him. I didn't want to admit to myself that he'd done these terrible things to me. I mean, what kind of a man molests his own daughter?

The months ahead were filled with tears as Angela mourned her father and her relationship with him.

> It is as if he has died, although he is very much alive. I haven't seen him for a couple of months, and I grieve him every day. Some days I just can't stop crying. It scares me. I'm afraid I'll never stop—that I'll go insane.

It is painful to come face-to-face with the reality that another human being could hurt and betray you the way your abuser did, especially if that person was someone you loved or admired. It is painful to realize that someone you cared for so deeply could be so callous, cruel, or selfish. And it is painful to remember how hurt you felt, how betrayed you felt, and how frightened you were.

Once you allow yourself to connect with your pain, the tears may gush in huge waves, as they did with Angela. These waves of sorrow may last for quite a long time, and you may become afraid that you will never stop crying. But as a very wise therapist once told me when I asked her, "How long am I going to cry like this?," "You will cry until you have no more tears." Although it can be scary when you end up crying for a long time, the good news is that your body will take care of you. Your sobs may cause you to cough and even choke momentarily at times—you may even need to throw up. But this is just your body's way of helping you to expel and clear both the physical and emotional reminders of the abuse. Your body will also not allow you to cry to the point where you are endangering yourself. You will either become short of breath and will need to stop to catch your breath, or you will become so exhausted that you fall asleep.

- *The fear of becoming so overwhelmed with grief that you become depressed.* Again, this is a very rational fear, but the truth is, you are more likely to become depressed if you do *not* allow yourself to express your pain and grief. Nevertheless, we don't want you to get stuck in your sadness and grief to the point that you can no longer experience any good in the world. I will teach you techniques that will help you move through your sadness instead of getting stuck in it. (Of course, if you feel you are getting stuck in your sadness or grief and are becoming deeply depressed, please consult a psychotherapist or medical doctor.)
- *The fear that you do not have the emotional strength to endure the pain.* You know yourself better than anyone else. You know how fragile you are at any given time. You may not feel strong enough at this moment to face your pain, and that is OK. But if your pain and grief come up on their own, organically, while you are reading this book, consider this: It has been my experience that clients aren't confronted with the truth about their abuse or the feelings that accompany it until they are ready. If you have been crying throughout this book, your body is telling you that you are sad and that you need to let out the tears. It is one thing to try to force yourself to grieve your losses associated with the abuse; it's another to hold back the tears once they start flowing spontaneously. And remember, you may be a lot stronger than you think. You may only need to consider what you have already survived to be reminded of just how strong you are.
- *The fear that you will get stuck in the past.* Although this is a valid fear, you can learn ways of grounding yourself in the present so that you don't stay stuck in your past feelings or in your past traumas.

Throughout this chapter I will provide techniques and strategies to help you make sure that your worst fears don't come true. I am confident that you can engage in these processes without being further traumatized. If, however, you feel too overwhelmed or traumatized, I recommend that you seek professional help.

One way of achieving balance is to allow yourself to face your pain, practice self-compassion, and then rest for a few days until you can build up enough strength to process another piece of an abuse experience or another incident of abuse.

As a victim of child sexual abuse, you have much to grieve—the loss of your innocence, the betrayal of trust, the loss of the belief that you were safe and protected, even the loss of the idea that the world was a safe place. Give yourself permission to grieve your losses.

Exercise: Write about Your Pain

- Begin by making a list of your sexual abuse experiences. Include your approximate age when the abuse began, the person who abused you, what this abuser did to you, and how long (months, years) the abuse lasted. This can be overwhelming, so take your time. If you were abused by multiple perpetrators, it may take you several sittings to complete your list. If you are in an especially fragile place right now, don't attempt to write about all of your traumas. Do the best you can even if it means you can only write about one abuse experience.

  Your description may be rather brief, as it was for my client Shana:

  When I was five years old, I was sexually abused by my grandfather during an entire summer when I stayed with him. He began by touching my genitals, but he progressed to inserting his finger inside me.

  On the other hand, if you were sexually abused by multiple abusers who performed numerous sexual acts on you, your description may be rather long, as it was for my client Chloe:

  My first abuser was my cousin when I was eight. He forced me to perform oral sex on him. This lasted most of my childhood whenever he came to visit until I became old enough and strong enough to say no to him.

  My second abuser was my uncle—the father of the cousin who abused me. It started when I was eleven. I figured out that this is where my cousin learned to abuse other people—I'm sure his father abused him. My uncle was more brutal than my cousin. He raped me and said horrible things to me like, 'You're worthless. This is the only thing you're good for.' This went on until I was in high school when I got strong enough to fight him off.

  My third abuser was my swimming coach in high school. I was already emotionally broken by my uncle, so I didn't put up a fight. He cornered me in the gym one night and forced me to have intercourse with him. It only happened once, because I quit the team.

- Pay attention to how you are feeling as you write your descriptions. If you notice you are becoming numb, dizzy, or disoriented, stop to ground yourself (refer to the instructions for grounding in chapter 1).

- Try to identify and connect with the emotions you felt with each incident of sexual abuse. You may notice that you are feeling shame, pain, fear, anger, or betrayal. Allow yourself to feel all these emotions.

Here is how Shana from the example above responded:

When my grandfather molested me, I felt so disappointed and so betrayed. Before he started touching me in this way, I loved him so much. I felt so special to him. But afterward I felt so sad. I no longer felt loved by him, and it was a huge loss in my life.

And here is how Chloe responded:

When my uncle raped me, I felt small and helpless. I was terrified. I think it was the first time in my life that I was confronted with the fact that there are people in the world who want to hurt you, people who actually get off on hurting you. Even though my cousin had already molested me, it felt different with my uncle. I didn't get the sense that my cousin wanted to hurt me. I naively thought that if I told my uncle he was hurting me, he'd stop. But he just laughed. Something inside me changed after that. My entire world view changed. I feel sad now just thinking about it. I wonder what my life would have been—who I would have been—if my uncle hadn't violated me in that way.

Notice that with both of these descriptions not only did the writer describe her emotions, but she expressed grief concerning what she lost.

ADDRESSING YOUR PAIN AND SUFFERING

Your pain doesn't go away because you ignore it. In fact, unexpressed emotions tend to fester and grow. Offering yourself self-compassion involves first acknowledging your pain and suffering and then comforting yourself.

Exercise: Talking to Your Pain and Suffering

1. Sit quietly with no distractions around you.
2. Take deep breaths.
3. See if you can find your pain by either visualizing it or noticing it in your body. You can imagine it to be an object, a color, or a shape.
4. Imagine that you are reaching inside and pulling out your pain.
5. Now imagine that you are placing your pain in the palm of your hand. Lift your palm up to your lips.

6. Whisper these words to your pain and suffering:

"I see you."

"I hear you."

"I'm so sorry you have suffered."

Once you have begun to acknowledge your pain and suffering, you have taken the first step toward offering yourself self-compassion. Most victims of sexual abuse have received very little if any compassion or empathy for the suffering they have endured. Many victims are so busy blaming and shaming themselves that they seldom if ever offer compassion for themselves. And because victims seldom tell anyone that they were abused, they miss opportunities for others to provide them with empathy and compassion. Even when they do tell, they aren't likely to receive compassion, but instead are questioned or even disbelieved.

Having self-compassion, connecting to one's own suffering, is a way of *validating* yourself, your feelings, your perception, and your experience. The sexual abuse you have suffered has done terrible things to you. It has damaged your self-esteem and self-confidence. It has made you feel so bad about yourself that you began to feel unworthy and unlovable. It caused you to behave in ways that harmed you and others. These and other consequences of sexual abuse are some of the ways you have suffered at the hands of your abuser(s). You need to acknowledge these wounds in order to heal them. If, on the other hand, you continue to minimize or deny how you have been harmed by the sexual abuse, not only will you not have the opportunity to heal your wounds, but you will be adding to them day after day.

LETTING IT ALL SINK IN

Think about how difficult it has been for you to have to live through the trauma of sexual abuse. Ask yourself: *Have I taken the time to acknowledge my own suffering? Or have I tried to just put it away—out of sight and out of mind?*

Take time now to let it really sink in: the pain, shame, and fear you are faced with every day. Allow yourself to feel compassion for what you have endured and for what you will likely continue to endure. Acknowledge all the pain you have endured due to the sexual abuse you experienced.

Exercise: Your Experiences of Abuse

Use the same descriptions of your experiences of sexual abuse that you wrote about earlier for this exercise.

- Read through one of your descriptions carefully. Take your time so that you can acknowledge how much you suffered because of what this person did to you.
- Now take a deep breath. This will allow you to absorb the fact that you suffered from this abuse experience.
- Allow yourself to experience whatever feelings arise in you. Don't hold back. Remember, acknowledging your feelings is a major part of healing.

Exercise: Self-Compassionate Words

1. Using the same list of incidents as before, say or write something that expresses compassion toward yourself for one of the incidents on your list. Do this as if someone outside you is saying the words. For example, "I'm so sorry that your grandfather betrayed you like he did. He took your love for him and turned it into something dirty and shameful," or "What your uncle did to you was horrible. It must have made you feel so lost and alone. And to learn the hard way, and at such as early age, that there are people in the world who deliberately want to hurt you— that must have been especially painful."
2. If you can't think of something to say to yourself, think of what a supportive friend or family member might say if you told them about how this person sexually abused you.

If at all possible, over time, go through this same process with each incidence of abuse that you wrote about—but don't rush it. Focus on one description at a time. If you feel overwhelmed, don't push yourself to move forward. Just stay with your feelings and take a rest.

Take time between processing each item on your list. The optimum would be to allow yourself to complete this process for each abuse experience you endured, but this may not be possible. You don't want to become so overwhelmed that it becomes traumatic or debilitating.

At a later time, think about the entirety of everything you have been through because of your sexual abuse experiences—all the pain, all the suffering. Say to yourself (out loud or silently) the words that will most comfort you regarding how you are suffering—*the words you most long to hear.* Again, if you experience difficulty, it might help if you imagine someone who has been kind and loving toward you saying the words. If words don't come to mind, say things to yourself such as:

"I'm so sorry you were mistreated in this way."
"No one should have to endure treatment like that."
"Oh, how horrible. That must have been so painful, so humiliating."
"I'm sorry you've had to endure this all alone."

- Get a cup of hot tea and sit quietly, letting it all sink in—all the pain, all the humiliation. Put your arms around your shoulders or across your stomach, as if someone is hugging you. Let yourself feel comforted. Let your tears flow if you feel sad. Know that the way you have been treated is not OK.
- Think about how much the abuse has damaged your self-confidence and self-esteem, how much it has affected your ability to trust, how much the abuse affected your ability to have healthy relationships, how much it affected your sexuality. Give yourself credit for how hard you have to work just to maintain your sanity. This acknowledgment and compassion for all you've suffered will help you gain the strength and courage to heal.

You've just offered yourself self-compassion. It isn't a complicated process to learn. It is just about acknowledging your suffering and attending to that suffering. It is just about treating yourself with the same kindness, understanding, and care you would give a wounded loved one.

EIGHT

GIVE YOURSELF PERMISSION TO BE ANGRY

Bitterness is like cancer. It eats upon the host. But anger is like fire. It burns it all clean.

—Maya Angelou

WHEREAS SELF-COMPASSION is the antidote to shame, anger comes in a close second when it comes to helping you alleviate shame. This is because when you allow yourself to become angry at your perpetrator, you automatically diminish the amount of shame you feel, primarily because you are not blaming yourself as much.

On the other hand, when you unfairly blame yourself for the sexual abuse, you continue to add to your shame. You take the anger that you should be feeling toward your abuser and you put it on yourself. Getting angry at the person who is truly responsible—the perpetrator—helps push your shame away.

Anger and shame go hand in hand. Therefore, it is important to understand how they interconnect. Anger is the opposite of shame and self-blame. For this reason, shifting from self-blame to anger is an extremely effective way to heal your shame. This is because feeling and expressing anger tend to empower victims whereas childhood sexual abuse robs victims of their power. Most former victims report that they felt completely powerless while the abuse was occurring. They felt overpowered and had no way to stop what was happening. This left them feeling vulnerable, helpless, and humiliated.

As difficult as it may have been to allow yourself to acknowledge your sadness, grief, and suffering about the fact that you were sexually abused, you may have as much or even more difficulty acknowledging your anger. *But there is no doubt about it; if you were sexually abused as a child, you are angry.* No one can be violated the way you were without feeling tremendous anger about it—anger because of the violation, the betrayal, the loss of your innocence, the multitude of problems it has caused in your life, and most of all, for the tremendous shame you have been shackled with.

Former victims of CSA cope with their anger in different ways. Many are unaware of their anger because it is buried—underneath their shame, underneath their fear, underneath their pain. If you are someone who has buried your anger, allowing yourself to find and then express this anger can sometimes be a difficult task, but in this chapter, I will offer you information and strategies to help you do so.

Others are aware of their anger, but they are afraid of it—afraid that once they begin to express it, their anger will get out of control. If you are one of these people, you probably were raised around violent people. You may have witnessed your mother or your father exploding in rage whenever they felt angry. A small argument often ended in physical violence. If this describes you, in this chapter I will help you get past your fear of anger and find safe ways to express it.

Still others don't have a problem finding their anger or expressing it. In fact, they are angry a great deal of the time. They are like a balloon filled with too much air. They are ready to burst at any minute. If this describes you, it doesn't take much for you to become impatient with other people, and you frequently feel insulted because people don't respect you. You don't have a problem letting people know when they aren't treating you the way you want to be treated. The problem with this is that you aren't really addressing your real issues. You are likely hiding your shame behind a wall of anger. In fact, you probably aren't connecting the fact that you feel so angry all the time with the amount of shame you are carrying. And you likely haven't even made the connection between the amount of anger you feel and the fact that you were sexually abused as a child or adolescent.

And, finally, some of you deal with your anger by projecting it on those around you. You take your anger out on your partner, your children, your employees. You constantly find fault in others and frequently become enraged when things don't go your way. In this chapter I will help you discover the real reasons for your anger so you can address it directly instead of projecting it onto others.

Whereas some of you have buried your anger, are afraid of it, or project it on those around you, others are keenly aware of their feelings of anger and know who they are really angry with—their abuser. You know you are angry for having to suffer all the problems you have had in your life. You know you are angry at the people who exposed you to the abuser or who didn't protect you. You are angry because you were blamed for the sexual abuse. You are angry because you are still accused of lying. If this describes your situation, you are ahead of the game. You just need to find healthy ways to release all that righteous anger. Later on in this chapter I provide an extensive list of ways to release your anger in safe and healthy ways.

It is completely understandable for you to be angry at having been sexually violated as a child or adolescent. Why wouldn't you be? It was a horrendous violation of your body, mind, and spirit. And in most cases, it was a tremendous betrayal by someone who was supposed to care about you. Unfortunately, you couldn't express that anger at the time because you were probably paralyzed with fear. And because of denial and confusion, you may not have been able to express that anger later on, when you realized what had happened to you. Now is the time to connect with your anger and find healthy ways to release it.

ANGER—POSITIVE OR NEGATIVE?

Anger can be either positive or negative. It is positive when you release your anger in constructive, safe ways. It is extremely healing to put your head in a pillow and scream at the top of your lungs. It can be healing when you find the courage to confront your past abusers by writing them letters (that you do not send) or by pretending you are speaking to them. Venting your righteous anger in healthy ways can mobilize, empower, and motivate you to become a stronger person.

Anger can also help you get past your fears. We cannot feel fear and anger at the same time. Anger tells our fear to go rest in the corner. It tells our fear that it will take over and protect us.

Research has shown that it is vital to help survivors process, uncover, and express anger, because anger can be used to help a client feel empowered, appropriately attribute responsibility, establish boundaries, and promote self-efficacy and power. Further, it has been shown that it helps survivors to reframe their anger into an emotion they can use to help define their rights and needs and help them to use their anger for productive action and behavior.

Anger can also be a negative force, of course, such as when we take out our anger on innocent people—romantic partners, friends, children, or other family members. Your anger needs to be directed at the source—at the person or persons who sexually violated you.

Anger is also negative when you bury it deep inside yourself where you can hardly find it rather than expressing it. Repressed anger (anger you unconsciously bury) or suppressed anger (anger you put aside consciously) can cause depression and self-hatred. It can make you feel hopeless and helpless.

Anger can hide out inside us for decades, primarily because it can feel like the riskiest emotion to express. This is especially true for those who were raised never to acknowledge or express anger. And it is true for those who sense on an unconscious level that if they ever acknowledge their anger, they will have to come out of denial—denial about just how deeply the sexual violations they've experienced damaged them.

Most important, anger is negative when you turn it against yourself. It is not only negative but unhealthy when you blame yourself for being sexually abused as a child. You need to become extremely clear that you have absolutely no responsibility for the abuse. You did not "ask for it" or encourage the perpetrator to abuse you. The only person who is responsible for the abuse is the abuser.

Anger is especially negative when you turn it into debilitating shame. Debilitating shame robs you of your power, your sense of efficacy and agency, your belief that you can, in fact, change your circumstances. Anger, on the other hand, empowers you, emboldens you, and motivates you to defend yourself and your rights.

YOU HAVE A RIGHT TO YOUR ANGER

Anger is a natural reaction to having been violated. And it is a natural reaction to being shamed and humiliated. This is why it is important to realize that you have a right to your anger even though it probably was not safe for you to express your anger or rage at the time.

Exercise: What Are You Angry About?

- Create a list of all the things you are angry about concerning the sexual abuse you suffered.
  Here are some examples of what clients have written:
  "I'm angry because the abuse caused me to distrust people. I have a terrible time getting close to anyone, especially males."
  "I'm angry because my relationship with my mother was never the same. I stayed away from her out of fear of her finding out and because I felt ashamed."
  "I'm angry that my abuser used the fact that I was lonely to manipulate me into doing things he wanted."
  "I'm angry that my father lied to me and told me that what he was doing to me was normal—that he was teaching me about sex."
- Continue writing your list until you can't think of any other responses.
- Now notice how you feel once you have acknowledged your anger in this way. Does it feel good to acknowledge your anger in this way, or do you feel afraid or guilty about doing it?

You also have a right to get angry at all the people who didn't protect you, who didn't believe you, who denied it happened, who turned a blind eye while you were being traumatized, who defended your abuser. Get angry at all of them for not being there for you in the ways that you needed. (Although it is OK, even healthy to get angry at all these people, always remember that only one person is responsible for the abuse—the abuser.)

- Now write a separate list that includes all the other people, in addition to the abuser, you are angry with and why.

Notice how it feels to acknowledge your anger in this way. Hopefully, you feel a sense of relief. You may even feel liberated and empowered. For others, however, it may have been a more difficult exercise. Even though you certainly have many good reasons to be angry, you may have felt at a loss for words; you may even have experienced a "brain freeze" in which you "forgot" how you've been mistreated or abused. Others may have felt like you were doing something wrong to acknowledge your anger in this way.

If you experienced any of these things while performing this exercise, spend some time writing about these feelings. Write about your fear of anger or your discomfort with it. Write about how you feel like you're doing something wrong.

STOP INTERNALIZING YOUR ANGER

We tend to either internalize or externalize our anger. Self-injurious behavior is the most common way of internalizing anger, whereas violent acts toward others are the most common way to externalize anger.

Internalizing anger not only makes people feel shame but can also cause them to punish themselves with negative relationships or self-destructive behavior (such as alcohol or drug abuse, starving yourself, overeating, or self-mutilation with razors, knives, pins, or cigarettes). Therefore, it is important to let all that self-hatred become righteous anger toward your abuser. Instead of taking your anger *out on* yourself, start taking it *out of* yourself.

It is especially important for those who internalized their anger (i.e., blamed themselves) to redirect that anger toward their abuser. After all, he or she is the appropriate target for your anger. By allowing yourself to get angry at your abuser, the vital force of anger will be moving in the right direction, outward instead of inward. Let all that self-hatred become righteous anger toward your abuser.

Releasing your anger at the abuser can also help you to give back the shame to the abuser—after all, it is his or her shame that was put on you. The following exercise will help you to do this.

Exercise: Giving Back Your Abuser's Shame

1. Ground yourself by placing your feet flat on the floor, taking deep breaths, and clearing your eyes.
2. Imagine that you are able to look inside your body. Scan your body and see if you can locate where the shame surrounding the abuse is located. Find any shame or feelings that you are "bad" inside your body.
3. Imagine that you are reaching inside your body and pulling out that dark, ugly stuff.
4. Now imagine that you are throwing all that dark ugliness at your abuser, where it belongs.
5. Open your eyes and make a throwing motion with your arms.
6. Say out loud as you do it, "There—take back your shame. It's yours, not mine."

This exercise may bring up more anger, or it may bring up sadness. Whatever emotions arise, allow yourself to express them freely.

GETTING PAST YOUR FEAR OF ANGER

Unfortunately, many former victims have difficulties giving themselves permission to express their righteous anger because they are afraid that if they start expressing it, they will lose control and harm someone. Those who were raised in violent households may be repulsed by any show of anger and may be so afraid of becoming like their abusive parent that they completely repress their own anger. And many girls are raised to believe that it is not OK for girls to get angry. It is common for girls to be taught that it is OK to cry, but not to yell, whereas boys are raised to believe the opposite.

Becoming comfortable with your own anger is a major step toward empowerment. Turning your fear into anger will help you stand up for yourself. Turning your feelings of helplessness and hopelessness into anger will motivate you to continue to value yourself enough to say "No!" to anything or anyone that will undercut your value and worth. Turning your shame into anger will help you stop blaming yourself for the sexual abuse and put the responsibility for it squarely at the feet of your abusers.

This is because when we express our anger, we connect with our power. It is similar to igniting a flame inside. If you don't light that match, you will never see the flame. You will never feel the heat. You will never feel the power of a bonfire inside of you.

OVERCOMING YOUR OBSTACLES TO RELEASING YOUR ANGER

My client Raven had been having a difficult time admitting that she was angry at her father, who had sexually abused her starting when she was five and continued until she was nine. She continued making excuses for him, telling me that he was an alcoholic and didn't even know what he had done. But avoiding her anger wasn't getting Raven anywhere in terms of her recovery. She remained passive, especially with men. She often complained that men used her for sex, that she wasn't able to say no to men, and that she hated herself for being so passive.

I suspected that the main reason Raven was resisting connecting with her anger was that she didn't want to connect with the pain underneath her denial. This is often the case with former victims. She didn't want to connect with the reality that her father, whom she loved dearly, had betrayed her, taken advantage of her, and let her down in an essential way by not being the father she deserved—a father who would protect her (even from himself), a father who would never put his selfish needs ahead of his own, a father who would take responsibility for putting his daughter at risk by being around her when he was drunk and by not seeking help for his drinking problem.

Exercise: What Are Your Obstacles?

- Buy a journal or write in an existing journal all your reasons for being afraid of or resistant to releasing your anger. Maybe you are afraid of losing control; maybe you are fearful of facing other feelings, such as sadness. Perhaps you were raised to never express anger. Whatever your reasons are, put them down on paper.
- Now let's go deeper. Think about your childhood and try to discover your reasons for being afraid of your anger or for your belief that anger is not supposed to be expressed. For example:

  Did one or both of your parents become verbally, emotionally, or physically abusive when he or she became angry?
  Do you think this caused you to be frightened to see or feel someone's anger?

As a child, did you come to believe that anger was a precursor to someone hurting you?

Were you given permission or encouragement to express your dislike of unfair situations, or were you given the message that you needed to keep quiet?

Now write about your beliefs about anger. For example, do you believe it's wrong to express your anger because you should always forgive people? Do you believe it is wrong for girls and women to express their anger? Do you believe expressing anger is unsafe? Do you believe expressing anger is a sign of weakness?

Answering these questions can help you understand yourself better when it comes to your feelings, fears, and beliefs about anger. Hopefully it will help you come to the conclusion that it is understandable that you have the feelings and beliefs you have. But this doesn't mean you can't change these feelings and beliefs. The following writing exercise can help you do just that.

Exercise: Write about the changes you need to make or beliefs you need to reject in order to give yourself permission to release your anger in healthy ways. For example:

- I need to stop feeling guilty about releasing my anger.
- I need to begin to believe I have a right to release my anger in healthy ways.
- I need to find safe ways to express my anger that don't hurt or damage myself or anyone else.

Write about whether you think there is such a thing as "healthy anger." If so, what is your definition of "healthy anger"? How does your anger expression need to change in order for you to become healthier?

Allowing yourself to feel and express your righteous anger at the abuser can take some work because victims feel so disempowered. This is what my client Jennifer shared with me:

Whenever I try to address my anger toward my father, I become terrified, just like I felt as a little girl.

And this was my response:

That's completely understandable—he made your life hell. He bullied you, physically tortured you, as well as raping you. You were afraid for your life. While the adult part of you is angry, the little girl in you is still terrified.

I recommended that Jennifer journal about her feelings of anger toward her father, that she give herself full permission to write down everything she wished she could say to him in person. I encouraged her to not hold back and to not censor herself and to allow herself to use the worst swear words she could think of if she felt like it.

This is what she reported at our next session:

> At first, I was even afraid to write my feelings down, like he was going to magically find out what I was doing and punish me somehow. But the more I wrote down my angry feelings, the angrier I became. The words just streamed out of me. I wrote for hours the first time. I felt like I was vomiting up all the hatred I had toward him, hatred I'd held in for years. It felt like an enormous relief to write all that down.

Writing down your feelings of anger is an especially safe and effective way of releasing your anger. No one else needs to know what you have written. It is just for you. It is both a way to acknowledge your anger and a way to release it.

Exercise: Journaling

- Write about your angry feelings toward your abuser. Using the sentence stem "I'm angry at my abuser because _____" is a good way to start.
  - "I'm angry at my abuser because _____."
  - "I'm angry at my abuser because _____."
  - "I'm angry at my abuser because _____."
- Now focus your anger on all the people who turned a blind eye to your trauma, all those who didn't protect you, all those who didn't believe you or defended the perpetrator. You can use the following sentence stem to get you going—"I'm angry at my mother because _____."
  - "I'm angry at my mother because _____."
  - "I'm angry at my mother because _____."
  - "I'm angry at my mother because _____."

Depending upon your history, trying to release your anger or even acknowledging your anger can be terrifying, just as it was with Jennifer. Speaking your anger out loud can be especially frightening. My client Cassie dissociated each time I asked her to speak her anger toward her sexually abusive mother out loud. I noticed this because her voice became weaker, to the point that I could hardly hear her. She'd lost all her power. When I asked her why she felt this happened she said:

As a child I tried to object to my mother's inappropriate touching or say no when she told me to do something to her sexually, but this just made her angrier and more determined to make me do it. It was like my objecting to doing something made her want it all the more. The worst incidences of abuse happened when I tried to say no. Now when I try to imagine telling her off, I get numb. I go away.

If you dissociate whenever you attempt to write about your anger toward your abuser, be sure to bring yourself back to the present by grounding yourself (see instructions in chapter 1).

GIVE YOURSELF PERMISSION TO BE ANGRY

Give yourself permission to feel and express the anger that you couldn't at the time—allow it to empower you and motivate you to continue on your healing journey.

- Get angry at your abuser for robbing you of your innocence.
- Get angry at him for putting his selfish and perverted needs ahead of your safety and welfare.
- Get angry at your abuser for manipulating you into doing things you didn't want to do.
- Get angry at him or her for forcing you to engage in sexual acts that were painful or repulsive to you.
- Get angry because your abuser caused you to hate your body.
- Get angry because he made you feel that sex was dirty.
- Get angry because he or she made you feel you were contaminated, damaged, or unlovable.
- Get angry because he or she caused you to have problems enjoying your sexuality.
- Get angry because your abuser projected his shame onto you.
- Get angry because he or she blamed you for the abuse.

SAFE WAYS TO RELEASE YOUR ANGER

As promised, the following are safe and healthy techniques that will help you release your anger without the fear of losing control, being punished, or being further shamed or abused. Consider any or all of the following depending on what seems most appealing to you:

1. Write down your angry feelings. Don't hold back; let all your feelings of anger and hurt come out on the page. Write a letter to your abuser that you do not send. Let him or her know how the abuse affected you.
2. Walk around your house (assuming you are alone) and talk out loud to yourself, expressing all the angry feelings you have toward the abuser. Don't censor yourself; say exactly what is on your mind, including swear words.
3. Imagine you are sitting across from one of your abusers and tell him or her exactly how you feel about what he or she did to you. Again, don't hold back and don't censor yourself. If you notice that you are afraid to confront your abuser in this way, imagine that your abuser is tied to the chair. If you don't want to see his or her eyes for fear of becoming intimidated, imagine that he or she is blindfolded. And if you are afraid of what he or she might say to you in response to your anger, imagine that he or she is gagged.
4. Put your head in a pillow and scream.
5. If you feel like you need to release your anger physically, ask your body what it needs to do. You might get the sense that you need to hit, kick, push, break things, or tear things. Honor that intuitive feeling by finding a way to release your anger in a safe but satisfying way. For example, it is safe to kneel down next to your bed and hit the bed with your fists. If you are alone and no one is around, you can let out sounds as you hit. You can lie on your bed and kick your legs, or you can stomp on egg cartons or other packaging. You can tear up old telephone books, or go to a deserted place and throw rocks or bottles.

Notice how you feel after releasing your anger in any of these ways. As my client Teresa expressed to me:

> I noticed that my rage felt cleansing. Like it burned away my shame and self-blame. I noticed that I had more and more energy the more I released my anger.

Releasing your anger, in addition to empowering you, will help you recognize that any sexual violation you've suffered was not your fault, and that you didn't deserve the abuse. In expressing your righteous anger, you will be drowning out the voices of shame inside you.

If you continue to have difficulty giving yourself permission to get angry or have fears of losing control if you were to get angry, please refer to my book

Honor Your Anger. I also write extensively about getting past your resistance to releasing anger in my book *The Right to Innocence: Healing the Trauma of Childhood Sexual Abuse.* Both these books will help you to work past your fears and resistance and offer you many more suggestions on how to release anger in constructive, safe ways.

WHAT IF I DON'T FEEL ANGRY?

Many former victims find it extremely difficult to even feel their anger, much less express it—even when they know they "should" be feeling it. If this is your situation, here are suggestions that might help you.

- Notice where you hold anger in your body on the occasions when you do feel angry. Is your jaw tight? Do you grind your teeth? Do you tend to clench your hands into fists? Are your muscles tight? Now, see whether at times you don't consciously feel angry, but you're experiencing at least one of these things. These body signals are telling you that even though you might not be aware of your anger, it is there, hiding in your body.
- Notice whether you are often irritated with others around you. This can also be an indication that you are angry without realizing it. Being consistently irritated, frustrated, or impatient with others is a sign that you are feeling a low level of anger almost all the time.
- Notice whether you are often angry or impatient with yourself. Do you have a powerful inner critic who is constantly finding fault in the things you do? Are you consistently disappointed in yourself? These are signs that you are angry, but your anger is not really at yourself.

Exercise: Priming the Pump

Even if you are not aware that you're angry about having been sexually abused, believe me, you are. It may be buried deep inside and covered with shame or fear. If you are a female, it may be hidden behind a facade of being a "nice girl." The following exercise can be like "priming the pump," in the sense that it might touch off or stimulate your buried or hidden anger.

First, find a private place where you won't be disturbed and where you will feel free to make noises without disturbing others or drawing attention to yourself. Ideal places can be your home (if no one is within earshot) or in your car, if you can drive to a secluded area.

Think of a particular incidence of sexual abuse. Say "no!" out loud while you continue to think about how you were violated. Gradually increase the volume of your *no!*s until you are yelling "No!" at the top of your lungs. Let yourself really feel your "no." Let your voice get louder and louder.

Now choose one the following sentences to say, again thinking of one of your experiences of being abused as a child or adolescent. Go with the sentence that has the most meaning to you. Allow your voice to get louder and louder:

- "Leave me alone!"
- "Stop touching me!"
- "Get off of me!"
- "Get away from me!"
- "I hate you!"

Repeat the phrase you chose over and over. Let your voice get louder and louder. Don't hold back; let yourself express your righteous anger. If a memory comes up, go with it and use it to fuel your anger and rage.

If you get in touch with some deep, unexpressed anger—brava! That's what we're aiming for. Notice how it feels to release this anger. If you really let yourself go, and you yelled loudly and for a long time, you might end up feeling exhausted, but you may also feel a sense of relief. If you start to feel scared of your anger, remind yourself that you are safe and that you are not hurting anyone. If releasing your anger uncovers more pain, let the tears flow. Tears don't weaken or diminish your anger—or power.

HEALTHY ANGER VERSUS UNHEALTHY ANGER: THE MASK OF RAGE

Whereas many of you reading this book need to work past your fear of releasing anger and allow yourself to express your righteous anger in healthy ways, some of you are quite comfortable expressing anger. As mentioned earlier, you vent your anger on everyone around you. Unfortunately, you may not be so comfortable when it comes to recognizing and expressing your anger about the fact that you were sexually abused. This is where rage comes in.

Rage is different from anger. Whereas anger can be constructive, rage tends to be destructive. Anger is usually a signal that something in your environment needs your attention—a problem that needs to be solved. It can also be a signal that you have been wronged. In addition, anger can serve the following purposes:

- Anger can be a signal that you need to speak up for yourself or right a wrong.
- Often anger can motivate us to make changes or to set boundaries.
- Anger can be seen as an act of self-preservation, as when someone attacks you emotionally or physically.
- By communicating your anger clearly and directly, you are more likely to have your needs met.

Whereas anger can serve a positive purpose by acting as a motivator or as a way to overcome personal difficulties, such as standing up for yourself, rage, on the other hand, can drive someone to physically attack another person, to destroy property, or to emotionally harm someone, as in the case of verbal abuse. When you use your anger to stand up for yourself or to change a situation, you are usually still in control of your emotions; but when you are feeling rage, you may not have any control over yourself and therefore can become destructive.

Rage is, indeed, an appropriate response to sexual violation. In fact, rage is one of the most spontaneous, naturally occurring reactions to shame. According to Gershen Kaufman, the author of *Shame: The Power of Caring*: "its presence serves a much-needed self-protective function by both insulating the self against exposure and actively keeping others away" (p. 84).

Unfortunately, victims of sexual abuse could not afford to express their rage at their abuser at the time of the assault. This unexpressed rage can cause a former victim to develop a personality defined by rage. It can also manifest itself either in hostility toward others or bitterness. Although this hostility or bitterness arises as a defense to protect the self from further experiences of shame, it becomes disconnected from its originating source and becomes a generalized reaction directed toward almost anyone who may approach.

Ironically, in this way rage can be a smokescreen that masks shame. Just as you may have built a wall to protect yourself against further exposure and experiences of shame and defend yourself against feeling vulnerable, rage can be a way to keep people away from you, a way to hide your shame. In this sense, rage is actively held onto and thereby prolonged—whether expressed or held inside.

My client Reuben was a good example of how someone can divert his attention away from his shame by being angry and defensive. When I first met Reuben, I was struck by how stiffly he held his body. It was as if he was braced for an attack. As soon as we began to talk, I experienced even more defensiveness in the way he answered my questions. He was extremely self-protective, often misunderstanding a question as an accusation. Even a simple observation seemed like criticism to him.

Reuben had sought therapy in order to save his marriage. "My wife says that I've been emotionally abusing her for years. She read your book on emotional abuse and says it made her realize that this is what has been happening in our marriage. She's threatening to leave me if I don't change."

"How does she say you emotionally abuse her?"

"She says I don't listen to her, that I always cut her off and dismiss what she says. She says I can't take any suggestions, that I'm always right—that I can never admit I am wrong. Oh yeah, and she says I constantly criticize her and yell at her a lot."

"And do you think she's right? Do you do these things?" I asked.

"Well, I admit I sometimes yell at her—but that's because she doesn't listen to me."

"So, would you say you have a need to control things?"

"No, I wouldn't say that. She gets to do whatever she wants. I don't tell her what to do."

"I didn't say you had a need to control your wife. I asked if you need to control things, like needing for things to be done in a certain way. That you generally need to feel in control of your life."

"Well, sure. Otherwise, things will just fall apart."

Reuben was a classic example of someone who had built a wall to protect himself from connecting with his shame and to avoid being shamed further. His need to be in control and his overall defensiveness were symptoms of underlying shame. If he could create a sense of being in control, he didn't have to feel his vulnerability; and if he never admitted he was wrong, he didn't have to feel shame.

I suspected that Reuben had been victimized in some way, probably in his childhood. When I took his history, my suspicion was borne out. Although he initially refused to admit he had ever been abused in any way, eventually he revealed that he had been physically and sexually abused by his uncle.

As I explained to Reuben, many people mask their shame with rage, and I thought this is what he had done. The abuse by his uncle needed to be healed, but that wouldn't happen if he continued to cover it with rage. Further, we needed to create a safe space for him to uncover his hidden shame so we could begin to heal it.

As Reuben discovered in our sessions, he was so shamed by his uncle's abusive behavior that he could barely handle it. "I felt so bad about myself, so ashamed of myself because I couldn't stop him," he shared with me.

And there was a sadistic element to his uncle's abuse that added to Reuben's unbearable shame. His uncle delighted in seeing him suffer. He sometimes tied him up and did painful things to his genitals. This is how Reuben described it:

> I felt like a little insect being toyed with by a bully. He could easily kill me, but he wanted to delay it so he could get more pleasure out of seeing me squirm.

The way that Reuben coped with the continual abuse (it went on for about four years—from the time he was six to when he was ten) and the enormous shame he felt was to become a bully himself:

> I started looking for weak boys on the schoolyard, kids I could intimidate— who wouldn't fight back. I despised their weakness, and this gave me a reason to bully them. The more they didn't fight back, the more I picked on them. It made me feel better.

When I attempted to get Reuben to connect with his anger toward his uncle, I encountered a huge roadblock. As defensive as he was, as aggressive as he was with others, Reuben could not feel angry at his uncle. He recognized that his uncle was a horrible person who preyed on the weak, but when it came to voicing his anger toward him for what he had done to him, he couldn't do it. His anger was buried underneath all the shame he felt due to the sexual abuse.

IDENTIFYING WITH THE AGGRESSOR

What Reuben had done was to "identify with the aggressor," a defense mechanism that involves taking the role of the aggressor and taking on his attributes, or imitating his aggressive actions. This most often occurs when a psychological trauma brings about the hopeless dilemma of being either a victim or abuser. We often see this occurring with children raised in households where there is domestic violence. Children witnessing such violence often feel like they must choose: Do I want to be like my father who is abusive yet strong and in control, or like my mother, a helpless victim who doesn't stand up for herself? Both choices are bad ones, but in a child's mind, these are the only two ways of being. Although their choice is certainly unconscious, it can dictate the rest of their lives.

In a more direct way, identifying with an aggressor can come out of a situation in which an individual identifies with someone who poses a threat. The identification may involve adopting the aggression or emulating other characteristics of the aggressor. A classic example is a child who goes to the doctor and gets a shot against his will. He then goes home and pretends to be the doctor giving a shot to a doll or stuffed animal, or perhaps a younger sibling. This counters his feelings and experience of being small, frightened, angry, subjected to pain, and helpless to do anything about it.

This is essentially what Reuben had done, but instead of pretending to be the doctor who had given him a shot against his will, he took on his abuser's bullying, sadistic behavior with the weaker boys at school.

Reuben continued his bullying behavior as an adult. As far as I know, he didn't reenact his uncle's sexual behavior, but he did surround himself with people he could control and bully, including his wife. In this way he could continue to avoid facing his feelings of shame, helplessness, and vulnerability that characterized his relationship with his uncle.

Now, we needed to make it safe enough for Reuben to face these more vulnerable feelings. I started by offering compassion for his pain and suffering. Even though Reuben found it difficult to let this in, he was eventually softened by my genuine concern for him. We then moved on to helping him practice self-compassion. He could do this more easily by remembering himself as a child, but eventually he could offer compassion for himself as an adult. This self-compassion freed Reuben to acknowledge just how horrible the sexual abuse had been:

> I didn't want to face it—I didn't think I could survive remembering it. It was just too much. But the more I allowed myself to acknowledge how bad it was, how really bad it was, the more I was amazed that I even survived it all.

But Reuben was still stuck when it came to allowing himself to feel angry at his uncle:

> In order to get angry with him, I had to recognize how much I had emulated him—how much I enjoyed being like him. I had to make the connection between my bullying behavior and the abuse. But the hardest part was that I had to make myself stop acting like that. Because it felt so much safer to operate like that in the world. I didn't have to feel my vulnerability—like how much I actually need my wife.
>
> And I had to learn how to have empathy for other people, especially my wife. That was the hardest thing to do because it involved facing how much I had hurt her. But the more I could have compassion and empathy for myself, the more I learned how to have it for others. Once I did that, I was finally free to get angry at my uncle.

THE CONTROVERSY OVER ANGER RELEASE

Some researchers and therapists believe that it isn't healthy to reinforce angry and violent behaviors (such as hitting your bed with a tennis racket, hitting a punching bag, or yelling). If you have a history of being violent, like hitting, pushing, or kicking people, I encourage you to release your anger in other ways, such as writing down your feelings, imagining you are confronting your abuser, or using art to express your rage. But for most victims of sexual abuse, expressing their anger, even doing so physically, doesn't make them violent. Instead, it empowers them to confront their fears and be more assertive. It also helps them release years of pent-up anger—anger they had never felt permission to express.

Other people may tell you that you shouldn't express your anger, that it is somehow more spiritual or moral to let your past go instead of releasing your anger. You ultimately need to be the one to decide whether this is true for you. But in my experience, traumas such as being sexually violated don't just "go away," and I don't believe you can truly "forgive" until you've released your anger. In any case, let your body and emotions determine what is right for you and your healing process.

My client Deborah shared with me how she had dealt with her anger:

> I was raised a Catholic and trained to believe we should forgive those who harmed us. After I was molested, I tried to put my beliefs into practice. I prayed and prayed for help in being able to forgive my father, but my anger just continued to come up. It wasn't just anger; it was rage. I finally went to a CSA support group and was encouraged to express my rage. We practiced stomping our feet and screaming, and it felt so good! They had a punching bag there, and after watching other women get their anger out on it, I took my turn. My hands weren't strong enough, so I used the wooden dowel they had there, and I began hitting that punching bag over and over, imagining my father's face on the bag. I could feel the amount of rage I had been holding in. I felt it streaming out of my arms and hands as I hit his face over and over.
>
> After it was over, I felt exhausted, but also invigorated. I felt strength in my heart that I've never felt before. I felt strong and determined to do everything within my power to never let that happen to me again. My rage didn't all go away in that one session, but after several times of working on the punching bag, I felt my rage was spent. After that I did feel more like forgiving the rapist.

FIGHT, FLIGHT, OR FREEZE

Peter Levine, the author of *Waking the Tiger*, has studied stress and trauma for thirty-five years. He has found that when a situation is perceived to be life-threatening, as in the case of sexual abuse or assault, both our mind and our body mobilize a vast amount of energy in preparation to fight or escape, often referred to as the "fight or flight" response. This is the same energy that can enable a mother to lift a car off her son's legs when he is trapped under a car. This kind of strength is created by a large increase in blood to the muscles and the release of stress hormones, such as cortisol and adrenaline.

In the act of lifting the two-thousand-pound car, the mother discharges most of the excess chemicals and energy she has mobilized in order to deal with the threat to her child. This discharge of energy from the body, when complete, informs the brain that the threat is over, and it is time to reduce the levels of stress hormones in the body.

If the message to normalize is not given, however, the brain just continues to release high levels of adrenaline and cortisol, and the body remains in a high-energy, ramped-up state. Unlike his mother, this is the situation the son faces. Unless he can find a way to discharge the excess energy brought on by the crisis, his body will continue responding as it did when he was helpless and his body was in pain.

Unfortunately, human beings don't know how to "blow off the stress" of a near-death experience the way animals do. For example, a captured bear that has been shot with a tranquilizer dart will come out of its state of shock once the tranquilizer wears off. It does this by beginning to tremble—lightly at first, and then at a steadily intensifying level until it peaks into a near-convulsive shaking, its limbs flailing seemingly at random. After the shaking stops, the animal takes deep, organic breaths that spread throughout its body.

What is even more interesting is that when the bear's response is viewed in slow motion, it becomes obvious that the seemingly random gyrations it is doing during this process are actually coordinated running movements. It is as if the bear is completing its escape by actively finishing the running movements that were interrupted when it was tranquilized by the dart. Then the bear shakes off the "frozen energy" as it surrenders in spontaneous, full-body breaths.

Researchers such as Levine explain that people do, in fact, possess the same built-in ability to shake off threat the way animals do—many of us have simply forgotten how to use it. Given the appropriate guidance, human beings can and do shake off the effects of overwhelming events such as sexual abuse using exactly the same procedures that animals use.

Levine says that the reason his program works is that trauma is primarily physiological. Trauma happens initially to our bodies and our instincts. Only afterward do its effects spread to our minds, emotions, and spirits.

Another reason why anger release is so important is that it helps former victims release the frozen energy trapped in their body after a physical attack. In other words, if you were sexually assaulted, you may have tried to fight off your attacker; you may have tried to escape. But in the end, he overpowered you. Now you likely have that unspent rage and fear trapped in your body. Discharging this energy informs the brain that it is time to reduce the levels of stress hormones in the body—that the threat is no longer present. Until the message to normalize is given, the brain just continues to release high levels of adrenaline and cortisol, the body holds on to its high-energy state, and you continue to feel pain and helplessness.

Releasing your anger in any of the following ways can help you "shake off" the stress associated with the attack. (Doing any of these exercises can act as a trigger, catapulting you back to the sexual assault. This is OK if you are imagining pushing, shoving, or kicking your attacker away and feeling empowered, but if you slip into feeling fear and helplessness, ground yourself and bring yourself back to the present. Stop doing the exercise until you are completely back in the present and back in your body.)

- Lie flat on your back on your bed, bend your knees, and place your feet flat on the bed. Now stomp your feet as hard as you can. You can also do this exercise by keeping your legs straight and alternating lifting each leg up and slamming it down hard on the bed. Say "No!" as you do this.
- Lie flat on your back on the floor, perpendicular to your bed. Place both your legs up against your mattress and push as hard as you can. Imagine you are pushing your abuser away with the power of your legs. Say "Get away from me!" or "Get off!"
- Stand in front of a sturdy door in your house. Put both arms straight out in front of you and place your palms flat against the door. As you push against the door as hard as you can, say "Get away!" or "Get out of here!"

CONFRONTING YOUR ABUSER(S)

If you feel like confronting your abuser in person, I encourage you to continue releasing your anger in healthy, constructive ways first so that you do not put yourself or the other person in danger. I also encourage you to carefully consider whether it is safe for you (emotionally and physically) to confront this person. Aside from the safety concerns of confronting a man or woman who is potentially violent, there is a chance that you will sustain psychological damage from the encounter. He or she could become physically or emotionally abusive toward you, thus causing you to be retraumatized. And just being in this person's presence may cause you to be retraumatized. Child molesters seldom, if ever, acknowledge their crime. Instead, he is likely to deny that he did anything wrong, insist that it was consensual, accuse you of lying, or, if he does admit any wrongdoing, blame you for his actions. This could cause you once again to begin to doubt yourself. (For more information on the pros and cons of direct confrontations, consider reading my books *Breaking the Cycle of Abuse* and *The Right to Innocence*.)

Exercise: Imagine Confronting Your Abuser

Even though it usually is not safe or recommended to confront your abuser, you can still have the experience of confronting him in your imagination. Many former victims report that imagining confronting their abuser felt almost as good as they imagined it would feel if they had done it in reality.

- Find words for what you want to say to your attacker. Examples: "I hate you!" "Don't touch me!" "Get the hell away from me!" "You disgust me!"
- Walk around your house and say these words out loud, or imagine you are facing your abuser as he sits in a chair across from you (imagine he is tied up, blindfolded, and gagged if you need to in order to feel safe).
- Say everything you always wanted to say to your abuser. Don't hold back and don't censor yourself. You will not be punished for saying exactly what you want to say.
- Notice how it feels to confront your abuser in this way. It may feel liberating and empowering, or it may feel frightening. If you feel more fear than freedom, repeat the exercise at another time when you may feel stronger.

Anger is an important aspect of healing your shame. For some of you, allowing yourself to become angry at your perpetrator and releasing your anger in healthy ways can help to empower you and diminish your shame. Others, namely those who hide or cover your shame with rage or by identifying with the aggressor, will need to learn that these avoidance strategies only perpetuate your shame.

Anger can either help you to heal your shame or it can help hide your shame from yourself, preventing you from healing it. We avoid our anger at the abuser by blaming ourselves or blaming others. When we internalize our shame, we hurt ourselves. When we externalize shame, we hurt others.

One of the major goals of this chapter has been to educate you about the benefits of releasing anger in healthy ways and to provide you with helpful suggestions about how you can go about it. Another goal has been to help you work past your resistance to owning and releasing your righteous anger over having been sexually violated in the past. And, finally, still another goal was to help you turn your fear and helplessness and hopelessness into empowerment. These are all tall orders, but all are within your grasp if you complete the exercises and practice the strategies recommended in the chapter.

NINE

TELL SOMEONE

There is no greater agony than bearing an untold story inside you.

—Maya Angelou

May your story find safe harbor in the presence of people who will honor both your vulnerability and resilience.

—K. J. Ramsey

IF YOU FELT A SENSE OF RELIEF from writing about your trauma, imagine the relief you might feel if you told someone about it. Although child sexual abuse can be difficult to disclose, it is imperative that you come to understand how vitally important it is for your emotional health and well-being. In fact, disclosing your abuse can be one of the most powerful ways to heal your shame.

CSA creates significant psychological wounds that are not only difficult to heal, but often worsen over time. The more these wounds are denied, neglected, or hidden, the more they fester and the more they make themselves known in physical, psychological, and relational symptoms. Keeping the abuse a secret creates a toxic environment that breeds shame, self-blame, and even self-loathing. In addition, when secrecy exists, your pain has to be borne alone. This isolation compounds the pain and confusion and shame that the abuse caused. Learning that you are not alone can help decrease this sense of shame and isolation.

As the twelve-step saying goes, "You are only as sick as your secrets." This saying refers to the fact that secrets create shame, and this shame makes us build walls between ourselves and others. In addition, not talking about the abuse makes it so much easier for victims to blame themselves and continue to be plagued by shame.

Ironically, the shame a former victim experiences can become a significant barrier to disclosing about their abuse, even when you would like to. In fact, a 2013 study found that 76 percent of participants reported shame as the most prominent reason for not disclosing their abuse and/or seeking help. This shame may prevent former victims from disclosing at all, or it may prevent them from disclosing again based on the shame and lack of support they have already encountered. Because shame is very much connected to a desire to hide a part of oneself (whether or not based on prior experience), as well as an awareness of the social taboos and stigmas that still surround sexual abuse in our society, both can factor into your fear or avoidance of disclosure. And even when a survivor knows that support from others is key to healing, they may feel convinced that they are undeserving of such support or healing and will continue to carry the weight of their trauma alone and in silence.

THE BENEFITS OF DISCLOSING

Learning about the many benefits of disclosing may help you get past your resistance to doing so. They include:

- Like a cancer, secrets can eat at us from inside, draining us of vital energy and good health. This is because keeping the secret creates shame. The secret of child sexual abuse is especially shaming. It can make you feel like something is radically wrong with you—that you are inferior or worthless. It makes you want to hide. In the extreme, it makes you not want to look other people in the eye for fear that they will discover who you really are and what you have done. You don't want to get too close to people for fear that they will find out your dark secret.
- Carrying around this secret isolates you from other people. It makes you feel different from others. It makes you feel alone. Telling someone about the abuse offers you the opportunity to gain support and understanding.
- Disclosing the abuse will help you to finally admit that it really happened. As long as you don't tell anyone about your abuse, you can continue to pretend it didn't happen or that it didn't really affect you. But once you tell someone, you make it real, you acknowledge to yourself and to the other person that you were, in fact, victimized, used, taken advantage of, traumatized, and harmed. By telling about what you went through, you are admitting how much the abuse affected you and how it impacted your life. We can't heal what we don't acknowledge.

REASONS VICTIMS KEEP QUIET

Just as disclosing can help heal your shame for several reasons, victims also keep quiet for good reasons. Like many victims of childhood abuse, you may have kept the secret because you blamed yourself rather than the person who abused you. And because many perpetrators threaten their victims in some way—to hurt them or someone they are close to, or to tell others that you seduced them—you may have still more reasons why you kept quiet.

Even years later, when they have become adults themselves, many victims dare not risk confiding in someone about what happened to them when they were a child. They are afraid of being judged, or not being believed, or in the case of males who were victimized, being seen as less of a man. For many former victims, only after many months or even years of therapy can they develop enough trust in someone to tell their secret. And unfortunately, many victims never make it to a therapist's office because they are so afraid of being judged or not believed, or because they insist on protecting the perpetrator.

You may feel that you shouldn't tell anyone until you are absolutely certain or until you get clearer memories. But this isn't the case. You certainly don't want to make an official "report" to the authorities when you aren't certain, but you could talk to a trusted friend about your suspicions. Talking to someone can help make things a lot clearer in your mind. And the chance is good that you have been minimizing what happened to you, so getting another person's perspective and feedback can be very helpful.

Male victims often have the most difficulty admitting that they were victimized because it makes them feel like a "loser," a "wimp," or not "macho" enough. My client Randy is a good example. This is what he shared with me:

> As long as I didn't tell anyone I had been abused, I could pretend it never happened. I wasn't willing to see myself as a victim, because that would mean that my abuser had 'won,' and I wasn't willing to let him do that to me. So, I blocked it out of my mind for years. I had a good life, a girlfriend who loved me, lots of friends. I told myself if I'd been abused, how could I have such a good life?
>
> But then my life started falling apart. I started waking up in the middle of the night because I was afraid someone had broken into my apartment. I got so scared I couldn't go back to sleep. I started drinking more at night so I could sleep. But it didn't really help. My girlfriend and I started arguing more and more, and our sex life went down the tubes. I just stopped feeling like having sex, and when she complained and I pushed myself to do it, it just got worse. Sometimes I couldn't even get an erection. My girlfriend accused me of not loving her anymore, and eventually we broke up.
>
> Then I started going out to the bars and drinking even more, and eventually I lost my job. That's when I decided I better get some help. I didn't want to admit I was having problems because of the sexual abuse, but deep inside I knew what was bothering me.

At first telling you felt like I was admitting that my father had won the battle. He wanted to humiliate me and break me, and while I was determined that he wasn't going to do it, the truth is, he did humiliate me, he did break me.

What I'm learning in therapy is that even though my father won the battle, he didn't win the war. I won the war, because I survived. He broke me as a kid, but I'm healing in my broken places. By getting help I'm getting stronger all the time. And admitting I was victimized is not the same as saying I'm not a man.

Of course, you don't have to begin therapy to disclose your abuse, but counseling can be the safest place for you to do so. If you aren't ready for counseling, or you are not willing to go into therapy, at least disclose to a trusted friend. Later in this chapter I provide more information about how to choose the right person to disclose to.

Exercise: Your Reasons for Keeping the Abuse a Secret

Think about your reasons for keeping the abuse a secret, even from your closest friends. Write a narrative about your reasons or list them.

OBSTACLES TO DISCLOSING

A main reason it is so difficult to tell anyone about the abuse is that you may be afraid of what the person you tell will think of you. If you are thinking of telling a partner or a friend, you may be especially worried that this person's image of you will be tainted, that he or she will look at you differently. For example, you may be afraid the person will now see you as "damaged goods" (especially if you are a female). You may be afraid the person will feel sorry for you and see you as weak, which may not be what you want (especially if you are a male). Or you may be afraid that a partner or a friend will secretly think that it was your fault, or at the very least that you wanted it or that you derived pleasure from it in some way and therefore you were not a total victim.

The truth is, this is your shame talking. You need to consider carefully who you tell, but most friends and romantic partners will not judge you. They will feel bad for you and will want to support you in getting the help you need. Even though you may be riddled with shame concerning the abuse, most people you tell will not blame you or feel that you had anything to do with causing it. They will be clear that the blame lies solely on the perpetrator, and that you were an innocent child who did not deserve the abuse.

When you don't share the secret of child sexual abuse, you don't have the opportunity to receive the support, understanding, and healing you so deserve.

You continue to feel alone and to blame yourself. You continue to be over-whelmed with shame.

Please don't let your shame, self-blame, and guilt stop you from telling someone about the abuse. You deserve to have someone hear your story. You deserve to be listened to and supported. Unless you tell someone what happened to you, you won't be able to receive any of these things.

Out of the Shadows

A tremendous amount of darkness is connected to child sexual abuse—the clandestine, sinister way it is accomplished, the manipulation and dishonesty surrounding it, the lies and deception used to keep it secret, the darkness and pain surrounding the violation of a child's most intimate parts of her body, and the violation of the child's integrity. Especially noteworthy is the darkness child sexual abuse brings into a child's life, the lifetime of pain, anguish, fear, and shame. Keeping the abuse a secret adds darkness to an already dark and sinister act. Telling someone will help bring you out of the darkness and into the light—the light of healing, acceptance, and support.

DECIDING WHO TO TELL

If you want to disclose for any of the reasons we have discussed, you will likely want to tell one of the following people: a good friend, your romantic/sexual partner, the people in your group or your twelve-step program, your minister or other church members, a trusted family member or friend of the family. Deciding who to tell to gain support can be difficult. You may be plagued with all kinds of questions and concerns: "Can I trust this person to not tell anyone else?" "If I tell this person, will it change his or her view of me?" "Will it change our relationship?" These are all good questions. Choosing who to tell is an important decision and should be considered carefully.

Ultimately, you want something positive to come out of your disclosure—at the very least, for you to feel less burdened by having to keep the secret. But in addition, you probably also hope to be believed and to receive some understanding and support. You certainly don't want to be doubted or disbelieved, and you don't want to be judged negatively.

Can I Trust This Person?

Let's address some of your concerns, starting with whether you can trust a particular person. One of the best ways to determine this is to ask yourself, "Has this person been trustworthy in the past?" A trustworthy person is someone who will keep what you tell them to themselves and not share it with others. Have you noticed that when you've told this person things in the past, she has kept your confidence, or has she told others, even after you asked her not to? If you've never told this person anything private before, notice whether she is the kind of person who gossips about others. If she has told you other people's secrets or tends to gossip about others, you can assume she will probably do the same with you.

Perhaps most important, choose someone who is compassionate and is able to feel and be sympathetic to other people's pain. For example, have you noticed that when other people have suffered, this person tends to feel bad for them or offers to help them? If this is the case, this person may be a good choice. On the other hand, if you know this person has a strong belief that people should "just get over" their problems and not "feel sorry for themselves," then this person might not be the best person to tell. They might play down what you went through, tell you to "move on," or even be critical of you for "making a big deal out of something that happened so long ago."

You may also want to be careful about telling someone who adheres to the metaphysical belief that there are no victims; that we all create our own destinies. This belief can be very "victim blaming," and it is not what you need to hear (quite apart from the fact that it isn't true).

As we've discussed, a very anti-victim mentality pervades our culture today. It is my personal belief that one reason for this is that it makes people feel more comfortable dealing with traumas such as sexual abuse of children if they can blame the victim. If they make victims and former victims believe that they had some responsibility for their victimization or that they shouldn't "wallow in their pain," then they don't have to grapple with the uncomfortable awareness that they or their children could become victims themselves. If you have experienced someone having a negative judgment about victims in general or an impatience when it comes to people talking about their problems, then this person is absolutely not the right person to tell.

You also don't want to tell someone you know will tend to protect, minimize, or make excuses for what the abuser did. This is especially true when it comes to telling family members. For example, telling a person who has turned a blind eye to your abuser's other negative behaviors (such as drinking too much or being abusive in other ways) is not a good idea. This is especially true concerning telling your abuser's mother or spouse, particularly if you suspect she already knows but refuses to believe that her loved one could do such a thing.

On the other hand, telling an intimate partner who has always been supportive and encouraging toward you and is the kind of person who seems to be sympathetic toward victims of abuse is probably a good person to tell.

Will It Change This Person's Perception of Me?

Although telling a supportive close friend or spouse can be an excellent choice when it comes to disclosing the abuse, this very person might be the hardest person to tell. You may be afraid that if you tell this person about your past abuse, it will change their opinion of you or change the way they perceive you. This may be true, but not in the way you probably imagine. Most of my clients who told a loved one reported that to their surprise, the person they told didn't lose respect for them but the exact opposite: they gained respect for them.

As one client said:

> My best friend told me she admired the courage it took for me to tell her. She said she thought I was so strong to have survived the abuse.

And another client shared:

> My husband told me he gained a tremendous amount of respect for me, because I trusted him enough to tell him. He said he knew it was difficult for me to tell him, and he admired me for doing something that was so difficult.

Will Telling Change My Relationship?

You may also worry that telling someone close to you will change your relationship with them. You may be afraid that it will create distance between you and your loved one. But this fear has also proven to be unwarranted overall.

This is what my client Mandy told me:

> Telling my husband actually brought us closer together. My husband told me he was relieved, because he always felt I was holding back in some way. And in the past, he always took it personally when I told him I needed space, but now he understands why.

Another client shared:

> Since I told my wife, we are so much closer. Now I feel like I have a real partner, someone who will stand by me as I go through my pain and my recovery. She's been more than understanding. She's been so loving and compassionate, too. Telling her is the best thing I ever did for myself and for my marriage.

Some people are afraid their sexual partners will get turned off and that it will repulse them to know that their partner was sexually abused as a child. But this seldom happens. Most partners recognize that you were an innocent child (or adolescent) and that what was done to you was a horrible, vile thing, but that you are neither horrible nor vile because of it.

This is what happened with my client Candice:

> I was surprised by my husband's reaction. I was afraid he'd see me as damaged goods and become turned off to me sexually, but telling him actually brought us closer together. After I told him about the abuse, he said I seemed to change—that I was able to get closer to him—to trust him more, and it's true.

In all my years of practice, I have only had two clients experience a negative reaction from their partner when they disclosed the abuse to them, and in both these cases those who did react negatively had problems of their own. One client's husband had a strong reaction and blamed her for her father abusing her. As my client was to find out later, her husband was in denial himself about having sexually abused his own daughter from a previous marriage. In the other situation, my client's girlfriend needed her man to be strong and macho; once she heard about his abuse, she couldn't continue to view him that way. Although my client was devastated by their breakup, he was eventually able to recognize that his ex clearly had an issue. In the end, the breakup turned out to be a good thing. My client needed a woman who was not turned off by a man who could be vulnerable, and I'm happy to report he found a woman who stuck by him as he healed from his trauma.

Exercise: Letting It In

Hopefully you will choose a person who can be compassionate toward you and will provide for you the love and support you deserve. If you do, in fact, receive this, I encourage you to allow this to be a healing experience.

- Take a deep breath and let in the supportive words of your friend or family member. Don't cut the person off by telling them that they shouldn't worry, you are OK now, or that it wasn't so bad.
- Don't take care of their feelings. This is your time to receive understanding, support, and compassion. If you are fortunate enough to receive these things from the person, view them as gifts—gifts that you deserve.

You deserve to be heard, believed, and supported. Unfortunately, no matter how careful you are about who you choose to disclose to, not every person will be able to offer you these things. Some won't be able to offer you support, because they are too threatened by the subject of child sexual abuse. It makes many people uncomfortable. Others may be in such denial about their own abuse that they simply can't be there for you. Surprisingly, the most startling responses can come from siblings. Even a sibling whom you know or suspect was also molested by the same perpetrator may deny her own abuse and get angry with you for falsely accusing the perpetrator. The fact that you may have even witnessed the abuse of a sibling or that a sibling may have even previously confided in you about their own abuse may bear no weight. In fact, *the most avid supporters* of the abuser are often the ones who were also victimized.

Because of the possibility that you don't get the support you need when you disclose, you need to promise yourself that if the first person you tell doesn't believe you and can't offer you support, then you will tell someone else.

THE BENEFITS OF DISCLOSING TO
A COUNSELOR OR THERAPIST

If you can't bring yourself to tell anyone you are close to, consider starting therapy if you haven't already done so. Although it can be difficult to reach out for help, the benefits of individual therapy outweigh the difficulties that can be involved in finding a good therapist. The benefits of therapy include:

- A good therapist is what we call a "compassionate witness" who will listen carefully and openly and not judge you. You are unlikely to be met with hurtful disbelief or insulting questions (and if you are, head for the door as fast as you can—this is not a good therapist). Instead, you are likely going to receive the words of compassion, support, and validation that you longed for and needed to hear, such as "I'm so sorry that happened to you," or "You endured such horrible abuse; what a strong person you are to have survived it."
- By disclosing to a therapist, you are also likely to hear, "It wasn't your fault," no matter what the circumstances. Although you may have heard this before, hearing it from a professional, especially one you have come to trust, can have a more significant impact on you, especially in terms of relieving your shame.

- Talking to a counselor will free you to get in touch with your pain, sadness, anger, and rage and encourage you to allow yourself to express these emotions in safe ways.
- Counseling will give you the space and safety to finally let down your barriers, to cry and grieve your lost childhood.

Note: if you disclose abuse to a therapist, this person may be required by law to report the abuse to the authorities. Even if you are an adult reporting past abuse, in some countries the therapist is also required to report to the authorities if he or she has concern that your abuser has access to other children. For example, if you report to a counselor that your abuser is currently babysitting your nieces and nephews, or that his grandchildren are now living with him, the therapist will need to report your past abuse to the authorities and notify them of the risk to other children in the family. If you are reporting abuse that occurred many years ago, and the abuser is dead or has no access to other family members, the therapist is not mandated to report to authorities.

The information in this chapter was intended to encourage you to reach out to tell someone, preferably a safe someone, about your abuse trauma. Some of you will feel encouraged and empowered by this information whereas others still may not be prepared to take this step. If this is your situation, practice self-compassion and tell yourself something like, "It is understandable that I would still be afraid to disclose the abuse. I will do so when I am ready."

PART III

FORGIVING YOURSELF

So far, we have explored four major strategies that you can use to rid your-self of the shame of childhood sexual abuse: face the truth, offer yourself self-compassion for your suffering, stop blaming yourself and get angry, and tell someone. Continuing to practice these four approaches can liberate you from the majority of shame you experience due to the sexual abuse. But one more important strategy is essential if you are to free yourself of this shame: self-forgiveness.

Everything you have read in this book so far, as well as all the processes and exercises you have completed, have all led to this important section. Self-forgiveness is the most powerful step you can take to rid yourself of your debilitating shame. And absolutely nothing is as important for your overall healing from the abuse and the effects of the abuse. It goes like this: the more shame you heal, the more you will be able to see yourself more clearly—the good and the bad. Instead of hardening your heart and pushing people away, you will be more receptive to others and to their feedback.

The more you heal your shame, the more capable you will be to have empathy for others, and this will cause your relationships to change and deepen. You will also have more compassion for yourself and your suffering, and you will be able to recognize and admit how you have harmed yourself and others. More important, your relationship with yourself will improve. You will be far less critical and self-loathing.

Whereas compassion is the antidote to shame—self-forgiveness is the healing medicine. Self-compassion acts to neutralize the poison of shame, to remove the toxins that shame creates. Self-forgiveness acts to soothe our body, mind, and soul of the pain that shame causes and facilitates the overall healing process.

What do you need to forgive? First and foremost, you need to forgive yourself for the abuse itself and stop making yourself a prisoner of your own making. As I've mentioned many times, victims tend to blame themselves for the abuse because it is preferable to feeling vulnerable and out of control. If you can continue to blame yourself for the abuse, you can continue to hold onto the illusion of control and avoid the feelings of helplessness that accompanied the abuse. And equally important, if you can continue to blame yourself for what your abuser did, you don't have to face the feelings of abandonment, betrayal, and disappointment that go hand in hand with facing the truth about someone you cared about.

Next, you need to forgive yourself for the ways you have hurt others as a consequence of the abuse you suffered. This includes all your "sins" and omissions—all the ways you have caused others damage.

Last, but not least, you need to forgive yourself for the ways you have harmed yourself because of the abuse.

Self-forgiveness is so important that I have divided it into two separate chapters: "Forgiving Yourself for the Ways You Have Harmed Others" and "Forgiving Yourself for the Ways You Have Harmed Yourself." I will guide you step-by-step through the process of completing each of these two tasks.

TEN

FORGIVING YOURSELF FOR THE
WAYS YOU HAVE HARMED OTHERS

True confession consists of telling our deed in such a way that our soul is changed in the telling it.

—Maude Petre

ALTHOUGH YOU MAY have been willing to work on forgiving yourself for your involvement in the abuse, you may not be as open to forgiving yourself for the ways you harmed others as a consequence of the abuse. You may ask, "Why should I forgive myself? It won't help those I've harmed." The most powerful reason: If you do not forgive yourself, the shame you carry will compel you to continue to act in harmful ways toward others and yourself. And forgiving yourself will help you to heal another layer of shame, freeing you to continue becoming a better human being. Without the burden of self-loathing that you have been carrying around, you can literally transform your life.

You may also resist self-forgiveness because you view it as "letting myself off the hook." You may even feel that judging yourself harshly for your negative past actions is the only way to improve. But as Kristin Neff so rightly stated:

Negative self-judgment and self-blaming can actually act as an obstacle to self-improvement. The more shame we feel about our past actions and behaviors, the more our self-esteem is lowered and the less likely it is we will feel motivated to change. And without self-forgiveness our level of shame will cause us to defend ourselves from taking on more shame by refusing to see our faults and not being open to criticism or correction.

More important, shame and self-blaming can interfere with you being able to feel self-compassionate.

FORGIVE YOURSELF FOR ANYTHING YOU
DID AS A CONSEQUENCE OF THE ABUSE

The good news is: You can resolve to change your behavior *and* forgive yourself at the same time. In fact, the more you forgive yourself, the more you will be motivated to change those things about yourself that are problematic. Self-forgiveness opens the door to change by lessening your resistance and deepening your connection to yourself.

In order to continue healing your shame, you need to forgive yourself for the ways you have hurt others as a result of the abuse you suffered, including all your "sins" and omissions—all the ways you have caused others damage. This can be extremely difficult, but it is important to know that you have several effective ways to go about it. In this chapter I will outline and discuss three strategies:

1. Self-understanding (making the connection between your actions and the abuse you experienced).
2. Common humanity. This is the idea that all human beings are fallible and that wrong choices and feelings of regret are inevitable. The truth is, we have all harmed others. *In fact, every single person on this planet has harmed at least one other person in ways that have shaped that person's life.* Knowing this and knowing that you are not alone can help you to have compassion for yourself and to forgive yourself.
3. Earning your forgiveness: This process includes taking responsibility, giving meaningful apologies, and making amends.

As you read about the following strategies, choose the methods and suggestions that you relate to or resonate with the most.

Self-Understanding

When it comes to forgiving yourself for the harm you have caused others, your most powerful strategy will always be self-understanding. In fact, you can't truly forgive yourself for the ways you have harmed others unless and until you achieve self-understanding. Once you come to understand yourself—including the motives and reasons for your more troubling behaviors—you will find it easier to practice self-compassion.

Without self-understanding, those who were sexually abused in childhood tend to continue putting themselves down for their mistakes and shortcomings instead of making the all-important connection between their current behavior and the abuse they experienced. I am not encouraging you to make excuses for problematic behavior, but without understanding why you have acted as you have, you will not only continue to experience debilitating shame, but you will have a more difficult time letting go of the troubling behaviors.

Those who were sexually abused tend to be particularly hard on themselves. They have unusually high expectations of themselves, and they chastise themselves unmercifully when they make a mistake, especially when their behavior harms another person. And they seldom, if ever, take the time to compassionately search for reasons why they may have behaved as they did. Instead, they tend to have a "no excuses" policy when it comes to their own behavior. (Interestingly, many victims do not have the same policy when it comes to the behavior of others; instead, they make frequent excuses for insensitive, even abusive behavior in others.)

This is very sad when you think about it. As a victim of childhood sexual abuse, you no doubt experienced sometimes horrendous pain and suffering, and yet you may find it difficult to allow yourself to acknowledge your suffering. Instead, you expect to walk away from the abuse unscathed. You expect to move on with your life without receiving any help or healing for your wounds.

Unfortunately, you pay a huge price for this way of thinking. First of all, if you were a victim of CSA, you were traumatized by the experience. You may not have been aware that you were traumatized at the time, but you were. And you may not be aware of how the trauma affected you, but it did. Think of it like this: Let's say you were the victim of a plane crash. Fortunately, you were able to walk away from the wreckage, albeit with some physical injuries. But the experience of the crash was in itself traumatic, wouldn't you agree? First were the moments leading up to the crash—the realization and panic that your life was in danger, the overwhelming fear of what could happen. Then came the crash itself, the terror associated with the physical impact and the sights, sounds, and smells that accompanied it.

So even though you were able to walk away from the crash, you would expect to carry the experience of the trauma with you, right? You'd expect yourself to probably replay the experience over and over in your head. You might expect to be in shock for hours, days, weeks, months, even years after the trauma. And as you no doubt have heard, you would probably expect to suffer for quite some time from what are commonly referred to as symptoms of post-traumatic stress disorder (PTSD) (e.g., nightmares, flashbacks, fear of airplanes, even terror responses when you hear airplanes passing overhead). The bottom line—you wouldn't have expected to walk away from that plane crash completely unscathed. You undoubtedly would have suffered physical injuries, and you would have suffered emotional and psychic wounds as well.

The same is true of those who experienced childhood sexual abuse. In addition to the debilitating shame that you have carried with you into your adult life because of the abuse, you have carried the memories of the trauma and the accompanying stress that these memories create. And these post-traumatic symptoms can take their toll.

Time after time I have found myself explaining to clients that I have never met a victim of CSA who didn't react to the abuse by behaving in problematic ways. These include abusing alcohol or drugs; sexual acting out, promiscuity, and sexual addiction; other addictions such as compulsive overeating; acting out against society (e.g., shoplifting); self-harm; abusive behavior toward others; or a pattern of staying in abusive relationships.

Instead of viewing yourself as a "bad person" because you have reacted to the sexual trauma in sometimes troubling ways, I hope that the following information will help you to understand yourself better and become less critical of yourself. And I especially hope that you will come to recognize that *the negative things you have done do not represent who you are at your core but are the ways that you learned to cope with the trauma you experienced.* In turn, I hope that this self-understanding will help you begin to treat yourself in far more compassionate ways.

Making the important connection between your past (and current) problematic behaviors and your trauma experiences will not only help you become more compassionate toward yourself, but be far less impatient, judgmental, and angry toward yourself. The following information hopefully will help you begin to understand why you have taken on certain behaviors and help you realize that it is not your fault but rather the typical after-effects of the trauma you experienced.

THE SINS OF CHILDHOOD

Children are compelled to repeat what happens to them as a way of processing events, especially traumatic ones. Watch children at play, and you will notice that they "act out" their experiences. For example, you'll see a child become their parent by holding a puppet or doll and having the doll voice the words of their parent, such as, "I told you to stop doing that!"

In addition to acting out the trauma of CSA in their play, former victims often act out their shame, pain, fear, and anger by reenacting the abuse with others or by breaking the law. If you did either of these things, I encourage you to forgive yourself for anything *you did as a child* that was a consequence of the abuse, such as lying and stealing after the abuse started; initiating sex with other children; bringing other children to the abuser; or hurting your pets. Remember, you were hurt and angry and full of shame. Unable to express your anger toward the perpetrator, you may have taken out your anger on those who were weaker and smaller than you. Because you likely hated yourself for being weak and helpless, you hated others who were weak as well. You may have also acted out your anger and hatred toward your abuser by becoming angry at authority figures. Or all that pent-up anger you felt toward the abuser may have been channeled into breaking the law.

For example, many people have memories of shoplifting when they were a child, but their forays into shoplifting were usually limited to stealing candy from a local store or shoplifting with a group of kids once or twice just to see if they could get away with it. But former victims of CSA often use shoplifting as a way of acting out their anger at authority figures.

This was my client Tiffany's situation:

> I started shoplifting right after I was abused. I did it at least once a week, sometimes more often. The more I got away with it, the more I did it. It got so I couldn't go into a store without stealing something. It was so exciting, and I got a rush every time I made it out the door. Looking back on it, I'm not sure why I did it. I've felt bad about it for years. I was raised in a very religious family, and stealing is one of the commandments, so I feel a lot of guilt and shame about it.

As Tiffany and I worked together, she came to realize that her shoplifting was a way to rebel. She viewed the owners of the stores as authority figures, and therefore, symbolic of the authority figure who had molested her—a teacher. Symbolically she was "getting even" with the teacher by stealing from the stores. In fact, it was rather dramatic the day she had this epiphany:

> I stole from them just like my teacher stole from me. He stole my innocence, he stole my trust in people, he stole my ability to respect authority figures.

Once Tiffany came to understand the reasons why she stole, she felt far less critical of herself for doing so and, most important, she felt less shame. This is how she explained it to me:

> I don't excuse what I did. It was wrong. But now that I understand the motive for my stealing, it makes sense to me. I can forgive myself.

Forgiving Yourself for the Harm You Caused Other Children

It is not unusual for victims of CSA to be pressured by their abuser to bring other children into the situation. This was the case with my client Clarke. Clarke was sexually abused by a man in his neighborhood who frequently invited young boys to his home after school to play video games. The man would slowly groom his victims by befriending them, plying them with sodas, snacks, and video games. This would lead to giving them beer and showing them pornographic films and eventually, to sexually abusing them.

Although he felt a great deal of shame about what his abuser did to him sexually, Clarke also loved the attention he got from him. His parents both worked, and in the past, he had to go home to an empty house every night and spend hours alone until his parents came home.

After several months of being abused, the man told Clarke that he wanted him to find another boy to bring back to the house. Clarke felt awkward and afraid about doing this, because he knew what would likely happen to anyone he brought into the molester's home, but he was afraid that if he didn't do what the man said, he would reject him. And so, Clarke brought a boy he had befriended at school back to the abuser's house.

Unfortunately, this wasn't the end of the story, but the beginning. Every few months the man insisted that Clarke bring home another boy. This went on for about six months. Finally, Clarke had had enough. He decided that he just couldn't take it anymore, he stopped bringing boys to the house, and in fact, stopped going there himself.

For years after, Clarke agonized over how many boys the man had molested, and he felt terrible about his part in it. He wanted to tell someone so the man would be forced to stop, but he was terribly afraid that he would be implicated in the crime. He finally told a counselor at a local Boy's Club, who referred Clarke to counseling.

As Clarke was to discover, he was not blamed for his role in the other boys' abuse but, instead, was appreciated for finally coming forward and telling authorities about the man. He was viewed by the police as a victim, not a perpetrator. Every authority involved, from the police to child protective services, recognized that he had been manipulated and coerced by the neighborhood man into not only becoming a victim himself, but to participating in bringing more boys to the home.

Although Clarke was relieved about not being arrested and for not being viewed as an offender, he still suffered from a great deal of shame. As he told me:

I'm glad I didn't get into trouble, but I still feel so bad about myself. Why couldn't I just walk away from that guy? Sure, I liked the perks, but they weren't worth putting all those boys in danger. I was just weak and selfish, and I'll never forgive myself for that.

I could see that we had our work cut out for us.

Forgive yourself for going back and for anything else you did as a child that was a consequence of the abuse. You were hurt and angry and full of shame.

UNDERSTANDING THE ROLE OF
POST-TRAUMATIC STRESS DISORDER

Although you may manage to understand that you were, in fact, a child and therefore be able to forgive yourself for your actions as a child, it can be even harder to forgive yourself for the harm you caused others as an adult. The following information should help you with this.

PTSD is a severe anxiety disorder with characteristic symptoms that develop after the experience of an extremely traumatic stressor such as the threat of severe injury or death to oneself or to someone else, or a violent assault on one's own or someone else's physical, sexual, or psychological integrity, overwhelming the ability to cope.

People who suffer from PTSD often relive the experience through nightmares and flashbacks, have difficulty sleeping, and feel detached and estranged, and these symptoms can be severe enough and last long enough to significantly impair the person's daily life. PTSD is marked by clear biological changes as well as psychological symptoms. It is complicated by the fact that it frequently occurs in conjunction with related disorders such as depression, substance abuse, and problems of memory and cognition.

PTSD symptoms tend to fall into three major categories. Circle or put a check mark next to the symptoms in each category that you suffer from.

1. Reexperiencing symptoms:
   - flashbacks—reliving the trauma over and over, often accompanied by physical symptoms such as a racing heart or sweating
   - bad dreams
   - frightening thoughts

2. Avoidance symptoms:
   - staying away from places, events, or objects that are reminders of the experience

- feeling emotionally numb
- feeling strong guilt, shame, depression, or worry
- losing interest in activities that were enjoyable in the past
- having trouble remembering the dangerous event

3. Hyper-arousal symptoms:
   - being easily startled
   - feeling tense or "on edge"
   - having difficulty sleeping and/or having angry outbursts

Many victims of childhood abuse can be diagnosed with PTSD. In fact, studies have shown that childhood abuse (particularly sexual abuse) is a strong predictor of the lifetime likelihood of PTSD.

You may have been suffering from PTSD for years without realizing it. As you read the list above, you may have been surprised to realize that many of the symptoms you suffer from are signs of PTSD, and this realization may bring you some comfort. You are finally able to understand your behavior and explain it to others. This can be the beginning of gaining self-compassion for your suffering.

Interestingly, in some cases, the symptoms of PTSD can become more debilitating than the trauma itself. For example, intrusive memories are mainly characterized by sensory episodes, rather than thoughts. These episodes aggravate and maintain PTSD symptoms because the individual reexperiences trauma as if it were happening in the present moment.

Many victims of childhood abuse are plagued by these sensory episodes. For example, my client Marjory frequently feels the presence of her father, who brutally sexually abused her starting when she was three years old. Sometimes she wakes up in the middle of the night in terror because she thinks she feels him coming into her bed. Other times she can be in the shower when she senses him come into the bathroom. Each time these episodes occur, Marjory is retraumatized by the experience. It is no wonder that those with PTSD find any way possible to cope with these sensory episodes, including self-medicating with alcohol or drugs, which is what Marjory did.

My client Donna came to understand that the reason she started drinking was to block out the feelings she frequently had in her vagina:

It felt like someone was touching me. It drove me crazy. I couldn't focus on anything else. It kept me awake at night. So, I started having a glass of wine before I went to sleep. One glass didn't always do the trick, so I had another, and another. Soon I became dependent on alcohol to go to sleep, and then I started drinking throughout the day. This led to neglecting my children, driving them around while I was drunk, and finally, to getting pulled over by the police and being taken to jail.

PTSD is also associated with impairment of a person's ability to function in social and family life, including occupational inability, marital problems and divorces, family discord, and difficulties in parenting. These factors in particular play a significant role in making those with PTSD particularly vulnerable to repeating the cycle of violence for the following reasons:

1. Many people with PTSD turn to alcohol or drugs in an attempt to escape their symptoms.

2. Some characteristics of PTSD can create abusive behavior, including:
   - Irritability—extreme irritation and reaction to noise or minor stimulants.
   - Explosive behavior and/or trouble modulating and controlling anger. Rage must go somewhere, either to the self or others.

3. Some characteristics of PTSD can create victim-like behavior, including:
   - Helplessness and passivity—an inability to look for and find problem-solving solutions
   - Self-blame and a sense of being tainted or evil
   - Attachment to trauma. Former victims seek out relationships that resemble the original trauma. Involvement with helping figures may end in an attempt to become one with the helper or in total rejection of the helper. A person with PTDS may vacillate between the two reactions.

Not all victims of childhood abuse suffer from PTSD, but those who have experienced interpersonal victimization at home or in the community have been shown to be at a very high risk for PTSD. If you have been diagnosed with PTSD or you suspect that you suffer from it, consider the strong possibility that it is at the core of any troubling behavior on your part such as addictive, abusive, or victim-like behavior.

Complex Trauma

Children who are exposed to multiple, chronic trauma, usually of an interpersonal nature, suffer a unique set of symptoms that can differ somewhat from those of PTSD. These children suffer from serious behavioral, interpersonal, and functional problems, such as a disrupted ability to regulate their emotions, behavior, and attention—a phenomenon or syndrome referred to as complex trauma. Like those who suffer from PTSD, victims of complex trauma often attempt to cope with their problems by self-medicating and thus often become alcoholics, drug abusers, compulsive overeaters, as well as suffer from other addictions. Those who have experienced such trauma often repeat the cycle of abuse—either becoming an abuser or continuing to be victimized.

Rates of major depression, anxiety disorders, substance abuse, and personality disorders are especially high among this group (even more so than those who suffer from PTSD). Unless victims are able to recover from the adverse effects of trauma, the effects may continue throughout their lives—most significantly in the area of interpersonal relationships.

In addition to suffering from most of the problems that those with PTSD suffer, victims of complex trauma tend to experience:

- extreme behaviors (self-injurious behaviors such as cutting, head banging)
- difficulties with sexual adjustment (confusion regarding gender or sexual preference)
- creating high-risk and painful situations in order to counteract feeling numb or dead inside (e.g., self-harm)
- sudden outbursts of anger
- suicide ideation or attempts
- extreme risk-taking behavior
- reenacting unhealthy relationships

If you suffered from multiple traumas in childhood (e.g., you were neglected or emotionally abused by your parents, you were also sexually abused as a young child, and you were raped when you were an adolescent) you likely suffer from complex trauma. The same is true if you were sexually abused for many years or by several perpetrators. Put a check mark next to the items from the list above that describe your symptoms.

Suffering from PTSD or complex trauma can explain much of your negative behavior that has harmed others, such as excessive drinking or violent outbursts. Again, this information is not intended to "excuse" your behavior, but understanding that you had a legitimate, *understandable* reason for the behavior can help you to have compassion for yourself, which hopefully will lead to self-forgiveness.

This was my client Tanya's experience:

I've carried so much shame about how I acted when I was drinking and drugging. When I was high, I always became belligerent, picking fights with my parents and friends. I would even get into physical fights with my siblings, and once I almost took out my sister's eye. I drove drunk and could have killed someone. In fact, I got into one car accident where the other driver was seriously injured. I felt terrible about it because it definitely was my fault because I was drunk driving. No one around me understood why I drank so much or took drugs and acted the way I did, but now I understand. Not only was I sexually abused, but my dad was physically abusive toward us kids and my mother. And I was bullied at school. It was all just too much to take. Now I understand that I was drinking and drugging to numb the pain of it all.

HOW TO FORGIVE YOURSELF FOR
THE HARM YOU CAUSED OTHERS

Forgiving yourself for the ways you have hurt or harmed others will probably be the hardest thing that you will ever do in order to heal your shame. In fact, it may be the hardest thing you ever do in your life. This is especially true if you have repeated the cycle of abuse by harming another person in the same ways that you were abused.

For example, it may seem impossible to forgive yourself for abusing a child, whether it be emotional, physical, or sexual. After all, you know firsthand how much child abuse damages a child. And you personally know how much the shame that accompanies abuse can devastate a person's life. Here are some examples of what clients have shared with me regarding the shame they felt for harming a child:

- "How could I possibly abuse my own child the way I was abused? I knew how much it devastated me to be beaten by my father. And yet I turned right around and did it to my own children. It's unforgivable."
- "I promised myself I would not treat my children the way I was treated. And yet to my horror, the very same words my mother said to me came out of my mouth. Those horrible, shaming, devastating words, 'I hate you. I wish you had never been born.' How can I forgive myself for saying those horrible words to the people I love most in the world?"
- "I feel like a monster. The shame I feel for molesting my daughter is so intense I can't even describe it. I couldn't have done anything worse to her. I've affected her life in such a horrible way. She must feel so betrayed. She must hate me, and I don't blame her."

UNDERSTANDING WHY YOU BECAME
A NEGLECTFUL OR ABUSIVE PARENT

Research shows that the long-term effects of trauma (such as abuse in child-hood) tend to be most obvious and prominent when people are stressed, in new situations, or in situations that remind them of the circumstances of their trauma. Unfortunately, becoming a parent creates all three of these circum-stances for someone who was abused in childhood. First-time parenthood, in particular, is stressful and almost always triggers memories of our own child-hood traumas. This sets the stage for child abuse.

In addition to being sexually abused, many former victims of CSA also experienced neglect and other forms of abuse, such as emotional and physical abuse. And the sad truth is that those who were abused or neglected in child-hood are more likely to become abusive or neglectful of their own children than someone who didn't have these experiences. There are certain traits that may have predisposed you to treat your children in abusive or neglectful ways. These include:

- an inability to have compassion toward your child
- a tendency to take things too personally (this may have caused you to overreact to your children's behavior by yelling, calling them names, or hitting them)
- being overly invested in your children looking good (and you looking good as their parent) because of your lack of self-confidence
- an insistence on your children "minding" you or respecting you to com-pensate for your shame or lack of confidence

And still another reason not often discussed that can cause a parent to become abusive is seeing your own weakness or vulnerability in your child. Those with a history of having been victimized often develop a tendency to hate or despise weakness. If you saw weakness in your child, you may have been reminded of your own vulnerability and victimization, which may have ignited your own self-hatred, thus causing you to lash out at your child.

IF YOU PASSED ON THE ABUSE TO OTHERS

Frank presented himself the way many abusers do—he was defensive to the point of being argumentative and seemed completely closed to any help I might offer, even though he insisted that he wanted to change to get his wife back. He was convinced that the reason he physically abused his wife was because she refused to listen to him, and that the solution to their problems was for her to begin doing what he told her. Although he understood that he had to stop physically abusing his wife if he was going to save his marriage, he couldn't see that it was wrong for him to treat his wife like property.

I suspected that underneath all Frank's defensiveness and bravado was a great deal of shame. It took a while, but Frank finally confessed to me that he had been bullied and sexually abused by a group of neighborhood boys when he was a child.

When I tried to get Frank to talk about the sexual trauma he experienced with the neighborhood boys, he just said, "It was no big deal. I'm tough. I got over it." But I was determined to help Frank begin to have self-compassion for what he had suffered at the hands of those boys. The best way I could do this was to show him compassion.

"I'm so sorry for what happened to you. No one should ever have to experience such a trauma. And I'm sorry that there was no one there to comfort you afterwards. It must have been so painful, and so humiliating."

But Frank couldn't let my words in. Instead he argued with me—"Na, it was no big deal. I was a tough kid. I could handle it."

"But you shouldn't have had to handle it. And you shouldn't have had to handle it all alone, no matter how tough you were," I explained.

Over the coming weeks I continued offering Frank compassion for his suffering. Eventually, he began to let down his walls and to feel his softer feelings—his vulnerability, his pain and sadness.

The next step was to encourage Frank to have compassion for himself. He began to recognize that he was, after all, just a little boy—an innocent, vulnerable little boy—when the rape occurred. He had survived the trauma, but at a price. He had defended himself from his pain and humiliation by taking on the role of an abuser.

Once he was able to offer himself some self-compassion, Frank could afford to see his wife in a more compassionate way and to look at his own behavior more honestly. It wasn't long after that that Frank began to see how he had passed on to his wife what had been done to him. He recognized that he insisted that his wife do everything he demanded because he needed to be in control. "I haven't realized it until now, but after what happened to me with those boys, I vowed to myself to never allow anyone to control me again. I needed to see myself as the man, as the boss. When she doesn't do things exactly the way I want, I feel out of control—just like I felt when those boys raped me."

The best part of this story was that by gaining self-understanding and connecting with his own suffering, Frank was able to have true compassion for his
wife's suffering. "Now I understand how my behavior hurt my wife. No one
wants to be controlled. It was like I had made my wife my prisoner. No wonder
she needed to get away from me."

If you have become abusive, I hope Frank's story has helped you. There is
always a reason someone becomes an abuser. In fact, I have never known an
abusive person who wasn't abused in some way. This isn't an excuse, just an
explanation. As you hopefully have begun to realize, being understood and
gaining self-understanding can be powerful healing tools.

Remember, the first step in preventing yourself from reenacting the abuse
that you experienced as a child or stopping behavior you have already begun is
to make a clear connection between your current behavior and the sexual abuse
you suffered. The second step is to gain self-compassion for your suffering.

THE LESS OBVIOUS LEGACIES OF CHILD SEXUAL ABUSE

In addition to coping with the sexual abuse by abusing alcohol and drugs or
continuing the cycle of abuse, child sexual abuse has other more subtle legacies.
For example, those with such a history are often unable to see their partner,
children, and even coworkers clearly. Instead, they see them through a distorted
lens of fear, distrust, anger, pain, and shame. They see ridicule, rejection, betrayal, and abandonment when it really isn't there. Their low self-esteem will
cause them to be hypersensitive and to take things far too personally. And they
will likely have control issues causing them to either need to dominate others
or be far too easily dominated by others.

Those with a history of CSA are often unable to trust their partners.
Instead, they often perceive their partner as an enemy instead of an ally. Those
who become parents find that it is difficult to see their own children's needs and
pain without being reminded of their own. They also find it difficult to allow
their children to make a mistake without taking it as a personal affront or a sign
that they are not a good parent. In work environments, past dramas with their
parents and siblings get reenacted with bosses and coworkers.

Exercise: Subtle Effects

Think about how the abuse you experienced has affected the way you view
yourself and others. Now complete the following sentences.

The abuse has affected the way I view myself in the following ways:

_____.

The abuse has affected the way I view others in the following ways:

_____.

WHERE DO YOU GO FROM HERE?

One of the primary goals of self-understanding is to stop the constant self-judgment and focus instead on understanding your faults and failures. Instead of blaming yourself for your mistakes or omissions, begin to believe that you had a good reason for your actions or inaction. This is a huge step to take, but one that is essential if you are to rid yourself of the debilitating shame that has haunted you most of your life.

Exercise: "It Is Understandable"

Whenever you become too critical of yourself for your current or past behavior, complete the following statement:

> Given all that I have experienced and suffered in my childhood, it is understandable that I would experience the following symptoms or take on the following behaviors _____.

As you've learned in this chapter, former victims tend to view symptoms of trauma with a lot of shame and impatience. And they tend to be self-critical and feel a lot of shame about how these symptoms have affected themselves and others. As you continue through the forgiveness process, remind yourself from time to time that the very behaviors you feel the most shame about are likely to be coping methods and survival skills.

No matter what your past or present mistakes, no matter whether you continue to be victimized or have become abusive, by practicing *self-understanding*—an important component of self-compassion—you can learn that your childhood environment likely set you up for your current behavior. By connecting through self-compassion with the suffering that you have experienced, you can gain *self-awareness*—and eventually *self-empowerment.*

COMMON HUMANITY AND GAINING
COMPASSION FOR YOURSELF

In Kristin Neff's construct of self-compassion, she names recognition of the common human experience—or what she calls "common humanity," as the second fundamental element of self-compassion. In her book, *Self-Compassion*, she states that "self-compassion honors the fact that all human beings are fallible, that wrong choices and feelings of regret are inevitable" (2011, p. 62).

The truth is, we have all harmed others. Knowing this, and knowing that you are not alone, can help you to have compassion for yourself and forgive yourself. Feeling compassion for yourself does not release you from taking responsibility for your actions. But it can release you from the self-hatred that prevents you from forgiving yourself and free you to respond to the situation with clarity. Rather than tormenting yourself with guilt and shame, having compassion for your own suffering and for the suffering of those you have harmed can help you achieve the clarity necessary for you to think of ways you can help those you have harmed (we will discuss making amends and repairing the harm later in the chapter).

When you examine your mistakes and failures, it becomes clear that you did not consciously choose to make them; even in rare cases when you did make a conscious choice, the motivation for your actions was colored by your abuse experiences. For example, because of the shame you have carried you closed your heart to others, you became blind to how your actions were harming others.

Exercise: Your Sins and Omissions

1. Write a list of the people you have harmed and the ways you have harmed them.

2. One by one, go through your list and write down the various causes and conditions that led you to this action or inaction. You've already made the connection between your harmful actions and the fact that you were abused or neglected. Now think of other precipitating factors, such as a family history of violence and a family history of addiction, as well as more subtle factors, such as stress due to financial problems or marital problems.

3. Now ask yourself why you didn't stop yourself from harming this person. For example, were you so checked out that you didn't even realize you were harming someone? Were you so full of rage that you couldn't control yourself? Did you hate yourself so much that you didn't care how much you hurt someone else? Had you built such a defensive wall that you couldn't have empathy or compassion for the person you harmed?

4. Now that you better understand the causes and conditions that led you to act as you did, see if you can apply the concept of common humanity (Neff, 2011) toward yourself: You were an imperfect, fallible human being and like all humans sometimes do, you acted in ways that hurt someone else. Honor the limitations of your human imperfection. Have compassion for yourself. Forgive yourself.

This exercise is an adaptation of a common humanity exercise created by Kristin Neff.

EARNING YOUR FORGIVENESS

If you continue to find yourself resisting forgiving yourself, ask yourself this question. "Why wouldn't I want to forgive myself?" Because you bought this book about ridding yourself of shame, why don't you want to complete one of the most important steps in this process? If your answer is "I don't deserve it," that is your shame talking. If you still feel like you don't *deserve* forgiveness, perhaps you believe you need to *earn* it.

Taking Responsibility

How do you earn forgiveness? First of all, you need to admit to yourself and others the wrongs you have committed. Unless you tell the complete truth about how you have harmed others, first to yourself and then to the person or persons you have harmed (if at all possible), you may not believe you deserve to be forgiven. (And incidentally, unless you admit what you did to harm the person or persons you have harmed, they may not be willing to forgive you.)

Dwelling on your mistakes does no one any good, including the person you harmed. But taking responsibility for your actions can do a lot of good— for you and the other person. When you take responsibility for your actions, you may feel more shame at the moment, but before long that feeling of shame will be replaced with a feeling of self-respect and of genuine pride (as opposed to false pride).

To prepare yourself for this process:

1. Spend time thinking seriously about how your actions or inaction have harmed the person. Completing the following sentence may help in this process:

   "I harmed _____ by _____."

2. Write down all the ways your action or inaction harmed this person.

"I caused _____ to suffer in the following ways _____

_____."

The next step is to face those you have harmed and admit what you have done to hurt them. If at all possible, do this in person. It will have far more impact on both you and the person you harmed than writing a letter, for example. Make certain, however, that you do not allow anyone to verbally abuse you or shame you.

Apologizing

Admitting what you did to harm others is doubly powerful if it is accompanied by a heartfelt, sincere apology. One of the most frequent comments that I hear from those who were abused in childhood is that they wish the offender would admit what he or she did and apologize to them for it.

Think of an incident when you felt wronged by another person. What did you want from that person in order to forgive him or her? Most people say they want an apology. But why is this the case? It isn't just the words "I'm sorry" that we need to hear. We need the wrongdoer to take responsibility for his or her action, and we need to know that the wrongdoer feels genuine regret or remorse for having harmed us.

Apology can help remove the cloak of shame that even the most remorseful person carries. On the other hand, if you don't experience enough shame when you wrong someone else, apology can help remind you of the harm you caused. The act of apologizing to someone usually causes us to feel humbled and humiliated. Remembering that humiliation the next time you are tempted to repeat the same act can discourage you from acting on your negative impulses.

When you are able to develop the courage to admit when you are wrong and to work past your fears and resistance to apologizing you develop a deep sense of respect for yourself. This self-respect can, in turn, affect your self-esteem, your self-confidence, and your overall outlook on life. When I apologize to you, I show you that I respect you and care about your feelings. I let you know that I did not intend to hurt you and that I intend to treat you fairly in the future. If you apologize for abusing or neglecting a child, even though that person is now grown, you will not only validate his or her experience but help the person to stop blaming himself or herself for the abuse.

How to Give a Meaningful Apology

A meaningful apology is one that communicates what I call the three R's—
regret, *responsibility*, and *remedy*.

1. A statement of *regret* for having caused the inconvenience, hurt, or damage. This includes an expression of empathy toward the other person showing that you understand how your action or inaction harmed him or her.
2. An acceptance of *responsibility* for your actions. For an apology to be effective it must be clear that you accept total responsibility for your actions or inaction. This means not blaming anyone else for what you did and not making excuses for your actions.
3. A statement of your willingness to take some action to *remedy* the situation. Although you can't go back and undo or redo the past, you can do everything within your power to repair the harm you caused. Therefore, a meaningful apology needs to include a statement in which you offer restitution in some way, an offer to help the other person, or a promise to take action so that you will not repeat the behavior. In the case of emotional, physical, or sexual abuse, you can enter therapy or a support group to make sure you do not abuse anyone again. You can offer to pay for your victim's therapy or you can donate your time or money to organizations that help victims of abuse.

For more information on how to give a meaningful apology refer to my book *The Power of Apology*.

If you have learned from your mistakes and do not wish to repeat them, then you no longer need to feel guilt or shame about it. If you need therapy to ensure that you will not repeat an offense, by all means give this to yourself. If you need to learn parenting skills, give this to yourself as well. Forgive yourself and let it go.

Criticizing and judging ourselves keeps us down, robs us of our confidence and motivation to change, and prevents us from learning from our mistakes. It encourages others to judge us and keeps us in negative situations and around negative people far longer than we should stay.

If you find you are still overwhelmed with guilt or shame about how your past behavior has affected someone, it will be important to realize and remember this truth: *The most effective method of self-forgiveness is to vow that you will not continue the same behavior and not hurt someone in the same way again.*

Forgiving yourself will do more for you in terms of healing your shame than almost anything you can do. Forgive yourself for the abuse itself. You were an innocent victim who did not deserve to be abused. Forgive yourself for the ways you reenacted the abuse. You were full of shame and, as you have learned, shame causes us to do horrendous things to ourselves and others. Forgive yourself for harming others. You probably didn't intend to hurt them, and you would take it back if you could. You were just trying to survive the pain and shame, sometimes unbearable, that you carried. Instead of wasting time chastising yourself for your past, look to the future. Learn from your mistakes. Promise yourself you will do everything in your power to become a better human being.

ELEVEN

FORGIVING YOURSELF FOR THE
WAYS YOU HAVE HARMED YOURSELF

Forgive yourself. The supreme act of forgiveness is when you can forgive
yourself for all the wounds you've created in your own life. Forgiveness is an
act of self-love. When you forgive yourself, self-acceptance begins and self-
love grows.

—Miguel Angel Ruiz Macias

AS WE HAVE FIRMLY ESTABLISHED, those who have been sexually abused tend
to be filled with shame, self-criticism, and self-loathing and to blame themselves for their own victimization. In turn, this can cause them to become
self-destructive by abusing their body with food, alcohol, drugs, cigarettes, and
self-mutilation; by sabotaging their success; or by eliciting punishment from
others. In addition, your shame can cause you to tenaciously hold onto your
problems and pain because it gives you the punishment you feel you deserve.
You may have spent your life punishing yourself with one bad relationship after
another or one illness after another.

The best way to rid yourself of this self-criticism and self-loathing is to
forgive yourself. Just as you needed to forgive yourself for the harm you caused
others, you need to forgive yourself for the harm you brought on yourself.

MAKING THE CONNECTION

As we have been discussing, self-understanding is beyond a doubt the most
powerful and effective way to accomplish self-forgiveness. Making the important connection between your behavior and your trauma experience will
help you become more self-compassionate and less impatient, judgmental, and
angry with yourself about your negative behavior. Below is a very short list
of troubling behaviors that are most common in victims of childhood sexual
abuse. This list is not comprehensive by any means but merely a way to begin
to understand the connection between troubling behaviors and the abuse you
experienced.

Eating disorders. Eating disorders such as bingeing, compulsive overeating, and emotional eating are especially common among those who were sexually abused, as well as those who were emotionally abused. These eating disorders arise as a way to cope with profound feelings of shame, emptiness, loneliness, depression, agitation, or other forms of distress.

Alcohol abuse and drug abuse. Alcohol abuse and drug abuse are common coping mechanisms for survivors of all forms of childhood abuse, including neglect and abandonment, verbal abuse, emotional abuse, physical abuse, and sexual abuse. However, more research has been done connecting alcohol and drug abuse to physical and sexual abuse than to other forms of abuse.

Self-injurious behavior. Self-injurious behavior such as cutting, intentionally self-inflicted cigarette burns, or head banging almost universally emerge originally as attempts to cope with severe abuse (e.g., long-term sexual abuse, sexual abuse by multiple perpetrators, severe neglect and abandonment, or sadistic or severe physical abuse).

Difficulties with sexual adjustment. Difficulties such as a tendency to sexualize relationships, becoming hypersexual, or avoiding sexual contact or alternating between these two extremes, usually stem from experiences of childhood sexual abuse.

The Connection between Eating Disorders and CSA

Many former victims of child sexual abuse suffer from eating disorders such as compulsive overeating, binge eating, and anorexia. My client Briana was a case in point. I had been seeing Briana for about two months. She initially came into therapy because she was severely depressed. Briana was twenty-eight years old and considerably overweight, but she had never talked about her weight until this session:

> I've just been diagnosed with pre-diabetes, and it's my own damn fault! The doctor tells me I have a chance to turn this thing around if I change my diet, but I know I won't stick with it. I never do. How stupid is that? I'd rather get diabetes than stop stuffing my face.

I'd been working on helping Briana notice how self-critical she was, so I pointed this out today. "Do you hear how harsh and critical you are being toward yourself?" I asked gently, not wanting to shame her.

"Yeah, I shouldn't be calling myself 'stupid,' but I've tried all kinds of diets and programs and nothing works for me. I just don't have any will power."

"Have you been overweight all your life?" I inquired.

"No, I didn't start gaining weight until I was around eleven years old."

"Did anything happen to you around that age? Any major changes in your life, any trauma?"

"Well, no—not anything I can think of."

"Were you getting along with your parents?" I asked.

"Yeah, no problems there."

"So why do you think you started gaining weight?"

"I don't know. It was like I suddenly couldn't get enough food. Before that, I ate normally. But I started eating so much that my stomach ballooned up, and I looked like I was pregnant."

"Had you started having sex?"

"No, no. I didn't have any interest in boys. Well, there was one thing that happened. I had a sexual experience with my counselor at summer camp." Briana said this matter-of-factly, like it was no big deal.

"Tell me about it," I said calmly.

Briana explained how her camp counselor had taken an interest in her, telling her he thought she was pretty and that she had a great body. He ended up sexually abusing her for the entire summer.

I didn't even realize until much later that what we did together was considered sexual abuse. I never told anyone about it and tried to go on with my life like nothing had happened. But honestly, I was never the same after that. I felt so dirty and ugly inside—I despised myself because I went along with it, you know? I could have run away; I could have told someone at the camp, or at the least told my parents when I got home. But I was too ashamed. I just kept my mouth shut the way he told me to.

"Could the molestation have been the reason why you started overeating?" I asked. "Could you have been overeating to comfort yourself?"

"Well, I never thought about that—it makes sense. I sure use food now whenever I'm upset."

"Do you remember how you felt when you started gaining weight?" I pursued.

"I hated myself even more."

"Any other feelings?"

"Well, in a way I was relieved. After what happened with Kevin, I always felt uncomfortable when boys or men paid attention to me. I was afraid that it would happen again, you know? But after I gained weight, men and boys stopped paying attention to me, and it was a huge relief."

"So, do you think that might be a factor in your weight issues today—in addition to the comfort factor?"

"Well, something about it seems important."

"Why don't you think about it?" I suggested. "Our time is up for today anyway."

Briana came into our next session looking brighter than I'd seen her before. It seemed she couldn't wait to talk to me.

> Remember the question you asked me last week about whether I might be trying to keep men away? Well, I thought about it, and the answer is yes! I definitely think that's what is going on. I have a pattern of losing weight, but as soon as I start getting comments about it, I gain the weight back! I never understood it before, but now I realize that when I lose weight, I also get more attention from men. I didn't realize that it makes me feel so uncomfortable, but it does. I never like men looking at me. It's not that I haven't had boyfriends because I have. But they are usually more passive men, not men who are flirtatious or aggressive in any way.

This insight on Briana's part was extremely important. It was a significant step toward her understanding herself.

"No wonder I continue to be overweight—I'm still trying to protect myself from further abuse," she shared with me. "Knowing this helps me to not feel so critical of myself about it. Now I just feel sad about what happened to me."

Using Substances to Manage the Impact of Trauma

A woman or man who has been sexually abused in childhood has to contend with powerful emotions and interpersonal chaos. Regrettably, some victims discover that they can ease the pain left by the trauma by abusing alcohol or taking certain drugs. If this is your situation, it can be helpful to see the connections between the feelings you are trying to manage and the substances you choose to use and abuse. The explanations that follow should not devolve into an "excuse for use" situation, but they can help you to place your substance use in context and help you consider alternative ways to manage some of your symptoms and feelings.

The following are common trauma symptoms and the drugs victims tend to use to manage them:

- *Depression.* Many former victims report feeling hopeless and despairing about their lives and their prospects for ever feeling good again. Drugs such as cocaine, which elevate mood even for a short time, may seem like a panacea for victims who experience prolonged bouts of depression.

- *Anxiety.* Trauma can leave victims feeling anxious and fearful. In the short term, they may be worried that more abuse will be forthcoming, and in the long term they may experience a pervasive sense of dis-ease and worry. Alcohol and some tranquilizers such as benzodiazepines can lessen the anxiety of a victim who feels chronically on edge.

- *Inner turmoil and pain.* Victims who are plagued by flashbacks and recurring memories of abuse may feel that the intensity of their experience is too great to bear. They may seek drugs that induce forgetting and tend to dull or numb all sensation. These victims are at especially high risk for choosing opiates or alcohol to dull the pain.

- *The absence of all feeling.* Although some victims feel too much, others report that the abuse left them unable to feel anything at all. They report an absence of all sensations, from sexual arousal to everyday feelings of happiness or sadness. For these former victims, any substance that produces an increase in sensation is appealing. They may find themselves drawn to cocaine or amphetamines for an immediate rush or to hallucinogens for a heightening of experiences.

- *Passivity.* A long-term consequence of the abuse for some former victims is the absence of any motivation or any ability to stand up for themselves. They may report that they see no choice other than to submit when someone is aggressive or intimidating toward them, and they wish that they could feel legitimate anger or assertiveness. Drugs such as alcohol or PCP that release and enhance anger may have a particular appeal for former victims who believe that they are "too passive."

- *Excessive anger and rage.* When former victims acknowledge what was done to them at the hands of an abuser, they may experience overwhelming feelings of anger coupled with a desire for retaliation. If the abuser is no longer living or is inaccessible due to illness or distance, a former victim may find that she feels angry but has no legitimate outlet for her rage. In some cases, she will turn to drugs that leave her feeling less angry and more accepting or mellow. She may choose alcohol, marijuana, or opiates to inhibit her feelings of anger and indignation.

If you have an alcohol or drug dependency, it is important to realize that it is very likely that you are using the substance to cope with some of the trauma symptoms listed earlier. This understanding can help you to be less critical of yourself as well as motivate you to discover and practice more effective ways of coping.

Self-Injurious Behaviors

> I've been a cutter for many years now. I'm so embarrassed about it—I wish I could stop, but it is a compulsion and a very strong one. I need help.

This is what Laura told me when she called to make an appointment.

I've worked with many clients who self-mutilate, and although it is a serious problem, I believed I could help her. I started by taking an extensive personal history. Laura revealed that she had been brutally sexually abused by her older brother for several years, starting when she was seven.

Not only did he rape and sodomize her, but he did so using objects such as pens, thermometers, toothbrushes, and eventually a hairbrush. The pain and fear Laura endured were horrendous. Because her brother was her parents' favorite and could do no wrong in their eyes, Laura knew they wouldn't believe her if she told them. In fact, she had tried telling them when he first started bullying her. Instead of making him stop, they accused her of making it up because she was jealous of him.

Laura started cutting herself when she was in high school.

> I didn't know why I was doing it. I just knew it made me feel better. I was terrified of anyone finding out, because I thought they'd think I was crazy. So, I always wore long sleeves, and I never undressed in front of anyone at the gym.

Even though Laura hadn't blocked out the memories of the horrendous abuse by her brother, she tried to put it out of her mind. She never made the connection between the cutting and the abuse by her brother.

> I just never put the two things together. The cutting wasn't a way of punishing myself, like you might think. It was more that I felt numb most of the time, and cutting myself made me feel something. I realize now it was my way of dealing with the trauma. When I cut myself, I felt pain, and that pain caused me to connect with myself—to feel alive. Most of the time I felt dead inside.

By the time we had worked together for many months, Laura reported that she only occasionally experienced the compulsion to cut herself. This was partly because she no longer needed to numb herself and was present in her body more often. And in therapy she had learned to experience her feelings of pain, anger, fear, and shame in safe ways.

FINDING MORE EFFECTIVE WAYS OF COPING

Safer and more effective ways of coping with shame and with stress can replace self-medicating with alcohol, drugs, food, self-harm, or other negative coping methods. Look over the following list of self-soothing practices and choose activities that sound good to you.

- Take a warm bath and allow yourself to sink into relaxation.
- Take a hot shower and enjoy the water falling on your skin.
- Massage your sore muscles with an oil that you especially like.
- Cuddle or pet your beloved pet.
- Practice yoga or meditation.
- Carry a photo of someone you love in your pocket, purse, or I-phone.
- Carry a smooth stone or soft piece of material in your pocket to touch when you need it.
- Suck on an ice cube or ice pop and enjoy the cool sensation.
- Drink your favorite beverage. Drink it very slowly and savor the flavors.
- Go for a leisurely walk in nature. Enjoy the sights, smells, and sounds all around you.
- Create a library of soothing music that you can listen to on your smartphone.
- Record a positive message to yourself that you can play on your smartphone.
- Listen to a recorded meditation.
- Think of a person who has been kind and loving, and imagine this person being with you in the present moment and caring for you.

Grounding

I introduced the practice of grounding in chapter 1. Below is more information on how to use grounding as a way of coping with symptoms such as flashbacks, dissociation, and panic episodes.

Grounding is a powerful yet simple strategy to help you manage and detach from emotional pain (such as memories of the trauma or flashbacks). The goal is to shift attention away from negative feelings toward the external world. Grounding is particularly powerful, because it can be applied to any situation where you are caught in emotional pain (e.g., triggered) and can be done anytime, anywhere, by oneself, without anyone noticing it.

Most victims report that they feel more "present" after practicing grounding. In fact, many are surprised to realize that they are "out of their body" (dissociated) more often than they realize. Practice grounding whenever you are extremely anxious, when you are having flashbacks or traumatic memories, and whenever you feel you are dissociated.

PUTTING YOUR SYMPTOMS IN THE CONTEXT OF YOUR ABUSE EXPERIENCE

Now that you have a better understanding of why you have adopted certain behaviors as a way of coping with the abuse you experienced, hopefully you will feel less shame about troubling or problematic behavior and will begin to feel less critical of yourself. The following exercise will help you in your attempts at self-understanding.

Exercise: Making the Connection between the Sexual Abuse and Your Behaviors

1. List your most troubling behaviors, the things that you have done that cause you the most shame (e.g., abusing alcohol or drugs, being sexually promiscuous, or other ways you have sexually acted out, abusive or victim-like behaviors).
2. Look at each of these behaviors and see whether you can find the connection between this behavior and your abuse experiences.
3. Once you have made this all-important connection, check to see whether you feel more compassion for yourself and for your suffering.
4. The next time you find yourself behaving in an unhealthy or self-destructive way (or having the desire to do so), instead of chastising yourself for the behavior use the sentence stem I introduced to you earlier:

   - "Given my history of sexual abuse it is understandable that I would behave like this."
   - Or simply say to yourself, "I understand why I'm acting like this."

5. Now find a healthier way to soothe yourself so that you don't need to resort to an unhealthy or dangerous way of coping. Don't expect yourself to make this transition right way. It will take practice and patience on your part to achieve this.

A PATTERN OF REVICTIMIZATION

Another reason you may need to forgive yourself is that you have stayed far too long in abusive relationships, or you have continually become involved with abusive people. As we have discussed, this is a common pattern for victims of child sexual abuse.

> I don't know what is wrong with me. I've put up with my husband physically abusing me for almost seven years now. He's put me in the hospital three times, and I lied to the doctors and the police each time. My family has completely given up on me—they've tried to help me so many times, but now they say it is just too painful to see my bruises. And my kids . . . God knows what I've done to them. My older son is as mean as his father, and he treats me just like his father does, ordering me around, criticizing everything I do. My youngest son is as afraid of my husband as I am, and he basically stays away from him. His older brother has been bullying and harassing him for years, and now he's even being bullied at school. He begs me to leave his father, but I still can't do it. I'm the poorest excuse for a mother.

This is how my client Ruby started her first session with me. As Ruby was to learn during our sessions, she had very good reasons why she could not leave her abusive husband, Adam. Research and experience now show that not only were most battered women victims of either emotional, physical, or sexual abuse in childhood, but most suffer from complex trauma, which we discussed earlier. This was the case with Ruby. She was severely sexually abused by her grandfather starting when she was only four years old and continuing until she was eleven. Because of the sexual abuse she suffered, Ruby had poor self-esteem, and because of this she lacked the internal resources to separate herself from her abusive partner. She also experienced difficulty trusting others, which prevented her from turning to others to obtain the help she so desperately needed. Finally, learned helplessness also played a role in her tolerance for the abuse by her husband, because, just as she felt with the sexual abuse, she believed that nothing could be done about the situation.

Over time, I was able to help Ruby understand why she stayed with Adam. Not only had Adam's continual abuse damaged her self-esteem even further, causing her to fear that she couldn't survive living without him, but she couldn't bear to leave the one person in her life who had understood her and supported her concerning the abuse she sustained at the hands of her grandfather. From the beginning of their relationship, Ruby had felt safe telling Adam about her childhood, just as he felt safe telling her about his. This had created a tremendous bond between them—what is sometimes called a "trauma bond." She felt sorry for him—she knew why he acted the way he did, and she knew he couldn't help it. How could she leave him?

Based on my experiences working with abused women and men for more than thirty-five years, they always have good reasons why they stay, and it typically has something to do with an abusive childhood. If you are currently the victim of emotional or physical abuse and have been unable to leave the situation, even though you know it is damaging to you and/or your children, I hope Ruby's story can help you understand yourself better. The following exercise may also help you in this endeavor:

Exercise: Why Can't I Leave?

- List all the reasons why you are unable to leave the situation or end the relationship (e.g., fear of being alone, fear of not being able to support your children, the belief that your partner will commit suicide if you leave him or her).
- Now focus specifically on your experience of sexual abuse. What role do you think it played in your choice of a partner?
- What role do you think the sexual abuse has concerning your inability to end the relationship? For example:
  - When my client Maura told her mother that her stepfather was sexually abusing her, she didn't believe her. She called her a liar and stopped talking to her. Now, whenever Maura thinks about telling someone that her husband is beating her, she hesitates, fearing she won't be believed or that she will alienate those closest to her.
  - My client Yolanda was afraid that her husband would commit suicide if she left him. We discovered that this fear originated from the fact that her father committed suicide when her mother left him.
  - My client Erin had still another reason for not leaving her abusive husband. This is what she shared with me during one of our sessions.

    My father sexually abused me throughout my childhood. I never told anyone because I felt so sorry for him, and he begged me not to tell. Every time he molested me, he'd break down and cry, asking me to forgive him, telling me he couldn't help himself. My husband does the same thing. After each episode of abuse, he comes to me begging for my forgiveness, telling me that he loves me but he just can't help himself. I can't believe I never saw the parallels before.

As I explained to Erin, some sex offenders (and some batterers) are good at making their victims feel sorry for them. They may break down and cry or threaten to commit suicide, putting the victim in the terrible position of feeling like they have to protect the very person who is harming them.

I guarantee that you have good reasons why you are unable to leave your abuser. Continue to work on finding the all-important connection between your reluctance and your childhood traumas, especially the sexual abuse.

FORGIVING YOUR BODY

As we have discussed, former victims of child abuse typically have a very negative relationship with their body. Many punish their body by starving themselves, eating unhealthy food, smoking, or self-mutilation such as burning or cutting themselves. And many hate their genitals, or consider them filthy or contaminated. It is not unusual for them to refuse to touch their genitals or to abuse them in some way. Some don't keep their genitals clean; some mutilate them by pinching them or having their genitals pierced.

Specifically, many former victims hate their body for the way it responded during the abuse. Many feel as if their body betrayed them, because it became aroused while they were being sexually abused. If you can relate to this, it is important to understand that our body responds to being touched, no matter who is doing the touching and no matter how much our *mind* fights it or feels repulsed by it. Some victims have experienced orgasms even though they were being traumatized, hated the perpetrator, or were terrified. This kind of experience can feel like your body betrayed you and can sometimes be the hardest to forgive. A child does not know that her body can respond without her consent, or even that it can respond in such a way. You may have felt that you must have wanted the sexual act; otherwise, why would your body feel pleasure? In addition, the perpetrator may have used the fact that your body responded to manipulate you into believing that you really wanted it.

If you can relate to the information above, as odd as it may sound, you need to forgive your body for responding. It is especially important to forgive those parts of your body that were directly involved in the sexual acts and the parts of your body that felt any pleasure. For example:

- Forgive your hands for touching his penis.
- Forgive your breasts for responding to his touch.
- Forgive your genitals for becoming stimulated.

Most important, understand that your body did not betray you. It was tricked just as you were.

In addition to and connected with the overwhelming feeling of shame that victims feel, they often feel dirty, tainted, spoiled, polluted, "ruined." This is what one client shared with me about how she felt about her body after she was abused:

After I was sexually abused by my uncle, I felt horribly ugly and dirty inside. I took dozens of baths hoping that I could wash away the dirtiness I felt, but it didn't work. I started becoming obsessed with washing my hands—the hands that touched his dirty, filthy penis. I brushed my teeth constantly trying to get the taste of his penis and his ejaculate out of my mouth. I changed my underwear several times a day because it always smelled like him.

If this is the way you feel about your body, my goal is to help you feel as if you have cleansed your body of the ugliness and dirtiness associated with the abuse. I want you to feel like you have stepped into a deliciously warm pool of water, water that has magical powers to cleanse and detoxify your entire body, inside and out.

Exercise: Forgiving and Cleansing Your Body

Self-healing rituals such as the one below can bring you a sense of being reborn, cleansed and refreshed. Combining them with the writing exercise can be a powerful way of working on forgiving your body:

- Soak in a hot bath or Jacuzzi. Imagine that all the residues of the abuse, especially your feelings of shame and self-blame, are being soaked *out* of you through your skin. Visualize the shame and impurities flowing out of your genitals, breasts, lips, mouth, anus—any part of your body that was "contaminated" by the abuser.
- For each part of your body that was involved in the sexual abuse, or that you feel betrayed you, complete the following sentence: I forgive you, _____, for _____.
- Now read over each of your forgiveness sentences and focus on taking in the words. Let your forgiveness words sink into your body, mind, and spirit.
- Imagine pouring compassion and loving energy *into* your body. Visualize yourself being reborn into a body that is wholesome, pure, and free of shame. Emerge from the water feeling cleansed, inside and out.

CONTAMINATION THOUGHTS

A recent study cited in *Behavior Modification* discusses a treatment that can help relieve feelings of intrusive body-hatred. This treatment appeals to both logic and emotion, via mental imagery.

Psychologists at Goethe University Frankfurt in Germany tested a brief treatment consisting of one session and a follow-up "booster" meeting. First, therapists and participants discussed the details of the participants' contamination thoughts—what it felt like, when and where it occurred, and how it affected their daily life. Then participants were instructed to research online how often human skin cells are rebuilt. They also calculated how many times the cells in their trauma-related body regions had been replaced since their last contact with their abusers. (Skin cells rebuild every four to six weeks; mucous membranes, more often.) The subjects discussed with the therapists what these facts mean—for instance, "not one of the dermal cells that cover my body now has been in contact with my abuser." Finally, they performed an exercise in which they imagined shedding their contaminated skin.

The researchers who conducted this study found that this treatment significantly decreased participants' feelings of being contaminated and also—to their surprise—their overall post-traumatic distress scores. Study author Kerstin Jung says the combination of factual information with mental imagery is key, because the information alone can leave a patient knowing the facts but not feeling that they are true on an emotional level. At that point, "we introduce the imagery technique as a vehicle to transport the rational information from the head to the heart," she says. "Images are much more powerful to change emotions than verbal information."

As I have stressed in this chapter, as important as it is to forgive yourself for the harm you have caused others, you also need to forgive yourself for the harm you have brought on yourself. Sometimes this harm is obvious—the harm you have done to your body due to excessive drinking, drugs, or cigarettes; overeating or eating unhealthy foods; purging and bingeing; self-mutilation; having unprotected sex or promiscuous sex. Forgive yourself for all these things. You didn't love and respect your body because of the massive amounts of shame you carried. You hated your body because it was a source of pain and shame. You starved your body because you had been starved of love, nurturing, and proper care when you were a child. You attacked your body because others had attacked it, and you felt that this was what it deserved. You were reckless with your body, because no one had cherished it when you were growing up. Forgive yourself.

Forgive yourself for the things you did that damaged your spirit, your image of yourself, and your integrity. For example, forgive yourself for overspending or stealing, for losing the family's house due to gambling debts, for prostituting yourself, for having sex with married people, for having sex with people you despised, for engaging in sex acts that felt repulsive or disgusting to you.

Often the harm you have caused yourself is more subtle than the obvious harm you did to your body or your self-image. We have touched upon some of these things throughout the book: For example, forgive yourself for pushing away people who loved you, for not trusting anyone. You pushed people away because you didn't believe you deserved to be loved. You didn't trust people because you were so deeply betrayed by the molester. Forgive yourself.

And there are even more subtle ways that you have harmed yourself for which you need to forgive yourself. Forgive yourself for being misunderstood so often by other people and by yourself. You were misunderstood because of layers of shame between you and other people, layers of shame that hid you from others, shame that prevented you from being yourself, from saying what you really meant, acting the way you really wanted to, layers of shame that made you appear one way when you really felt another way, layers of shame that made you say one thing when you really meant another. Forgive yourself for being misunderstood. It was the last thing you wanted. You wanted people to know the real you and to be accepted for who you are. You wanted your feelings and your perceptions validated. You wanted to be seen and heard. Forgive yourself for not knowing how to show people who you really are and for not knowing how to express yourself in the way that others could understand the real you.

Exercise: Self-Forgiveness Letter

- Write a letter asking yourself for forgiveness. Include all the ways you have harmed yourself, including ways that you have neglected and abused your body.
- Don't expect to write this letter in one sitting. It may take several days or even weeks to complete it. Take your time and really consider the many ways you have harmed yourself.
- As you write, bring up all the self-compassion you can muster. If you begin to feel self-critical, stop writing. Either do one of the other self-compassion exercises in the book or reread a portion of the book that will remind you of why you acted the way you did. Then go back to your letter with self-compassion in your heart and mind.
- This exercise, in addition to the following heart meditation, should make it easier to forgive yourself for the harm you caused yourself.

Heart Meditation: Forgiving Yourself for the Ways You Have Harmed Yourself

- Sit comfortably, allowing your eyes to close and your breath to be natural and easy.
- Let your body and mind relax.
- Breathing gently into the area of your heart, let yourself feel all the barriers you have erected and the emotions that you have carried because you haven't forgiven yourself.
- Let your heart feel the pain of keeping your heart closed.
- Breathing softly, begin extending forgiveness toward yourself, reciting the following words: "There are many ways that I have hurt or harmed myself. I have betrayed or abandoned myself many times through thought, word, or deed, knowingly or unknowingly."
- Feel your own precious body and life. Let yourself see the ways you have hurt or harmed yourself.
- Repeat to yourself: "For the ways I have hurt myself through action or inaction, out of shame, fear, pain, or anger, I now extend a full and heartfelt forgiveness. I forgive myself; I forgive myself."

PART IV

MOVING FORWARD:
ELIMINATING SHAMING BEHAVIOR

Even though hopefully you have been able to remove a great deal of the shame you've experienced due to the actual abuse, and have even forgiven yourself for the ways you have harmed others or yourself in the past, shame is such an insidious and pervasive emotion that you will need to be on the lookout for it to rear its ugly head. This includes noticing any *current* behavior on your part that creates shame. In the next section, I will name typical behaviors that cause shame and make suggestions as to how to avoid these behaviors.

TWELVE

AVOIDING UNHEALTHY
SHAME-INDUCING BEHAVIORS

Lack of forgiveness causes almost all of our self-sabotaging behavior.

—Mark Victor Hansen

The law is simple. Every experience is repeated or suffered till you experience it properly and fully the first time.

—Ben Okri, *Astonishing the Gods*

BY THE TIME YOU REACH THIS CHAPTER, most of you have stopped blaming yourself for the sexual abuse and are making progress when it comes to ridding yourself of negative beliefs such as "I'm damaged," "I'm worthless," and "I don't deserve anything good." Now you need to learn ways to eliminate behaviors that are likely to continue to create shame. This will include learning ways to work toward more self-acceptance and begin practicing self-kindness.

You haven't done all this work on healing your shame to just create more shame. In this chapter I will discuss the three most common ways that former victims continue to produce shame in themselves, along with strategies to help you avoid them. This includes:

- self-sabotage
- reenacting aspects of the abuse
- distress reduction behaviors (DRB)

SELF-SABOTAGE

My client Adrianne exclaimed:

I can't believe I just blew up my life like this! Everything was going so well. I just got that promotion at work, my husband and I had worked through most of our trust issues, and my kids were doing great. So why did I have to go and ruin everything?

The sad truth is that Adrianne's story is common for survivors of sexual abuse. In fact, it is at the time when things have turned around for the better, when things are going extremely well, that CSA survivors are often most vulnerable to self-sabotage. It is so true that sometimes I even warn my clients to be on the lookout for this tendency. For example, I've had clients who had a breakthrough in therapy one day, a breakthrough that gave them a great sense of hope, only to get into a car accident on the way home, or walk into a glass window and seriously cut themselves, or go home and start a horrendous fight with their spouse. Self-sabotage is nothing to play around with.

In Adrianne's case, not only had she received a promotion at work and mended her relationship with her husband, but she was feeling exceedingly good about herself. In the past two years of therapy, she was able to sever her relationship with her father, who had sexually abused her for a great deal of her childhood; and confront her mother, who had been complicit in the abuse. She had become clear that the abuse was not her fault and had forgiven herself for the ways she had acted out as a teenager, including being sexually promiscuous, being expelled from school, and being arrested for shoplifting. And although she had almost gone down a very dark path as a young woman, she was experiencing some healthy pride in the fact that she had managed to pull herself together.

But Adrianne clearly had more work to do, including coming to understand why she had sabotaged herself in such a dramatic way. I hope her story will act as both a warning and a lesson about how very vulnerable you still may be, no matter how much you feel you have healed your shame.

> I can't even believe I did what I did. It's absolutely shocking to me. I got to a place where I didn't even recognize myself. It started with what I thought was an innocent flirtation with a man at work. I was turning forty and felt complimented by his attention. But suddenly I felt this intense sexual attraction to him, something I just couldn't ignore. I tried to resist him but before I knew it, we were in this mad love affair. It was like I couldn't help myself—I couldn't stop seeing him. I began to lie to my husband, something I never did before, something I didn't believe in. For most of my life, I've had an issue with being able to trust people, but I had finally begun to trust my husband after many years of marriage. Now here I was lying and betraying him! I didn't even recognize myself.
>
> To cut to the chase, the affair went on for three months, and during that time I risked losing my job because we were forbidden to get involved with other employees, and because I was so preoccupied with thinking about my lover that my work suffered. And I became distant with my husband and kids. In the end I lost my husband and almost lost my job. And my kids aren't speaking to me.

Adrianne had stopped therapy with me six months prior to returning on this day. At the time she felt she no longer needed therapy; and although I still believed that she had more work to do, I didn't try to talk her out of leaving. I've often found that clients need to discontinue therapy for a time in order to fully integrate what they have learned and to appreciate the changes they have made. And I never want a client to become dependent on me or on therapy. I want clients to begin to take charge of their own healing.

Nevertheless, I wasn't surprised that self-sabotage had reared its ugly head, nor was I surprised that Adrianne knew enough to return for help. As I told her on the day she returned, we had work to do. We needed to help her understand why she had acted as she did and then help her forgive herself for her mistake. And I needed to offer her strategies to help prevent such self-sabotage in the future.

As Adrianne soon wondered:

> You know, I have a feeling that I didn't think I deserved all the good things that were happening to me at the time—the promotion, getting closer to my husband, having my kids doing so well. Do you think the affair was a way for me to sabotage myself?

Self-sabotage is a common shame-inducing behavior, a behavior clearly connected to the amount of shame the person continues to experience. Those who are shame-ridden typically have an extremely difficult time tolerating happiness or success in any form. Because of the shame they carry, they don't believe they deserve good things. So, whether it is a healthy relationship, a promotion at work, winning a contest, or receiving accolades from others, they need to sabotage their success as soon as possible to become more comfortable.

It is common for those in a healthy relationship to sabotage it by becoming critical of their partner or by being unfaithful; common for those who are promoted at work to follow up on the promotion by making a huge mistake that will require censure or even termination. Even feeling successful in therapy can cause former victims to self-sabotage by pushing the therapist away; because this is unconscious behavior, the act of making the behavior conscious can be the first step toward change.

This is how another client, Cathy, described her sabotaging behavior:

> Every time I'm in a good relationship, I do something to sabotage it. I get jealous, I become critical, I start fights. I used to assume I was choosing the wrong guys, but I've realized that most of the men I've been with were really good guys. In fact, when I look back on it, the nicer the guy was, the more I pushed him away.

Strategies to Help Prevent Self-Sabotaging

As it was with Cathy, when good things happen to them, many former victims feel uncomfortable because they don't believe they deserve it. This is not usually a conscious thought, but it is a powerful one nevertheless. They have such low self-esteem and so much self-hatred that they can't take in the good.

Exercise: Taking in the Good

The next time you experience something good (a great night out with your partner, a fabulous vacation) or receive something good, whether it be a compliment, a gift, or an accolade, pay attention to how you feel and how you react. For example:

- How do you react when you have a positive experience? Do you savor the experience, think about it again and again and remember the good feelings, or do you find something wrong with the experience and focus on any negative aspects of it?
- How do you usually react to a compliment? Do you graciously thank the person and allow yourself to feel the good feelings that can come with being praised, or do you push the compliment away with a statement such as, "Oh, this old thing, I've had it for years," or "If you'd been doing this as long as I have, you'd do it well, too."
- How do you react when someone is especially nice or loving toward you? Do you let yourself enjoy the good feelings? Or do you brush it off with thoughts such as, "She's probably that nice to everyone"? Or worse yet, become suspicious that the person wants something from you?

The next time any of these situations happen to you, try doing the following:

1. Instead of numbing yourself or countering the positive message or experience, try allowing yourself to consciously take in the good thing.
2. Start by taking a deep breath. Now imagine the positive comment or the good experience and the good feelings attached to it flowing into your body.
3. Take another deep breath and again, imagine the good thing coming into your body. Notice whether a feeling is attached to the good feeling. Repeat this several times.
4. If you noticed resistance to taking in the good thing, take another deep breath and tell yourself, "I worked hard for this," or "I deserve this," or "I'm going to consciously work on believing that I deserve this."

Practice this "taking in the good" process every time you experience something positive. This is not an overnight fix. You may continue to experience resistance to taking in the good, but if you continue to practice this exercise, in time it will become easier and easier.

Another Way to Take in the Good

Below is yet another way to practice taking in the good. This strategy is based on the evidence-based therapy method developed by Francine Shapiro known as EMDR (eye movement desensitization and reprocessing). "Tapping in the good" uses bilateral stimulation to reinforce feel-good moments, times when you connect to a positive feeling. Slow bilateral tapping helps strengthen and grow neuropathways in your brain that can take you to a calm, feel-good state. Along with the tapping, simply staying a while with the feel-good moment makes these neurons more likely to fire together in the future.

Exercise: Tapping in the Good

- Choose a time to tap when you are feeling good—when you have received a compliment, when you feel a moment of joy, when you feel connected to nature—any time you have a reason for feeling good about yourself or experience a positive feeling that you want to take in.
- Place your right hand on your left shoulder and your left hand on your right shoulder.
- Gently tap your left shoulder, then tap your right one, then back to your left and so on.
- Go slowly, about one tap a second or slower, until you have tapped a total of seven or more times on each shoulder.

By practicing this method, you are literally tapping in the good feelings. Over time, you will be teaching your brain to take in good things. In addition, you will actively be promoting a state of calm and relaxation by staying longer with your positive moments. This, in turn, can counteract a tendency for the neurons in your brain to move toward and intensify anxiety.

COUNTERING YOUR SABOTEUR WITH SELF-ACCEPTANCE

Practicing self-acceptance and self-kindness are especially powerful tools to help you to avoid continuing to shame yourself with self-sabotage. Self-acceptance isn't the same as excusing our behavior or giving ourselves permission to continue negative, unhealthy, or dangerous behaviors. Instead, it is an *open-heartedness* to all our shortcomings and faults. It is essentially saying to ourselves, "I recognize that I am not perfect, but I accept myself anyway."

Unfortunately, those who have been deeply shamed often find it almost impossible to view themselves in this way. Although you may rid yourself of self-blame and negative self-beliefs regarding your past abusive or shaming experiences, and may even forgive yourself for your past behavior, if you continue to be self-critical, you will continue to accumulate shame.

Therefore, a major step toward obtaining self-acceptance is to quiet your critical inner voice. Everyone has a critical inner voice, but people with low self-worth and those who were deeply shamed or abused tend to have a more vicious and vocal inner critic. This type of loud, verbose inner critic is enormously poisonous to our psychological health—more so, in fact, than any trauma or deprivation we have experienced. This is because we can often heal our wounds and recover from our losses, but the critic is always with us, judging us, blaming us, finding fault in us.

One of the most effective tools in developing self-acceptance is to begin to turn off your critical inner voice and to install a more nurturing one. The following processes and exercises will help you in this regard.

Exercise: Installing a Nurturing Inner Voice

- Take a deep breath and begin going inside and consciously creating an intimate connection with yourself. Many people don't know how to do this. Others are afraid to do it because their inner life seems like a cold, empty, or uninviting place. Tell yourself that whatever you find inside is OK. Continue to focus inside anyway. (Start by simply asking yourself, "How do I feel?" as many times a day as you can think of it. You may need to prompt yourself to go inside by leaving yourself written reminders such as "check in with yourself" or "how are you feeling?")
- You may become aware of a wall of anger, sadness, fear, or guilt; or you may feel a void inside. If you notice a wall of thoughts, step over the wall and begin to sink into yourself more deeply.
- Focus inside and see if you can find even a fledgling sense of connection with yourself.
- See if you can bring up a nurturing inner voice, one that is deeply connected to the inherent strength, goodness, and wisdom within you (your essence). This is not a harsh, critical, or depriving voice, and it is not an overly sweet, indulging voice. It is a warm, kind voice that cherishes you and accepts you for who you are. In time, this voice will become your own, but for now, it can be any voice that meets your needs. Some

people are readily able to find such a voice, whereas others have more difficulty. If this is your situation, begin speaking to yourself in the voice you use when you talk to a small child or beloved pet. Or adopt the voice of someone you know who is nurturing but strong (your therapist, a sponsor, a loving friend).

- Whenever you find you are criticizing yourself or being hard on yourself, consciously switch to this more nurturing voice. This is especially important for those who were highly criticized by a parent. If this applies to you, work on replacing your parent's critical, negative voice with a more nurturing, compassionate inner voice.

(This exercise is an adaptation of an "Imagine" from *Solutions Training* by Laurel Mellin.)

Countering Your Saboteur with Compassion

Compassion is the greatest antidote to the poison of your inner critic. Compassion is the essence of self-esteem. When you have compassion for yourself, you understand yourself. You accept yourself the way you are. You tend to see yourself as basically good. If you make a mistake, you forgive yourself. You have reasonable expectations of yourself. You set attainable goals.

Compassion is a skill. That means that you can improve it if you already have it, or you can acquire it if you don't. The next time you hear your inner critic chastising you about something you did or did not do, counter this negativity by telling yourself something like, "I'm doing the best I can," or "Given my circumstances, this is all I am capable of at this time."

Unfortunately, to some extent people with a strong inner critic will always be shackled to a negative inner voice. Your job is to diminish the intensity of self-attacks while practicing ways of healthy self-talk. Although you may never be entirely free of an inner voice that says, "What's wrong with you?" or "You're an idiot" whenever you make a mistake, you can create and reinforce the growth of a parallel and even stronger voice that says, "I did the best I could," or "I'm just fine the way I am." You will discover that as your healthy inner voice grows stronger it will respond more quickly, more forcefully, and more believably to the attacks of your critic.

Practicing Self-Kindness

As the shame from the abuse continues to lift, you will undoubtedly become more open to providing yourself with self-kindness, but I do understand that it will be especially difficult for some of you. If you haven't had much experience of being treated kindly thus far, it can be difficult to learn how to treat yourself in this way.

Self-kindness involves providing for yourself the patience, acceptance, and caring that you so desperately need. But it is so much more. Self-kindness involves generating feelings of care and comfort toward oneself. And it also involves learning simple tools for giving yourself the support you need whenever you suffer, fail, or feel inadequate.

One such tool is *self-soothing*. I introduced the concept of self-soothing as an alternative to self-destructive behavior in the chapters on self-forgiveness. Research shows that the power of self-kindness is not just some feel-good idea that doesn't really change things. For example, one important way that self-soothing works is by triggering the release of oxytocin—what researchers have dubbed the "hormone of love and bonding." It has been shown that increased levels of oxytocin strongly increase feelings of trust, calm, safety, generosity, and connectedness and facilitate the ability to feel warmth and compassion for ourselves. This is especially true when you self-soothe by touching your body in a gentle way because physical touch releases oxytocin, which has been shown to reduce fear and anxiety and can counteract the increased blood pressure and cortisol associated with stress.

You can physically soothe yourself in many ways. Many of my clients find that softly stroking their cheek or gently stroking their arms is especially comforting. I encourage you to find a way that works for you in order to soothe yourself when you are anxious, triggered, feeling alone, or feeling hopeless. In the previous chapter, I shared some self-soothing techniques my clients have reported being especially effective in producing positive and comforting sensory experiences. Refer back to this list for some suggestions.

All the strategies and information in this chapter can help you to prevent self-sabotage. But the most efficient and powerful way to deal with self-sabotage is self-forgiveness. In fact, if you are sabotaging your happiness or success, it indicates that you have not completely forgiven yourself. Please reread the chapters on self-forgiveness and, if you haven't already done so, complete all the exercises. Past readers have consistently reported that completing the exercises in my books made all the difference for them.

In summary, in order to prevent self-sabotage, I encourage you to do all the following:

- Practice "taking in the good."
- Work on discontinuing behaviors that induce shame, including being self-critical, being perfectionistic, and comparing yourself with others.

- Recognize that we all have weaknesses, shortcomings, and character flaws—this is part of being human. This does not mean that we stop trying to become a better person, but that we come to *recognize the difference between what we are able to change and what we need to accept.*
- Confront the belief that you should be good all the time, never makes mistakes, never hurt anyone's feelings, and never break the rules. The reason this is so important is that by adhering to these beliefs you set yourself up for continual shaming.
- Work on accepting yourself in spite of the fact that you are likely to continue to make mistakes or poor choices at times. If you have been able to forgive yourself for your past mistakes, it will be ludicrous for you to continue criticizing yourself for mistakes you will likely continue to make in spite of your best intentions.
- Practice self-compassion, self-kindness, and self-soothing.
- Continue to work on self-forgiveness.

REENACTMENTS

Another common behavior that continues to create shame in survivors' lives is the tendency to reenact or relive past trauma. These phenomena have been called reenactments. *Trauma reenactments* occur when people expose themselves to situations reminiscent of the original trauma, placing themselves at emotional risk or in physical danger in a compulsive mimicking of the past.

Ongoing reenactments often indicate that survivors are emotionally stuck. They are attempting to work through some aspect of the trauma by repeating it with another person hoping that this time the result will be different. In addition, reenactments often lead to revictimization and with it, related feelings of shame, helplessness, and hopelessness. For example, it has been found that women who were sexually abused as children are more likely to be sexually or physically abused in their marriages. Therefore, gaining an understanding and control of reenactments is a primary way to avoid further shaming.

Reenactments are caused in part by powerful unconscious forces that must be eventually verbalized and understood. Thus, in order to address reenactments and break their repetitiveness, the survivor needs to understand why they occur. Several ideas have been suggested to explain the phenomenon of reenactments.

- Many experts understand reenactments as an attempt to achieve mastery. This means that a traumatized individual reenacts a trauma in order to remember, assimilate, integrate, understand, and heal from the traumatic experience.

- Some experts perceive reenactments as spontaneous behavioral repetitions of past traumatic events that have never been verbalized or even remembered. For example, Freud noted that individuals who do not remember past traumatic events are "obliged to repeat the repressed material as a contemporary experience instead of . . . remembering it as something belonging in the past."

- Others suggest that reenactments result from the psychological vulnerabilities characteristic of trauma survivors. For example, as a result of a range of ego deficits and poor coping strategies, trauma survivors can become easy prey for victimizers.

Reenactments as an Attempt to Achieve Mastery

Individuals may actively reenact elements of past traumatic experience as a way of coping with and mastering it. Freud called this behavior "the repetition compulsion." At times, the attempt is an *adaptive* process that facilitates the successful resolution and working through of the earlier trauma. In other cases, the effort to master the trauma is a *maladaptive* mechanism, and the strategy results in continued revictimization and distress for the individual. Although the individual may have adequately mastered certain aspects of the trauma, in other areas the resolution may be less than adequate. For example, an individual who was violently beaten as a child may have adaptively mastered this trauma by becoming a homicide detective. However, his intimate relationships may be marked by detachment and underlying terror.

Reenactments Indicative of Adaptation

It has been suggested that actively reenacting a past trauma can provide an opportunity for an individual to integrate and work through the terror, helplessness, and other feelings and beliefs surrounding the original trauma. Freud posited that mastery could be achieved by actively repeating a past uncontrollable and unpleasant experience. Control can slowly be reestablished by repeatedly experiencing what once had to be endured.

For example, my client Melody was sexually abused from age six to age thirteen. Because of this, she was terrified of physical contact. In fact, when she first came into therapy at age twenty-five, she was still a virgin. "I not only have never had sex; I cringe whenever a man tries to touch me in a romantic or intimate way."

In the past, I had witnessed several clients overcoming their fear, discomfort, or repulsion of touch by going to a trauma-informed massage therapist or by training in massage therapy. In the cases where my clients went to trauma-informed massage therapists, they had the opportunity to slowly experience safe touch to a nonthreatening part of their body and then discuss their feelings and reactions with the therapist. They could then slowly advance to more threatening parts of their body. For the few who studied massage therapy, the process was similar, but they had the added advantage of being able to be the one in control and of learning about how the body functions. Both groups of clients were able to work through their overwhelming feelings of fear related to their past sexual abuse as well as diminish their fear of physical contact. In the next chapter, I will share with you still another method for overcoming fear of touch—sensate focus.

Reenactments Indicative of Maladaptation

In many cases, actively reenacting a past trauma reflects a more *maladaptive* defense posture than an adaptive one. For example, many victims of CSA become abusers themselves. In these cases, reenacting past abuse is a defensive stance that ensures that they don't reexperience the terror and helplessness related to the past traumatic experience or relationship. In addition, the abusive act allows the individual to express and direct rage at others. (This is important because a child victim is seldom ever able to direct his or her rage toward the abuser.) This way of being in the world is an attempt to master the previous trauma, but it is a maladaptive one because it does not result in a reworking and integration of the person's traumatic past, and it victimizes others in the process.

Another example of a maladaptive way of reenacting abuse is the phenomenon of CSA victims becoming prostitutes. Many women (and men) who become either prostitutes or strippers try to explain their choice to reenact in this manner as a way for them to control men though sex. In their minds they are turning the tables on men. Although this may sound like they are now controlling rather than being controlled, the old drama is still being played out in the present. An adaptive mastery of the earlier trauma has not been achieved; men are still feared, they still need to be controlled, and revictimization often continues to occur.

Still another example of a maladaptive way of reenacting past abuse is to unconsciously seek out a person who is similar to a past abuser and reenact the past traumatic relationship. The unconscious desire is to get the abuser to treat her well, which, if successful, would ameliorate her feelings of self-blame and badness. This is, unfortunately, an all-too-common way for former victims to feel like they have gained mastery.

Maladaptive reenactments can also occur because a person seeks out and "chooses" a powerful, caretaking (and sometimes abusive) person in order to solidify a shaky self-concept and a fragile sense of self. In addition, survivors who suffer from self-hatred, an internal sense of badness, and a sense that they deserve mistreatment may gravitate to others who resonate with their negative self-concept, and past experience can then be repeated.

This is what occurred with my client Mason. Mason was sadistically sexually abused when he was a teenager by a much older man. Even though he had experienced a lot of healing in the past several years, he continued to be attracted to older men who ended up treating him poorly. Each time this happened he ended up feeling terrible shame.

How Reenactments Can Be Addressed in Therapy

I highly recommend individual therapy if you continue to suffer from reenactments, because it is a clear sign that you have not adequately processed the trauma. Allowing yourself to experience the intensity of the old traumatic feelings within the safety of a therapeutic relationship will provide the opportunity to integrate the entire traumatic experience. This is where one-on-one therapy in which a positive therapeutic alliance has been established is ideal. Once the trauma has been integrated, your feelings will be less intense and more manageable, and you will be able to exercise better judgment as well as less rigid defenses.

Although some former victims may not have the ego strength or desire to explore early traumatization, therapy can still be of considerable benefit. Even without a full reworking of the individual's past traumatization, reenactments can be stopped by helping the patient to respond differently in the world through behavioral and cognitive change.

This is what my client Lily and I decided to focus on. Lily came to see me because she had just ended another abusive relationship, one of several that she had experienced in the past several years. "I want to find out why I continue to choose partners who are abusive. I don't know if I just don't pay attention to red flags, or if there is something I am doing to bring this out in men."

Although I made it clear that it was never her fault that her partners abused her emotionally and physically, I did agree to explore her history with her and see if we could find some connections between her history and her pattern. As it turned out, Lily had a long history of childhood sexual abuse involving several perpetrators. She had sought therapy several years ago for help to heal the abuse, and she found the work very healing.

In spite of her previous therapy, I noticed that Lily seemed rather timid and frail, and I wondered how this might contribute to how others treated her. I started by asking her how she imagined others viewed her.

"I don't know. I really haven't thought about it."

"Do you think you come across as someone who is confident?" I pressed.

"Well, maybe not. I guess I could work on appearing more confident."

"Why might this be important?"

"Well, I don't want to be a target to abusive men."

"And why would appearing more confident help in that regard?"

"Well, if I come off as someone who isn't confident, or someone who is rather passive, men might think I can be easily controlled."

I was delighted that she was making this connection so readily and so soon. "What could you do to change the way you come across?"

"I guess I can start by just paying attention to the way I present myself."

"Absolutely."

Although you need to remain clear that being bullied, harassed, abused, or sexually violated is never your fault, presenting yourself to others as someone who is strong and assertive will likely invite fewer attacks and can affect the way you perceive yourself. The following exercise can help you do this.

Exercise: Changing Your Posture

- Begin this exercise by grounding yourself.
- Notice your posture. Are you slumping or are you sitting up straight? Try purposely slumping and notice how you feel. Describe this feeling if you can. Now sit up straight and pull your shoulders up and back. Again, notice how you feel emotionally.
- Now lengthen your spine by imagining that you are increasing the space between the vertebrae in the lower to middle part of your back.
- Slowly lift and move your shoulders back. Notice how this feels.
- Gradually lift your chin and head, and again, notice how this feels.
- Gently bring up your gaze and focus on something at eye level.

Now notice how you feel with your body in this position. Hopefully, you will notice that you are a little less fearful, a little calmer, even a little more confident. Continue to pay attention to your posture until you notice that you are standing up straighter and appearing more confident. It may take time and attention to change your posture permanently, but it will be worth it.

DISTRESS REDUCTION BEHAVIORS—
PROBLEMATIC AVOIDANCE BEHAVIORS

So far, we have discussed self-sabotage and reenactments as examples of ongoing shame-inducing behaviors. You also need to be on the lookout for a third major category of shame-inducing behaviors—*problematic avoidance behaviors.* We began our discussion of these behaviors in chapter 3. John Briere, in his book *Treating Risky and Compulsive Behaviors in Trauma Survivors,* refers to these behaviors as distress reduction behaviors (DRB). DRBs can include problematic substance use, food bingeing and purging, compulsive gambling, shoplifting, thrill or sensation seeking, self-injury, and risky or compulsive sexual behaviors. For a complete list of DRBs, refer to chapter 3.

In the self-forgiveness chapters, we also discussed the idea that it is common for former victims to use various unhealthy behaviors such as alcohol or drug abuse or self-harm to cope with their shame and other painful emotions. Problematic avoidance behavior is just another name for these unhealthy and often destructive coping behaviors. Almost any behavior can be a DRB if it is used in an attempt to reduce internal distress. All of the above behaviors and the ones listed in chapter 3 have been shown in scientific research as *avoidance mechanisms,* thought to operate by:

- diverting attention away from painful emotions,
- "blocking" unwanted memories,
- providing distress-incompatible feelings,
- reducing unwanted dissociation, or
- otherwise altering awareness of painful internal states.

DRBs are triggered by phenomena in the person's current environment (e.g., perceived rejection or danger) that are reminiscent of early adverse events. Unfortunately, DRBs are only temporarily effective and do not permanently eliminate the individual's painful emotions or negative thoughts, including shame, nor do they alter the presence of triggers in the environment. Further, the DRB itself may produce additional shame or guilt.

Ways to Reduce or Eliminate Distress Reduction Behaviors

The key to reducing or eliminating problematic avoidance strategies, including DRBs, suicidality, dissociation, or problematic substance use is threefold:

1. Identify your triggers.
2. Discover the function of your particular DRB.

3. Learn and practice some emotional regulation skills. By increasing your ability to internally "handle" negative emotional states, you can decrease your need for external avoidance strategies.

Identifying Your Triggers

DRBs usually occur after you have encountered a trigger in your current environment. We began our discussion of triggers in chapter 5. Many triggers are interpersonal, for example: perceived rejection, abandonment, criticism, boundary violations, yelling, or maltreatment. Others may be nonpersonal, such as certain sounds, smells, tastes. They can be anything your mind perceives as similar to the traumatic event such as a location, a tone of voice, a topic of conversation, a scene in a movie.

Because people usually use DRBs after they have been triggered, it is vitally important that you discover exactly what your triggers are. If you have been working on creating a list of triggers, you can now use it to help you work with your DRBs. If you haven't created such a list, do so now. Earlier (in chapter 5) I listed the most common triggers for those who have been sexually abused. Here is a more extensive list of triggers. These aren't necessarily focused on sexual abuse but, rather, on child abuse and neglect in general.

Read the list carefully and put a check mark next to each item that tends to trigger you:

- feeling abandoned or rejected
- the sound of someone crying
- criticism
- someone being very angry
- someone saying mean or abusive things to you
- someone yelling at you
- someone raising a hand or fist near you
- someone threatening to hurt you
- mean or dirty looks
- seeing violence on TV, at the movies, or on the internet
- people in authority
- competition
- being lied to
- someone acting like they are better than you
- someone who reminds you of your mother
- someone who reminds you of your father
- being let down by someone

- being laughed at
- being accused of something you didn't do
- being ignored
- feeling alone

Knowing your particular triggers can help you to better understand yourself and your reactions. In particular it can help you understand why you may sabotage yourself with DRBs.

Discovering Your Triggers Associated with Shame

Some triggers not only remind you of the abuse itself but remind you of the shame you experienced at the time of the abuse. The following exercise will help you to identify the triggers associated with shame.

Exercise: Your Shame Triggers

Begin this exercise by asking yourself, "What were the most shaming aspects of the sexual abuse?" For example: Was it the fact that you didn't resist? That you returned to the abuser? That you didn't tell anyone? That you experienced some pleasure? That you introduced other children to sex?

These shaming aspects can give you hints concerning your specific triggers regarding the sexual abuse. For example, let's say that one of the most shaming aspects of the abuse was that you didn't resist. If you are a male, it can be particularly shaming to think about the fact that you didn't fight back, and you may carry a great deal of shame because of it. This memory can become a trigger under each of these circumstances: whenever you are afraid to stand up for yourself, whenever you are dealing with a person who has more power than you do, whenever someone is forcing you to do something you don't want to do; in other words, whenever you feel you are being exposed as weak or powerless, or you fear such exposure.

Let's look at another common shaming aspect of sexual abuse—the fact that you didn't tell anyone. In this case, you may be triggered whenever you are asked to keep a secret or you are involved with something clandestine—something hidden, illegal, secretive.

I think you can see how this works—certain aspects of the abuse remind you of the shame you felt and trigger you. These triggers represent your vulnerabilities—areas where you need to do more work. *Triggers point you in the direction of what needs healing.*

DISCOVER THE FUNCTION OF YOUR
DISTRESS REDUCTION BEHAVIOR (DRB)

Whether or not you realize it, your DRBs serve a function in your life. Even though this same behavior creates more shame in your life, it provides you with something important. Discovering what it provides will help you to avoid shaming yourself when you behave in a self-destructive way. And once you understand why you use this DRB, you will then be able to provide alternative ways of coping with the problem.

For example, if you are involved in compulsive sexual behavior, this might indicate that sexual DRBs distract you from upsetting memories, soothe triggered distress, and lessen feelings of emptiness. Discovering the reasons why any given DRB is being used potentially highlights the best intervention. For example, self-injury blocks memories, distracts from triggered angry feelings, and lessens dissociation. The most helpful interventions might include emotional processing of specific memories, learning self-soothing or self-grounding skills so that dissociation is less likely, and problem solving what you might do instead of self-injury that would still address your immediate needs.

Trigger Management Activities

The activities list below, if engaged in immediately following a triggering event, can reduce subsequent distress and therefore lessen the need for DRBs or other avoidance reactions. They include:

Grounding

Grounding usually involves learning to focus on the immediate external environment, as well as the present moment as a way to pull attention away from escalating internal states associated with painful memories. See chapters 1 and 11 for instructions on how to ground yourself.

Self-Talk

It helps if you can remind yourself that a painful memory has been triggered, causing your body to react as if you are in danger, but that the trauma is not occurring now. You are safe.

- Say the following words to remind yourself of this: "Now, in this moment, as I ground and center myself, I know that I am safe."
- Breathe deeply and take in these words: "I am safe. I am empowered. I will take care of my needs."

Self-Soothing

As we have discussed, self-soothing can increase feelings of calm and well-being. Many former victims of CSA report that engaging in activities that are self-nurturing diminishes the emotional effects of triggered memories. Refer to chapter 11 for examples of self-soothing behaviors.

Also, to soothe your nervous system and calm fearful thoughts try the following exercise.

Exercise: Comforting Your Heart

- Tenderly place your hands on your heart.
- Say the following words to yourself: "In this moment I am safe."

Strategic Distraction

The goal of strategic distraction is to pull attention away from the activated internal state for a sufficient period of time so that it fades due to lack of reinforcement. Examples of strategic distraction include:

- exercise
- interacting or cuddling with a pet
- conversations with safe, supportive others
- listening to music
- reading or watching TV
- writing or journaling
- going for a walk
- engaging in yoga

Harm Reduction

Harm reduction is based on the idea that most people who engage in unsafe behaviors are not intentionally trying to harm themselves or others but, instead, are unable or unwilling to stop a given behavior as a result of previous trauma.

Harm reduction approaches to DRBs involve:

- Attempting to delay avoidance behaviors for as long as possible after the onset of a trigger so that the associated distress decreases or fades in time and the person has the opportunity to sit with and develop greater emotional tolerance for unwanted emotional states.
- When a behavior seems necessary, replacing dangerous DRBs with less detrimental ones. For example, holding ice cubes until it hurts your

hands instead of self-cutting. Such replacement activities should only be used when absolutely necessary because they model self-harm.

- If the original DRB is impossible to avoid, consciously engaging in the behavior for the least amount of time as possible (e.g., bingeing for ten minutes rather than for an hour, trying to limit sexual behavior to flirting as opposed to intercourse), so that the harmfulness of the behavior is reduced.

Safety interventions, lessening trigger-related distress, and harm reduction activities can offer an opportunity to understand and de-pathologize what have typically been experienced as shameful behaviors, increase your immediate safety, and begin to stabilize your internal environment.

The following are still further strategies for defusing a trigger.

- Stand up, stretch, move around, and shake off the trigger.
- Wash your face with cold water, dip your hands in a bowl of ice, or hold an ice cube to your forehead or the back of your neck.
- Sip a cup of warm tea, or wrap a blanket around yourself. Weighted blankets have proved to help alleviate anxiety.
- Put a pillow up against your stomach; hug a stuffed animal; or if you have a cat or small dog, pick it up and hold it.
- Clear your eyes, take a deep breath, and focus on an object in the room. Notice every detail as if you were going to sketch or paint it.
- Focus on listening to the sounds in the room or environment you are in.
- Get involved in another activity such as taking a walk while at the same time staying aware of the sensations, feelings, and thoughts you are experiencing.
- Journal about your experience.

BE ON THE LOOKOUT FOR OLD
SHAME-INDUCING HABITS AND BELIEFS

You can't spend a lifetime practicing negative habits and believing shame-inducing beliefs and not expect them to rear their ugly heads from time to time. So, be prepared. Typically, former victims of CSA tend to have certain behaviors that continue to create shame in their lives. The primary ways of doing this include:

- addictive behaviors such as alcohol or drug abuse
- self-abuse (cutting, starving themselves)

- shoplifting or stealing from others
- involvement in abusive relationships, either as the abuser or the victim
- self-sabotaging behavior
- problematic ways of treating others
- being neglectful or abusive toward their children

In this chapter I have addressed shame-inducing behaviors such as self-sabotage, reenactments, and distress reduction behaviors (DRBs) and offered suggestions for how to change them. Now it is time for you to identify your own shame-inducing behaviors and come to understand why you are prone to them. For example, shoplifting or stealing from others is a common problem with former victims of CSA, particularly for females. A typical motivating factor for this phenomenon is a need for power to make up for the feeling of helplessness and powerlessness experienced due to the sexual abuse. Those who shoplift often describe experiencing a feeling of exhilaration as they walk out the door of a store, or when they realize they got away with stealing. This feeling of exhilaration can be likened to the feeling of power. Once former victims become aware of this motivating factor, they can begin to look for healthier ways to experience the feeling of empowerment, such as participating in sports if they are athletic, or finding a hobby that they can excel in.

If you continue to have a need to reenact the sexual abuse, think about the most powerful elements surrounding the sexual abuse: your fear; your sense of betrayal; your shame because you couldn't defend yourself, couldn't run away, or couldn't tell anyone. We have discussed all these scenarios in the book to help you better understand what happened and in order for you to forgive yourself. If you continue to reenact the sexual abuse, it is because you are still stuck in some way—stuck in blaming yourself, stuck in not being willing to face the truth about your abuser or face your pain about what happened to you.

SWITCHING FROM UNHEALTHY TO HEALTHY HABITS

Once you've identified your potential problem areas, the best way to prevent yourself from repeating them is to practice healthy habits and cultivate healthy beliefs. Examples of healthy habits include:

- Be aware of your triggers. When you suddenly feel shame, anger, fear, or sadness, ask yourself if you have been triggered.
- Stay away from triggering situations whenever possible.
- "Check in" with your feelings (see chapter 7 for instructions).

- Have equal relationships—choose partners and friends carefully.
- Practice "taking in the good" to prevent self-sabotage.
- Practice self-compassion and self-kindness.
- Install a more nurturing inner voice to replace your critical inner voice.
- Continue to heal your emotional wounds.
- Continue to forgive yourself.

A NEW HABIT: CONNECTING WITH YOUR FEELINGS

If you aren't in touch with your emotions and your body, you have a greater chance of becoming overstressed and reverting to unhealthy ways to soothe yourself. For this reason, it is important to check in with your body and your emotions on at least a daily basis, if not more often. In chapter 7, I introduced a process for doing this. Please refer to the specific instructions for doing a daily "check-in."

MAKING THE CONNECTION BETWEEN NEEDS AND FEELINGS

As we have been discussing, instead of reverting to an unhealthy or even destructive way of coping with triggers and other uncomfortable situations, it is important to find healthier ways of self-soothing. But it is equally important to discover your real needs. For example, instead of believing that you need alcohol or drugs to numb yourself of your pain and/or shame, look for your real need. One way of discovering your needs at any given time is to check in with your feelings. They will tell you what you need if you pay close attention. The following exercise, based on a process by Laurel Mellin in her *Solutions Program*, will help you make this important connection.

Exercise: Feelings and Needs

1. Check in with yourself several times a day by going inside and asking yourself what you are feeling.
2. When you find a feeling, look for the corresponding need. Ask yourself, "What do I need?" Often the answer will be "feel my feeling and let it fade." Answer in the simplest way instead of confusing the issue with too many details or complexities. For example, if you are hungry, you need food. When you feel guilty, you need to apologize.
3. It may take trying on several needs before you find the one that is true for you at the time. You may also have many needs attached to one

feeling. For example, you may feel *lonely* and your *need* may be to call a friend, get a hug from your partner, or find a way to connect with yourself (journal, take a walk alone, and try to connect with what you are feeling).

4. Be on the alert for answers that are not truly responsive to you. For example, I feel sad, I need some candy, I feel angry, I need to hit him. Tap into your inherent wisdom and relax into a more logical, self-nurturing answer. Ask yourself, "OK, what do I really need?" For example, "express myself" (write, sing), "get physical" (walk, stomp), "develop a plan," "learn from it" (next time I will).

If you find that you sometimes continue lifetime compulsive behaviors, make sure you don't shame yourself for them. These behaviors have likely been a lifesaver for you, helping you to cope with the most horrendous pain, fear, and shame. You will need to slowly wean yourself of these behaviors by practicing self-soothing and other healthier ways of coping.

In the next chapter, we will focus on how to change shaming sexual behavior.

THIRTEEN

TAKING THE SHAME OUT OF YOUR SEXUAL RELATIONSHIPS

Intimacy is not something that just happens between two people; it is a way of being alive. At any moment, we are choosing either to reveal ourselves or to protect ourselves, to value ourselves or to diminish ourselves, to tell the truth, or to hide. To dive into life or to avoid it. Intimacy is making the choice to be connected to, rather than isolated from, our deepest truth at that moment.

—Geneen Roth

IT SHOULD COME AS NO SURPRISE that former victims of child sexual abuse too often suffer from a tremendous amount of sexual shame. When your first experiences of sex are characterized by shame, humiliation, secretiveness, exploitation, control, and manipulation, it is not difficult to understand how shame can permeate your sexual experiences from that time forward.

For this reason, for many of you, this will be one of the most important chapters in the book. This is because child sexual abuse, more than any other factor, can literally shape a survivor's sexual personality. For many former victims it can be almost impossible to engage in sexual activities without subjecting themselves to shame. For others, shame occurs due to the choices they make and the circumstances surrounding their current sexual experiences.

Many people experience shame because they suffer from sexual dysfunction such as an inability to achieve orgasm or painful intercourse in women, or erectile dysfunction or premature or delayed ejaculation in men. And many former victims are very restricted when it comes to where they can be touched, how they want to be touched, and what kinds of sexual acts they can tolerate. To make matters worse, some former victims suffer from destructive sexual obsessions and fantasies that cause them to feel enormous shame.

In this chapter, we will focus primarily on active steps you can take to minimize or eliminate many of the sexual behaviors that continue to bring shame into your life. We will also touch on identifying how the shame of child sexual abuse can shape a former victim's feelings, experiences, preferences, beliefs, and fantasies regarding sex. You will be encouraged to be understanding and forgiving of the ways you have come to view sex even when they are problematic.

The ultimate goal is to help you take the shame out of sex as much as possible. If you continue to practice shame-inducing behaviors and to think about sex in shame-inducing ways, you will constantly subject yourself to shame and, in essence, retraumatize yourself.

THE MOST COMMON SEXUAL PROBLEMS EXPERIENCED BY FORMER VICTIMS

Let's begin by identifying the various sexual problems former victims experience. Put a check mark next to each item that applies to you.

- lack of sexual desire
- sexual aversion
- inability to enjoy sex or to have an orgasm
- sexual dysfunctions such as painful intercourse or vaginismus (an involuntary contraction of the vaginal muscle) in women; erectile dysfunction, premature ejaculation, or delayed ejaculation (with no medical explanation) in men
- an inability to enjoy certain types of sex (can't be penetrated but can engage in oral sex, can't be fondled but can be penetrated, can't be touched on certain parts of the body)
- promiscuity; continuing to be a sexual object
- a pattern of sexual revictimization
- gynecological issues, including menstrual irregularities and severe menstrual cramps, pelvic and genital pain, external and internal scarring as a consequence of the abuse, chronic yeast infections or sexually transmitted diseases from the abuse as well as frequent urinary tract infections
- problems with sexual identity (questioning whether you are gay, straight, or bisexual)
- attraction to "illicit" sexual activities such as pornography and prostitution
- sexual manipulation, including using seductiveness or other forms of sexual manipulation to get what you want in your marital, social, or business relationships
- sexualizing all relationships (which can cause victims to become sexual victimizers)
- sexual addiction
- pornography addiction
- attraction to kinky or public sex

If you identify with a certain item or items on that list, you probably feel a great deal of shame about it. If so, remind yourself, as you learned in previous chapters, that it is *understandable* that you would suffer from these issues and that it is *not your fault*. Also know that you are not alone—many former victims of CSA suffer from these same sexual issues as a result of having been sexually abused.

You may have been struggling with one or more of these problems for quite some time without understanding why. The following information hopefully will help you to understand the origin of your sexual issues and thus feel some self-compassion as well as hope about changing them.

Lack of sexual desire. When your earliest experiences of sex were being manipulated, coerced, or forced to do things you did not want to do, nor were emotionally equipped to handle, it can induce an indelible memory of sex that is not only undesirable but traumatic, painful, and shaming. You may have become numb to your sexual feelings and desires as a way of protecting yourself from these painful memories. And if you feel shame because you experienced sexual pleasure during the sexual abuse, anytime you feel sexual desire or pleasure it may reignite that feeling of shame.

Sexual aversion. It is not uncommon for former victims to go through a period of sexual aversion, also known as sexual anorexia. The trauma inflicted by CSA causes some former victims to shut down their sexuality to avoid feelings of shame, fear, and betrayal associated with the trauma. Unconsciously turning off sexual desire, numbing your body (including the pelvic floor for women), or dissociating to avoid having to deal with the trauma's painful triggers and flashbacks are all signs of aversion.

Inability to enjoy sex or have an orgasm. Due to the traumatic memories surrounding sex, as well as the fact that you likely dissociated from your body during the sexual trauma, causing you to be numb to your body and its normal reactions, sex may not be enjoyable for you. Instead of experiencing sexual pleasure, it is normal for a former victim to either feel nothing—to be numb—or to feel very little sensation in their sexual organs. This numbness and dissociation make it almost impossible to achieve an orgasm.

Sexual dysfunction. In most cases, a CSA victim's first sexual experience was the sexual abuse they suffered. Instead of being an experience characterized by curiosity, exploration, and tenderness, this initiation was one of exploitation and violence. It is extremely difficult for a victim to overcome this violation to make sexuality a positive experience. Each subsequent sexual experience, even when the former victim chooses his or her partner and enters into the experience willingly, can be accompanied by memories and flashbacks of the abuse

and the abuser. Common sexual dysfunctions suffered by child sexual abuse
victims include:

For females:
- painful intercourse or vaginismus (an involuntary contraction of the
  vaginal muscles making penetration difficult or painful)
- inability to feel sexual sensations (includes inadequate vaginal lubrica-
  tion before and during intercourse)
- inability to achieve orgasm

For males:
- erectile dysfunction (an inability to achieve or maintain an erection suit-
  able for intercourse)
- early or premature ejaculation (an inability to control the timing of
  ejaculation or to maintain an erection for more than a few minutes or
  even seconds before ejaculating)
- absent or delayed ejaculation (an inability to climax despite enough
  sexual stimulation, or needing to have intercourse [or other stimulation]
  for an unusual amount of time before ejaculation can occur)

For males and females:
- lack of interest in or desire for sex
- inability to become aroused
- sexual aversion
- pain with intercourse

An inability to enjoy certain types of sex. Due to the trauma of sexual abuse,
it is very common for former victims to be turned off to certain types of sex.
Typically, these are the sexual activities that were involved in the abuse. This
may be as general as not liking to be in a passive position to more specific activities such as oral sex (giving or receiving), touching your partner's genitals, or
having them touch yours.

Gynecological difficulties. Problems are common due to chronic tension
throughout the pelvic area due to the intrusion, as well as tensing and pulling
away from the abuser. This tension can become habitual and chronic and can
cause unexplained pain. Chronic tension in the pelvic area can cause a con-
striction of blood flow throughout the pelvic area and a decrease in physical
sensations.

Problems with sexual identity. Males who are sexually abused by another male often suffer from confusion about whether they are homosexual: "Why was a male attracted to me?" "Sometimes I enjoyed it; does that mean I am gay?" Another cause for confusion may be that the former victim (male or female) has a sexual attraction to both males and females. For example, a female may be compulsively attracted to reenacting sex with males (sometimes even males who remind them of their abuser) while feeling more emotionally attracted to (and safer with) females.

Promiscuity, continuing to be a sex object. Promiscuity is very common among former victims. You may have come to believe that being sexual with someone is the only way to gain their love or attention, or you may feel like damaged goods, so you see no reason to be discriminating regarding with whom you have sex.

A pattern of sexual revictimization. As we have discussed, reenactments of sexual abuse are very common among former victims. This unconscious drive will cause you to be attracted to abusive partners and may cause you to be reckless sexually, putting yourself in dangerous situations.

Attraction to illicit sexual activities. It is extremely common for former victims to develop a pattern of involvement with forbidden or illicit sexual activities such as prostitution, public sex, cheating on your partner, getting involved with married people, being attracted to partners who are under age, and so forth. This can be a clear reenactment of the sexual abuse, which was characterized by secrecy, fear of being exposed, and feelings of shame about your involvement in the act.

Sexual manipulation. Child molesters are incredibly manipulative. They are experts in getting the child to do what they want them to do, even when the child is frightened, repulsed, or completely disinterested in the sexual activity. In this sense, former victims learned from the experts how to manipulate others into doing their bidding. This is another clear example of reenactment, only now the former victim has all the power and control.

Sexual compulsion. Having a sexual compulsion means that you experience an inability to control your behavior when it comes to sex. Often paired with sexual fantasy, the person with a particular sexual compulsion (e.g., to expose himself) usually has obsessive thoughts and fantasies about doing so before he acts on it. These thoughts and fantasies often feel as if they come out of nowhere and can be quite troubling and distracting.

Sexual addiction. Closely related to sexual compulsion, sexual addiction is defined as a lack of control over sexual thoughts, urges, and impulses. Sexual addiction refers to behaviors that are done in excess and that significantly impact one's life in a negative way. Persons with a sexual addiction may have a compulsive need to be sexually stimulated—so much so that it interferes with their daily life. Sexual addiction can take many forms, including an addiction to sexual acts, prostitution, watching pornography, masturbation or sexual fantasy, exhibitionism, or voyeurism.

The cornerstones of sexual addiction are compulsivity, shame, and despair. Sexual addiction can begin early in childhood. Because they were sexualized early in life, some victims become addicted to masturbation as a way of alleviating anxiety and comforting themselves. This continues into adulthood when the need to keep emotional pain at bay leads to mental preoccupation with sex. When someone is struggling with intrusive thoughts of their sexual abuse or insidious negative self-talk as a result of their abuse, the lure of escape through addictive patterns of behavior is not only compelling, but sometimes a means of psychological preservation. The result of this addictive cycle often includes feelings of shame, regret, depression, isolation, anxiety, alienation from loved ones, a breaking of one's own value system, and secrecy—all things that often increase feelings of despair and a yearning to escape and repeat the abuse.

Pornography addiction. Despite the increasing worldwide availability and social acceptance of pornography, evidence indicates that pornography can become a source of distress and tension. It can have a negative effect on one's emotional well-being, can lead to conflicts with partners, and can put relationships at risk. In addition, research shows a correlation (85 percent) between viewing child pornography and participating in sexual relations with children (Bourke & Hernandez). And a recent meta-analysis by Hald et al. strongly supports and clarifies previous data demonstrating the fact that pornography can induce violent attitudes against women. Specifically, what is abundantly clear is that watching pornography can be a dangerous and extremely unhealthy thing for former victims of child sexual abuse to do.

An attraction to public, risky, or kinky sex. This can include exhibitionism, public sex, sex without protection, sex with prostitutes, or becoming a stripper or prostitute oneself. These acts can be reenactments of the sexual abuse or self-punishing acts. Fringe or kinky sex such as bondage and discipline and sadomasochism can become extremely attractive to former victims of CSA. With these practices, depending upon the role they take—passive or aggressive—former victims can either turn the tables and become the one in power or reenact the shame and humiliation they felt due to the sexual abuse. Either way, this is another clear example of reenactment and as such, ends up creating more shame.

Other behaviors that can result from sexual abuse are:

- an inability to initiate sex
- an inability to say no to sex
- a tendency to fake sexual enjoyment
- has sex when he or she really doesn't want to
- feels she or he has no physical boundaries when it comes to sex
- needs to be under the influence of alcohol or drugs to enjoy sex
- allows sex to be forced on her or him
- is confused as to what is appropriate and inappropriate touch in dating
- uses sex to help her or him to feel better when feeling down
- uses sexual fantasies that are reenactments of the sexual abuse

Any or all of these sexual problems and issues can elicit shame in someone. Our sexuality is an extremely fragile aspect of ourselves and one that can cause us to feel enormously vulnerable. Males are especially vulnerable when it comes to their sexuality because they tend to rely on it for a sense of self-esteem and power. If they can't function sexually in the way they want to, they can feel emasculated and like a failure. Females can also rely on their sexuality to gain attention, approval, and love. If they can't perform the way they would like to, they also feel less than, which can affect their self-esteem and self-image.

THE SPECIFIC IMPACT ON THE SEXUALITY OF INCEST VICTIMS

Most victims of incest (sexual activity between those who are related to one another or whose relationship with one another resembles that of relatives) suffer from the same sexual issues that any victim of child abuse does. In addition, recent research has found that in comparison to non-incest controls, survivors of incest experienced:

- sexual intercourse earlier
- had more sex partners
- were more likely to have casual sex with those outside their primary relationships
- were more likely to engage in sex for money

Thus, survivors of incest are at increased risk for revictimization, often without a conscious realization that they are being abused, because the line between involuntary and voluntary participation in sexual behavior is blurred.

SEXUAL REENACTMENTS

As we discussed in the previous chapter, reenactments are patterns of behavior that are often unconscious attempts to reconcile, reframe, or repair the abuse that occurred in your childhood. Unfortunately, they do not always accomplish this task and can result in perpetual psychological and emotional damage.

In the previous chapter, we discussed adaptive and maladaptive reenactments. In this chapter we will discuss passive reenactments versus active or aggressive reenactments.

Passive Reenactments

Although those involved in reenactments typically are unaware of what they are doing, those who are involved with passive reenactments are particularly unconscious when it comes to realizing that they are reenacting previous abuse. They go about their lives, putting themselves in risky if not dangerous situations, completely oblivious to their motive—replaying the trauma of child sexual abuse, hoping for a different outcome.

Passive behavior is basically continuing to view sex from a victim's perspective and, therefore, can become a reenactment of the abuse. Behaving in any of these ways causes you to feel ashamed of yourself and to continue to lose respect for yourself. Even more troubling, behaving in these passive ways is often retraumatizing.

Examples of passive reenactments can include:

- not being able to say no to someone who comes on to you or to getting involved with sexual activities that you are not interested in or are even repulsed by
- allowing someone to pressure you into sex or demand sex of you
- being involved with domineering/abusive partners
- being involved with shame-inducing behaviors—sexual activities that cause you to feel ashamed of yourself during or after sex (e.g., someone humiliating you sexually or saying derogatory things to you during or after sex)
- practicing risky behaviors such as drinking too much or taking drugs at bars or parties, especially when out alone or where you don't know anyone (e.g., not watching your drink or leaving your drink to go to the restroom; not insisting that a man wear a condom)

Aggressive Reenactments

As we've discussed throughout the book, those who identified with the aggressor or hid their shame behind a wall of arrogance or bravado can re-create the abuse by being aggressive sexually. This can include:

- being sexually inappropriate (standing too close to a stranger; touching a stranger in an intimate way, such as putting a hand on their leg, hip, back, or behind)
- being sexually coercive or demanding
- humiliating and degrading your sexual partners
- being emotionally, physically, or sexually abusive toward your partner

SHAME-INDUCING SEXUAL COMPULSIONS

If things weren't bad enough for former victims, some find themselves locked into compulsive sexual behavior that can perpetuate feelings of helplessness, a sense of being bad, or out of control, resulting in further suffering. These sexual compulsions happen outside of conscious awareness and are often characterized by dissociation of thoughts, emotions, and sensations related to the traumatic event. Remind yourself of this when you begin to be self-critical for engaging in these compulsive practices.

Males, more than females, tend to reenact the abuse through negative compulsive behaviors. This is partially due to the fact that, as research has found, male survivors are less likely to report or discuss their trauma and more likely to externalize their responses to CSA by engaging in compulsive sexual behavior. Even today, men and boys are still provided with narrow cultural and familial messages about what it means to be masculine. This narrative includes such things as devaluing expression and vulnerability while prioritizing promiscuity and maintaining control.

Listed below are some of the most common shame-inducing sexual compulsions—sexual activities that can cause you repeatedly to reenact the pain, fear, or humiliation of the sexual trauma (either as the one in power or as the victim).

- engaging in humiliating sexual practices (sadomasochism, sex with animals)
- combining sex with physical or emotional abuse or pain
- frequently using abusive sexual fantasies (either seeing oneself as the abuser or the abused)

- engaging in promiscuous sex (many sexual relationships at the same time or in a row)
- visiting prostitutes
- charging money for sex
- having anonymous sex (in restrooms, adult bookstores, telephone sex services, internet sex)
- acting out sexually in ways that are harmful to others (forcing someone to have sex)
- acting out in ways that are harmful to you (allow yourself to be tied up or humiliated during sex)
- manipulating others into having sex with you
- demanding sex from others
- using rape or other types of fantasies to gain sexual arousal or increase sexual arousal
- committing sexual offenses (voyeurism, exhibitionism, molestation, sex with minors, incest, rape)
- feeling addictively drawn to certain unhealthy sexual behaviors (sado-masochism)
- continually using sexual slurs or degrading sexual comments to humiliate your partner
- engaging in secretive or illicit sexual activities
- relying on abusive pornography to become aroused

Other sexual compulsions can be less obvious reenactments of the trauma of child sexual abuse and are more likely to be ways to cope with stress or self-punishing behaviors such as:

- engaging in compulsive masturbation
- engaging in risky sexual behavior (not using protection against disease or pregnancy)
- being dishonest about sexual relationships (has more than one partner but professes to be monogamous)
- engaging in sexual behavior that has caused problems in your primary relationship, at work, or with your health

ELIMINATING SHAME-INDUCING BEHAVIOR

As you probably noticed, many if not most of the items listed above elicit shame and, therefore, need to be removed from your sexual repertoire if you wish to eliminate or decrease the amount of shame you experience. The most extreme, and therefore the most shaming of these behaviors include talking to or treating your partner in degrading ways or asking to be talked to or treated in these ways; demanding sex or forcing someone to have sex; watching violent pornography; engaging in violent sex; prostitution (either charging for sex or paying for sex); sadomasochism. These activities are all examples of extreme shame-inducing behaviors and are often re-enactments of the abuse. Therefore, it is vitally important that you make a special effort to identify and then eliminate these particular behaviors from your sexual repertoire. Once again, I have divided those who practice these shame-inducing behaviors into two categories: passive reenactors and aggressive reenactors.

Passive Reenactors

- being easily manipulated into having sex you don't want or with a partner to whom you aren't attracted
- having an attraction to "forbidden" sex such as public sex or getting involved with unavailable partners (married men, your boss, an underage partner)
- a need to be overpowered (need to be ordered around, held down, tied up)
- a desire to be humiliated (urinated on, defecated on)
- a desire to be tortured (sadomasochism, bondage, and discipline)

Aggressive Reenactors

- a need to be in control or dominate (needs to always be the initiator, sex with a less powerful or submissive person)
- a desire to humiliate partners
- a desire to physically harm partners

Eliminating or decreasing the number of shame-inducing behaviors from your sexual repertoire can be difficult but very possible. Fortunately, you can begin to make specific changes to eliminate these shame-producing behaviors and attitudes that may have dictated your sexual life.

REMEDIES FOR PASSIVE REENACTORS

The following information and suggestions are specifically for those who re-enact the abuse by being passive.

Step 1—Learn How to Deal with Sexual Coercion

Sexual coercion is unwanted sexual activity that occurs after someone is pressured, tricked, or forced in a nonphysical way. Sexual coercion can include being egged on or persuaded to have unwanted sex (on one end of the continuum) or being forced to have sexual contact (on the other end of the continuum). Social and emotional pressure to force a person (man or woman) into sexual activity when they don't want it can take many forms—from pressure and flattery, to threats of violence. It often comes in the form of statements that make you feel pressured, guilty, or ashamed.

If you have sex because you cannot say "No," you have been coerced. If you are pressured to have a type of sex that repels you, you have been coerced. If you have unprotected sex because your partner doesn't want to use a condom, you have been coerced. If you have sex because of a guilt trip your partner has laid on you, you have been coerced.

No one should ever feel forced into any type of sexual activity that they are not comfortable with or don't feel like doing. And yet countless former victims are pressured to have sex every day—by a date, a boyfriend or girlfriend, by a spouse, or even by a stranger. This is especially dangerous, because it is a reenactment of the sexual abuse they suffered. Being coerced as an adult is the same as being groomed by a child molester as a child. The results are similar—you end up feeling used, manipulated, and stupid for going along with it, and all these feelings cause you to feel shame.

Although I am mostly addressing women in this section, many males who were victims of CSA suffer from the same problem of being easily coerced. Female partners can often be aggressive about pressuring their male partners for sex, which can be especially difficult for former male victims to deal with. They often feel their masculinity is in question, and they often feel terrible shame if they hesitate to do what their partner is asking them to do.

And sexual coercion doesn't only occur in heterosexual relationships. Gay men and lesbian women report being fondled and pressured for sex at bars and parties, and partners of gay men and lesbian women often feel coerced into having sex.

One reason that so many women get into sexual situations where the other person goes too far is because of a reasoning process that goes something like this: "It's no big deal if he touches my breasts (or vagina). He likes it, and it doesn't hurt me."

It may seem like it doesn't hurt you if you allow someone to do things to your body that you don't really want him to do, but the truth is, *it does hurt you.* It lowers your self-esteem, because it causes you to begin to *lose respect* for yourself. And it can *humiliate* you and add to the shame you already feel about your body or your sexuality. Most important, it is a reenactment of the sexual abuse you experienced as a child or adolescent. In essence, you are being retraumatized each time you are coerced into sex you don't want.

In some situations, sexual pressure crosses the line into sexual harassment:

- Threatening your job, home, or school career ("I really respect your work here. I'd hate to have to let you go." "Don't worry about the rent. There are other things you can do." "You work so hard, it'd be a shame for you not to get an A.")
- Threatening your children or other family members ("I'll do this to your daughter [or sister] if you don't do it with me.")

Former victims deal with sexual pressure not only from dates and acquaintances, but also in their ongoing intimate relationships. Here are some common tactics used to pressure an intimate partner into having sex:

- Wearing you down by asking for sex again and again, or making you feel bad, guilty, or obligated ("If you really loved me, you'd do it.").
- Playing on the fact that you're in a relationship ("Having sex with me is the way to prove your love for me.")
- Threatening to get sex from someone else unless you give in ("If I don't get sex from you, I'll get it somewhere else.")
- Reacting negatively by becoming angry, resentful, or depressed if you say no or don't immediately agree to have sex or have sex in a certain way ("I hate it when you reject me like this. It reminds me of being rejected as a child.")
- Trying to normalize his sexual expectations ("I need sex. I'm a man.")

Like rape, sexual coercion is never OK (some consider coercion to be a subset of rape). Your body is your own, and no one else has a right to it. You don't owe anybody sex, no matter how they feel, what they want, what they've done for you in the past, or if you've had sex with them before. This can be hard to believe, especially if you don't have a healthy sense of self-esteem—but remember, you are the only person with a right over your body and over your decisions concerning with whom to share it.

This is especially important for you, a former victim of CSA, to understand. Because all of the above examples can feel exactly like the ways the perpetrator manipulated you or threatened you, it is vital that you learn how to handle these situations in a healthy, assertive way. You can easily become triggered or dissociate when you are being coerced, which makes it even more important that you be prepared for each scenario and practice what you are going to say.

In my book *I'm Saying No!: Standing up to Sexual Assault, Sexual Harassment and Sexual Pressure*, I focus on the importance of women being able to say "no" to unwanted sexual attention from men. Although it may seem obvious that saying no is important and necessary, many women don't know they have the right to do so. It is also true that even more women don't know *how* to say it. *I'm Saying No!* teaches women literally how to say "no" in a strong, assertive manner—but perhaps even more important, it will give you *permission* to say it, not just with your words, but also with your actions and attitude. It will help you to understand, on a deep emotional level, that you have a right to expect that your body is off limits to anyone you don't want touching you. If you continue to have difficulty dealing with sexual coercion, I recommend that you read the book.

Here is one exercise that I offer in the book. Practicing it will help you become stronger in your resolve to stop allowing men (or women) to pressure you sexually.

No! Exercise

- Think of a situation in which someone recently disrespected, invaded, or abused your body.
- Imagine that you are saying "No!" to this person.
- Now say it out loud. Say "No!" as many times as you feel like it. Notice how good it feels to say it.
- If you'd like, in addition to saying "No!" add any other words you feel like saying. For example, "No! You can't do those things to me." "No! I don't want you to touch me like that!"

Practicing saying "No!" will help you gain the needed courage to say it when you need to—whenever someone is trying to coerce you into sex when you don't want it.

Step 2—Know What Is Healthy for You and What Is Off Limits

This step is especially crucial for former victims of CSA. In many cases, this goes beyond sexual "preferences" to sexual *needs*. For example, if the person who molested you fondled your breasts as a part of the molestation, you may have an aversion to having your breasts touched. This is a common scenario and is completely understandable. On the other hand, if the perpetrator did everything else *but* touch your breasts, that may be a "safe zone" for you, a place on your body where you are not retraumatized and from which you can actually derive some pleasure. If the perpetrator did not penetrate your vagina with his finger, his penis, or another object, having vaginal intercourse may be your "safe zone" and may be quite pleasurable. A fairly common scenario is for former victims of child sexual abuse to be able to enjoy having their partner touch those parts of their body that *were not* touched by the abuser, as well as enjoying engaging in sexual activities that the abuser did not impose on them.

We need to focus here on another important issue. Although I am not making a judgment about this, certain sexual activities that you may enjoy or find exciting may not be good for you in the sense that they may be reenactments. For example, if you and your partner have been engaging in bondage and discipline or sadomasochism, I encourage you to seriously think about whether it is healthy for you to continue these practices because you are likely reenacting the abuse and being retraumatized. If you prefer the "top" or the domineering role as an aspect of sexual excitement, it may be that you like "turning the tables" and feeling what it is like to be the one in power. It is understandable that you might want to experience this, but think about a healthier way of feeling in control or expressing your anger at having been sexually violated. If you are being dominated, it may feel familiar and thus comfortable or arousing, but it most certainly is a reenactment of the abuse you suffered and is likely causing you to be retraumatized each time you engage in this behavior.

Exercise: What's Off Limits

- Make a list of *the parts of your body* you find uncomfortable to have someone touch. Don't worry if you end up listing many parts of your body. This is common for former victims and is a reminder of just how traumatic the abuse was.
- Try to find the reason why someone touching a particular part of your body is uncomfortable for you. It probably is due to the fact that this part of your body was involved in the sexual abuse in some way.
- Now list the *sexual activities* that are uncomfortable, shaming, or triggering for you. Try to be as honest as you can, even if it means listing activities you believe you "should" like to do or have been doing.

- Write about the reasons why you think these sexual activities are uncomfortable, shaming, or triggering for you. The more connections you can make, the more in charge of your sexuality you will become.
- Finally, list the parts of *other people's body* that you find uncomfortable to touch.
- Think of the possible reasons why these body parts are uncomfortable for you to touch.
- Now complete the following sentences:
   o Some parts of my body are just off-limits. These are: _____

   _____.

   o I am triggered by (have a post-traumatic response to) certain sex acts. These are: _____

   _____.

   o I am not comfortable looking at, touching, or feeling some parts of another person's body. These are: _____

   _____.

Step 3—Learn to Communicate Your Preferences

Although it is vitally important that you know what you like and don't like, it is equally important to be able to communicate your preferences to your partner(s). Ideally this conversation should be a direct one, with your partner agreeing to listen to you without interrupting you. You can also do this in writing.

Telling your partner one time what is off limits should be enough, but it rarely is. He or she can legitimately forget what you've said and make the mistake of touching you in an area of your body or in a way that you find uncomfortable or even threatening. But if he or she continues to "forget," this is more serious. He or she may be the kind of person who can't take no for an answer because he or she needs to be in control.

You may need to set a boundary several times before you have made it clear that you are not interested in an activity. Do so clearly, calmly, firmly, and respectfully. And do it in as few words as possible. *Do not justify, get angry about, or apologize for* the boundary you are setting.

If you are having a lot of difficulty communicating your off-limits lists to your partner, you may choose to give him or her a copy of the list you created. This can also serve as a reminder to your partner in case he or she is forgetful or resistant.

You are not responsible for the other person's reaction to the boundary you are setting. You are only responsible for communicating your boundary in a respectful manner. If it upsets them, know that it is their problem. Some people, especially those who are accustomed to controlling, dominating, abusing, or manipulating others, might test you. If this feels like it is happening, remain firm and make sure your behavior matches your words. You cannot successfully establish a clear boundary if you send mixed messages by apologizing for being too rigid or for not meeting your partner's needs.

It is common to feel selfish, guilty, or embarrassed when you set a boundary, but do it anyway. Remind yourself that your needs are important and that you deserve to protect and care for yourself. Setting boundaries takes practice. Don't let your fear, discomfort, anxiety, or guilt or shame prevent you from taking care of yourself.

Remind yourself that you have rights when it comes to your sexuality, including the right

- to choose your sexual partner(s) instead of having this imposed on you
- to choose when you want to have sex
- to choose the place where you have sex
- to choose what parts of your body you want to be touched
- to choose what particular sexual activities you want to engage in
- to say no to any sexual advance that scares you, offends you, or repulses you

Learning to set boundaries, to say "No!" in an assertive, strong way takes time and practice. Don't get discouraged, and don't become critical of yourself. Just do the best you can.

Step 4—Keep Your Wits about You: Booze and Drugs

Alcohol and drug consumption are important issues when it comes to remaining safe, avoiding rape, and avoiding shame-inducing behaviors. It is especially important for you to stay alert when on a date, at a bar, or at a party. The association between alcohol consumption and sexual assault is an important one, and it's one that both women and men need to be aware of. Here are some important things to know:

- Because intoxication lowers inhibitions and decreases mental awareness, women and men using drugs or alcohol are at a much greater risk of being sexually assaulted. Those who tend to become aggressive sexually are also more prone to this behavior when they are intoxicated or using drugs.

- Some 43 percent of sexual victimization incidents involve alcohol consumption by victims.
- One study found that 55 percent of those raped by an acquaintance had been using drugs or alcohol immediately prior to the assault.
- Women need to not only watch how much alcohol they consume, but how much their date is consuming. One out of three sexual assaults is perpetrated by those who are intoxicated.

If you are drunk or high, you cannot be aware of your environment and be alert to the dangers around you. For those who tend to become aggressive sexually, the danger may be your own behavior. If you consume too much alcohol or drugs when on a date, at a bar, or at a party, you are taking a huge risk.

REMEDIES FOR AGGRESSIVE REENACTORS

Just like those who reenact the abuse by being passive, many former victims react to past abuse by being aggressive. As we have discussed, these people attempt to avoid further shaming by building a wall of protection to insulate themselves from the criticism of others. These same people often become bullies—attacking others before they have a chance to criticize them. But behind that aggression, behind that need to dominate or humiliate others, is a little child who is still shaking in his boots. Pretending to be tough and strong isn't really solving the problem. And shaming and humiliating others before they have a chance to do it to you doesn't help either. What will help is to take off your mask, tear down that wall, and face the truth. You are just as vulnerable, just as hurt as any other victim of child sexual abuse, and you need to address your pain, humiliation, and fear instead of hiding it from yourself. Start by doing the following:

- Instead of insisting on sex or compulsively masturbating or watching pornography, ask yourself if sex is really what you need. Young children who were sexually abused often discover, perhaps for the first time, that their sexual organs can provide good feelings. This can be the start of compulsive masturbation or a sexual addiction as the child, and later the adult, grows to rely on sexual pleasure and sexual release in order to cope with feelings of shame, anxiety, fear, and anger. When you begin to obsess about sex, it may be a signal that you are feeling shame or that you are feeling anxious, afraid, or angry. You may use sex as a way of avoiding your feelings and staying dissociated. For many former victims, sex becomes one of the only ways they can feel worthy or interact with another person. In other words, you may be having sex to fill needs that are not necessarily sexual, such as needs for physical contact, intimacy, and self-worth. You may be seeking sex because you need to be held. Many former victims don't feel loved unless they are engaging in sex with someone.

- Learn what your triggers are—what emotions or circumstances catapult you back in the past to memories of the abuse. If you haven't made a trigger list, do so now.

- Check to see whether you have been triggered by shame. Shame is an especially powerful yet common trigger. For example, if you have been triggered by shame (your partner complains about the fact that you don't make more money), offer yourself some self-compassion. Compassion is the antidote to shame, so tell yourself something like, "It is understandable that I would feel shame about not making more money. But I am doing the best I can under the circumstances. I don't feel good enough about myself to go out and try to find a better paying job, but eventually I will." This is also where self-soothing strategies come in. Instead of using sex or sexual fantasies to soothe yourself, find soothing strategies that work for you (refer to chapter 11 for self-soothing suggestions).

- If you discover that you are using sex or fantasies of sex to cope with shame, anxiety, fear, or anger, find other, healthier ways of coping.

- Ask yourself what sexual activity or sexual compulsion does for you. For example, what needs are you trying to fill when you have sex? Is sex the only way you can connect with other people? Is it the only way you think you can be loved? What painful emotions does the compulsion help you avoid? One of my clients answered the question in this way, *"Having a lot of sex makes me feel powerful. It keeps me from feeling how helpless and powerless I felt when I was being abused by my father."*

- If you tend to be sexually controlling or demanding, practice taking a more passive-receptive role. At first this will likely feel uncomfortable or even scary. You took on an aggressive stance in order to avoid feeling small or vulnerable. But if you can practice being more passive a little at a time (i.e., turning over so that you are on the bottom and your partner is on top), you will likely discover that it feels good to allow sexual feelings to rise up inside of you instead of always pushing yourself and your partners to experience sexual feelings.

- Allow yourself to be more vulnerable with your sexual partners. If a partner has opened up to you and shared information about their childhood, see if you can do the same. You don't have to tell the person that you were sexually abused, but test how it feels to share other information about your childhood that you don't normally share with others. Opening up and becoming vulnerable will feel risky at first, but if you choose wisely who you reveal yourself to, you will likely discover that it feels good to be more open.

- Avoid exposure to things that reinforce or replicate the sexual abuse. This includes television programs, movies, books, magazines, websites, and other influences that portray sex as manipulation, coercion, domination, or violence.

- Avoid pornography or work toward weaning yourself of pornography if you use it regularly or feel you might be addicted. For former victims of CSA, watching pornography can feel like a safe sexual experience. However, pornography can be problematic, reenacting an abusive dynamic that disengages you from yourself and opportunities for respectful sexual relationships. Pornography has aspects of sexual abuse that can be replicated: secrecy, shame, and dominance—all tied up with sexual arousal. Pornography is especially harmful to sexual healing, because it is often a depiction of sex as one person dominating another (usually a male dominating a female), which is a reenactment of child sexual abuse. Specific problems that watching pornography causes include:

  o Those who were sexually abused are often inundated with feelings of shame and try to distract themselves from these feelings by watching porno. But after viewing pornography and masturbating to it, it is common for former victims to feel shame, disgust, and failure—the very feelings they have been trying to get relief from in the first place.
  o Former victims tend to keep their pornography watching a secret from their partners. This can mirror the way sexual abuse was kept a secret, and in that sense can be a reenactment. When their partner finds out, their sense of betrayal can be overwhelming.
  o Experts have found that the secrecy, deception, and sense of betrayal that partners feel when they find out that their partner is using porn can cause as much harm to the relationship as the pornography itself.

More than one-quarter of women viewed pornography watching as a kind of affair and reported that the impact of their partner's pornography use created the following:

1. adverse effects on sex life
2. negative effects on their relationship
3. lowered self-esteem
4. feeling less attractive and desirable
5. feeling insecure

- o Women who use pornography are most likely to do so with a partner, usually due to pressure put on them by their partner. This in itself can be retraumatizing to the woman, especially if she is a former victim of CSA.
- o Male partners can also pressure their partners to engage in sexual activities that they view on the internet, such as anal sex. Because most women report that anal sex is not enjoyable and often painful, this sexual pressure can cause problems in the relationship.
- o Viewing pornography is, generally speaking, not about connection, intimacy, and affection, but a blurring of boundaries around acceptable sexual behaviors, especially when it includes overtly humiliating or degrading practices. Researchers have found that more than 80 percent of pornography includes acts of physical aggression toward women; almost 50 percent includes verbal aggression. Only 10 percent of scenes contained positive caring behaviors such as kissing, embracing, or laughter.
- o Research also shows that viewing pornography can influence the viewer's sexual interests and practices. A 2011 study found that people who watched violent pornographic material were more likely to report that they had done something sexually violent or aggressive. Another study found that men who watch violent pornography or are frequent viewers of pornography are more likely to say they would rape a woman if they could get away with it.

- Use healthier, more positive language when referring to sex. The way a person talks about sex can influence how he or she thinks about it. Avoid slang terms such as screwing, banging, getting a piece, and so forth. Instead, use terms such as making love, being physically intimate. Stop using words for sex parts such as prick, dick, boobs, tits, cunt, and asshole. Instead, use accurate anatomically correct terms such as penis, breasts, vagina, and anus.

- Learn more about healthy sex. Read books about healthy sex, attend classes or workshops that present healthy models for sex.
- Tell someone about the abuse. (Reread chapter 9 to remind yourself why it is important and what are its benefits.) The most important benefit of disclosing is that you will be allowing yourself to be vulnerable and to admit how much you were hurt. This will help you lower your defenses and not always have to be the one in charge.
- Enter psychotherapy or join a survivor's group. This can be especially difficult for males. Research has found that male survivors are less likely to report or discuss their trauma and more likely to externalize their responses to CSA by engaging in compulsive sexual behavior.

ALLOW EMPATHY TO HELP YOU EXTINGUISH BEHAVIORS THAT HURT OTHERS

Unfortunately, aggressive reenactors are often either oblivious or in denial about the harm they are causing others, as well as the harm they are causing themselves. One of the best ways to become more aware of the consequences of your actions is to learn to be more empathetic.

Not only does engaging in activities such as humiliating your sexual partners, forcing your partners to have sex, frequenting prostitutes, and watching violent pornography create more shame in you, but it has an effect on your very humanity. You may have become so numb, so defended, that you can do these things without feeling shame. But ironically, on some level, the shame comes seeping through. It rises up in you like oil deep inside the earth, suddenly exploding in a torrent. This shame can cause you to explode in a rage against those you care about, to become emotionally or physically abusive to those around you, or to become self-destructive.

We've all heard the saying, "Power corrupts." The more power a person has, the more likely he or she will abuse that power by taking advantage of others, throwing his or her weight around, disregarding the needs of others, and always placing his or her needs first. But in addition to corrupting people, research now shows that power can rob us of our empathy. As psychologists see it, empathy includes:

- taking perspective—viewing the world through the eyes of others
- experiencing what other people feel

- an attempt to understand what others feel and why (*cognitive empathy*)
- feeling concerned for what others are going through and a desire for them to feel better

As you've learned throughout this book, being a victim of CSA messes with your head. It can make you believe that you only have two choices—to continue to be a victim or to become an aggressor or abuser. Females often come out of the trauma with a tendency to be more passive than they were before they were abused, often believing they have no choice but to "go along" with males or those in charge and to accept their "lot in life." Males, on the other hand, often come out of their trauma experience bent on making sure they will never be abused, attacked, or shamed again.

Those males (and some females) who take the "no one's going to hurt me again" route tend to look down on those who take the more passive route, thinking them either stupid, weak, or unworthy of their respect. But everything isn't so black and white. It is a continuum—with passive people on one end of the continuum and aggressive people on the other. Between these two extremes lie many other options. For example, you can defend yourself from future attacks without taking on the behavior of your abuser. Just as important, you can learn to have empathy for those who are not as strong as you. This empathy will help you stop taking advantage of females or those you perceive as weaker than you.

Current research has found that empathy and power have an inverse relationship. According to *The War for Kindness* by Jamil Zaki, the more powerful people are, the less likely they are to have empathy, because they're less likely to need other people. This especially may explain why women are more inclined to cooperate rather than rebel, why female victims tend to be more passive. For example, people who are lower in status and power tend to practice or work on their ability to understand other people (a component of empathy).

Females in our culture (and every culture in the world) still suffer from the inequity of males having more power, control, status, and money. Because of their lower status, they realize that the skill of connecting with others is very important, because they often don't have the resources to make it on their own. In other words, they realize they need others—thus their ability to empathize is stronger.

When someone realizes that they are the cause of the pain someone else is experiencing, this can be a threat to them. We want to view ourselves as good people, but when we're forced to see ourselves as a perpetrator, our ability to view ourselves in this way is damaged. When this happens, we strive for any way that we can recover our sense of being good. Unfortunately, one of the most effective ways is to blame victims or to dehumanize them.

You may have been successful in numbing yourself sufficiently or in denying and blocking out what you are doing to others so that you don't feel your shame. You may have taken the focus off of the wrongs you have committed by blaming the victim. Or you may have been able to deny or pretend that you have the right to control or abuse others. But the truth is—you don't. Not only do you harm others when you humiliate, control, take advantage of others—you harm yourself.

You do not have to be in a position of power to experience this phenomenon. By closing off your heart and building a defensive wall, you can convince yourself that you do not need anyone—therefore, you do not need to have empathy for them.

How to Become More Empathetic

- When you are talking to other people, especially those who are close to you, make eye contact. Also, make a real effort to listen to what they are saying. You may have to feign interest at first, because you are so accustomed to blocking people out, but the more you use your empathy muscle, the stronger it will get, and you will find that you are more interested in others.
- Have equal relationships, especially equal sexual relationships. Research shows that personal power interferes with our ability to empathize. This means that if you choose partners who allow you to control or abuse them, you lessen your ability to have empathy toward others (evidence shows that power can change how the brain functions).
- Stop frequenting prostitutes/strip clubs, and pornographic sites. You may think that visiting prostitutes and strip clubs or watching pornography doesn't harm you or others, but you are wrong. First of all, doing these things hurts you. It prevents you from developing or maintaining a healthy intimate relationship with a woman (or man). Second, whether or not you are aware of it, continuing to do these things adds to your shame and robs you of your ability to have empathy. Third, women (and men) who work in the sex industry typically are often victims of child sexual abuse themselves. They are usually reenacting their abuse or punishing themselves. Further, by frequenting prostitutes or porn sites you are contributing to industries that use and abuse women.

  This is what a male client of mine who came into therapy because of a sex addiction that included frequenting prostitutes shared with me:

I was recently arrested for soliciting prostitution, and I was required to go to what they call a 'John School' where they educate men about this so-called victimless crime. Man, did I learn a lot. I'd heard that most prostitutes had been sexually abused, but I never really took the time to think about what this meant. These women are often reenacting the abuse they experienced, and many of them are addicted to drugs as a way of coping with the effects of the abuse they experienced. Many of them are revictimized by their pimps by being violently raped and beaten. When I learned this, it broke my heart. I also learned that by going to prostitutes, I was contributing to an industry that is known for its corruption and cruelty toward women. I don't want to be a part of this anymore. Please help me so I won't feel compelled to continue.

- Work on becoming more vulnerable, on letting others in. Allow others to see your pain. You don't have to be the tough one all the time. The more vulnerable you become, the less you will need to pretend that you are always in control, that you are always strong. The more you soften, the less need you will have for that defensive wall—the very same wall that keeps you from truly connecting with others and having empathy for others.
- Think of empathy as a skill or a muscle. The more you practice it, the stronger it will become.

GENERAL WAYS TO STOP SHAME-INDUCING SEXUAL BEHAVIORS

The following suggestions can be powerful strategies for change whether you tend to passively or aggressively reenact the abuse.

- Make the all-important connection between your negative sexual behavior and your sexual trauma. For example, allowing yourself to be coerced into sex when you don't want it is similar to a perpetrator grooming you and tricking you into sexual activities you did not want to participate in and were ill equipped to handle. Your attraction to "illicit" sex (having an extramarital affair, having sex in public places, having sex with an underaged partner) are usually reenactments of sexual abuse. Think about it: childhood sexual abuse involves secrecy and engaging in the forbidden.
- Get clear as to why you want to stop the shame-inducing behavior. For passive reenactors, although it may seem difficult to be able to stand

up to someone who is pressuring you for sex, the effort will be worth it. Each time you give in, you are going against yourself, going against your well-being and being revictimized. For aggressive reenactors, your powerful drive to turn the tables and be in the aggressor's position in an attempt to reduce or eliminate your shame is not only ineffective, but ironically, it adds to your shame.

- Get support to stop harmful sex (sexual addiction, an attraction or compulsion to engage in dangerous or illicit sex, unprotected sex). This may include participating in a twelve-step program such as Sex Addicts Anonymous, or seeking individual therapy with someone who specializes in trauma and/or sexual healing. Many forms of therapy are particularly effective for those who suffer from sexual compulsions or addictions, including one-on-one therapy with a psychotherapist who specializes in trauma, child sexual abuse recovery and sexual compulsion/addiction recovery, cognitive-behavioral therapy (CBT), eye movement desensitization and reprocessing (EMDR), and somatic therapy.

If you feel like you are addicted to internet pornography, these strategies can help you in your endeavor:

- Put the computer in a "public" area of the house.
- Apply safety controls (filters, etc.) and ask someone else to set the passwords.
- Use an older model mobile phone that makes accessing online content more difficult or impossible.
- Put a picture of your partner and family near your computer, or as a screen saver.
- Work on connecting with your body and being present instead of being numb or dissociating. Somatic therapies are especially positive in helping former victims connect with their bodies and releasing traumatic emotions.
- Be patient and realistic about making changes. This includes not setting unreasonable expectations, but being self-compassionate and allowing yourself to feel proud when you make a significant change.
- Take a break from sex. This will give you a chance to "reset" your sexuality as you work to resolve your issues with sex that are related to the abuse.
- Learn new approaches to relationships and touch. In the next chapter, I will offer you effective and powerful strategies to help you trade your unhealthy ways of viewing sex for more positive, healthy, and healing ways to view and express your sexuality.

Remember: You are not to blame for the ways you have attempted to cope with the abuse you experienced, nor are you to blame for the ways that the sexual abuse shaped your sexual preferences. I've never met a sexual abuse victim who didn't have sexual issues—whether it is the two extremes of avoiding sex or being sexually promiscuous; having feelings of fear or repulsion about certain sexual behaviors or parts of the body; or inappropriate or even dangerous sexual fantasies or compulsions. But this doesn't mean that it isn't possible to confront and heal these unhealthy ideas and practices. I hope you have been able to learn about and begin to change those aspects of your sexuality that are based on shame, fear, a need to punish yourself, or a need to have power and control overs others.

In the next chapter, I will offer still more information and strategies to help you continue your transformation—from desiring to engage in sex that is based on and characterized by shame to one that is based on connection, passion, and mutuality.

FOURTEEN

REPLACING SHAME-INDUCING SEX WITH HEALTHY SEX

Be in your fingers and hands as if your whole being, your whole soul, is there.

—Osho

REPLACING SHAME-INDUCING SEX with healthy sex may not be easy, but it is doable. The information and strategies offered in this chapter will help you to create a healthier sexual environment for yourself, one that can replace the shame-filled atmosphere you have surrounded yourself with. This includes reconnecting with your body, your senses, and your desire, as well as learning healthy ways to connect with your partner.

WHAT IS HEALTHY SEX?

Although you may at times continue to be triggered by memories of the abuse, memories that can certainly elicit shame, in general, having healthy sex doesn't create shame in you when you engage in it. Having healthy sex also means that you don't engage in sex for the purpose of shaming yourself or the other person. And finally, it can also mean that you don't engage in sex when you are experiencing shame or as a way of avoiding a shame trigger.

So, what do you need to do in order to experience shame-free healthy sex? Here are a few components of healthy sex:

- safety
- awareness and connection with your body
- connection with your partner
- equality and mutuality
- open communication

Safety

Previously we discussed ways to ensure your physical and emotional safety when you are connecting with a potential sexual partner. These strategies apply the most to women and those who have a more passive way of relating to others, but they also apply to men and those who have a more aggressive stance in life. Although you may feel perfectly safe when you dominate and control others, remember that a fragile, wounded part of you is hiding inside you and needs to feel safe and protected.

First of all, make sure you don't passively or aggressively set up situations where you are re-wounded or retraumatized. This includes weaning yourself from past or present partners who have been rejecting, humiliating, or abusive toward you. It also includes choosing partners who have a healthy outlook concerning sexuality and who are able to be emotionally intimate and focused on receiving and giving physical pleasure instead of focusing primarily on techniques, performance, domination, and control.

Awareness and Connection with Your Body

Healthy sex is the ability to create an "embodied" sexuality, in which you are in your body, present for the sexual experience, and doing what you enjoy and desire, based on your individual needs. In order to facilitate this, it is essential to break your habit of dissociating. This is especially important for those who have taken on a more passive or victim-like style. If you aren't in your body, you won't know when you are in a dangerous or unhealthy situation and you won't know when to say no. You need to be in the present and in your body to make sure you aren't unconsciously reenacting the sexual abuse. And just as important, you need to be in your body in order to connect with an intimate partner.

Each time you have a sexual encounter, make sure you do the following:

- *Breathe.* Notice when you hold your breath and when you are breathing naturally. Make sure your breathing isn't too shallow but is filling your belly and chest.
- *Stay in your body.* Make sure you can feel sensations in your chest, arms, legs. Move around if you need to. Being connected to how your body feels is your reference point for knowing what you want and where your boundaries are.
- *Be present.* Notice your surroundings. Make sure you aren't dissociated; if you are, ground yourself so that you will come back to the room and to the present. Look at your partner and connect with him or her.
- *Have your wits about you.* This means not being too drunk or too high or too dissociated to be able to protect and defend yourself.

For those with a more aggressive style, it is important to be more aware of how you are feeling to detect any anger or need for power that you are feeling and acting out. If you aren't in the present and in your body, you are more likely to unconsciously act out the abuse—for example, taking out your anger at your abuser on your sexual partner. The more you are in your body and in the present, the more you have an opportunity to open up and be more vulnerable with your sexual partners and ironically, the more physical pleasure you will receive.

Earlier in the book (chapter 7), I taught you how to do a "check-in" exercise to help you determine what you are feeling at any given time. This is also an effective way to break your habit of dissociating or becoming numb to your emotions, so practice it daily if you notice you have a tendency to dissociate.

Connection with a Partner

The more you are present with yourself, the easier it will be to be present with your partner. All too often former victims get in the habit of distancing themselves from their partner while engaging in sex. It is as if their body is present, but their mind is somewhere else. An additional problem is when you become triggered while having sex and are no longer in the present but in the past, being sexually abused by your perpetrator. When this happens, I suggest that you do the following:

- Stop all movement.
- Tell your partner you need a time out (the optimum would be that you discuss this plan with your partner ahead of time).
- Open your eyes.
- Look around the room and notice where you are.
- Look at your partner's face and notice that he or she is not your abuser.
- Don't resume sex until you are clear that you are not with your abuser.

Truly connecting with your partner involves intimacy, which requires being willing to be vulnerable and transparent with your partner. Lasting intimacy is built over time and involves allowing yourself to be known to your partner. This includes:

- taking your time to get to know a potential partner
- communicating your sexual preferences and especially the things you don't enjoy

- deciding whether you wish to disclose the fact that you were sexually abused
- exploring alternative ways of touching and being together before engaging in oral sex or penetration (see instructions for sensate focus later in the chapter)
- showing your partner how you like to be touched (guide his hand by letting it rest on yours)
- focusing on being in the present and in your body when you begin to share physical intimacy
- practicing being able to pay attention to your own sensations and being attentive to your partner at the same time

Equality and Mutuality

One of the best ways to reduce and eliminate shame from your sexual relationships is to ensure equality and mutuality between you. Equality means that neither of you is controlling, dominating, or abusing the other. Mutuality means that you and your sexual partner reach consensus on what kinds of sexual activities you will engage in prior to beginning the activity and that you agree to end the activity when either wants to stop. To achieve these two things, you naturally will need to learn how to communicate with one another.

Open Communication

Open communication runs counter to the dynamics that existed in the sexual abuse—the secrecy, silence, shame, manipulation, and victimization. When you are communicating with your partner your wants, needs, and desires, you are no longer being a victim who has to give in to your abuser's demands. And you are doing the opposite of having to remain silent and having to keep a secret. When you are communicating openly, you are stepping out of the victim role and are instead an equal and willing participant.

By communicating openly with one another, you build emotional intimacy with your partner. To achieve open communication, you and your partner will need to create a climate in which open communication feels safe. A number of good books can help you learn to communicate with one another as a couple; some are included in the recommended reading section of this book.

SENSUAL SEX

The best way to connect with your partner and stay connected throughout the sexual encounter is to engage in sensual sex. Sensual sex is more about awakening your senses and connecting with your partner than focusing on your performance; it is more about helping you to sink into sensation rather than trying to impress or even please your partner; more about encouraging you to bask in the exquisite pleasure of touch than on expending your energy trying to reach an orgasm.

Most important, sensual sex is not goal oriented. It does not include a push for orgasm. It is slow and relaxed, more like a lazy river than a tumultuous ocean. Passion is present, but the kind that builds slowly, gaining momentum with time. Sensual sex is far more fulfilling and far more intimate than routine sex. By taking the time to really take in and enjoy your partner's body, you will satisfy not only your desire for an orgasm but also your desire for deep intimacy.

Sensual sex is flowing, spontaneous, exploratory. Instead of following the same old routine, you allow the next feeling and touch to unfold. Most important, sensual sex focuses on the present. This makes it less probable that you will have flashbacks or be reminded of the sexual abuse, thus making it possible to explore your sexual feelings free of the past trauma.

The premise of sensual sex is that by focusing more on pleasure than on performance, by slowing down and taking time to connect more intimately, you can enjoy a deeply satisfying relationship with your partner that goes beyond orgasms, performance, and striving for perfection often brought on by shame.

HOW TO BEGIN CONNECTING WITH YOUR PARTNER

You can learn to reconnect with your body and establish intimate trust with your partner through the use of a series of innovative touching and sensuality exercises. The following experiences, taken from my book *Sensual Sex: Arousing Your Senses and Deepening the Passion in Your Relationships*, can help you to connect with a new partner or reconnect with an existing partner emotionally and physically, especially if you have not been able to feel safe enough to do so for quite some time. Pick and choose the experiences that feel safest for you— and the most enjoyable. If an experience reminds you of the sexual abuse you experienced, do not feel pressured to engage in it.

SYNCHRONIZED DEEP BREATHING

Couples often talk about their desire to flow together and to get in rhythm with each other. There is no better way to achieve this than to practice synchronized breathing, which can increase your feelings of connection and harmony with your partner.

Breathing together is also a beautiful way to communicate nonverbally. Synchronized deep breathing at any stage of lovemaking will intensify both your feelings and your energy level. And deep breathing together as you are approaching orgasm can help create an incredibly exciting experience.

Note: Hearing someone breathe fast can be a trigger for many former victims, because it reminds them of hearing the abuser's breath deepen as he or she became sexually aroused or reached orgasm. If you are triggered by the mere idea of breathing with your partner, do not engage in this exercise.

Partners can breathe together in two ways. You can breathe in and out as one, or you can alternate like two pistons, with one breathing in as the other breathes out. The first is breathing simultaneously, the second is breathing in tandem.

Try this technique:

- Sit facing each other. Make eye contact and begin to breathe together, inhaling and exhaling at the same time. Now decide who will be the leader and who will be the follower. The leader will begin breathing very slowly and deeply, and the follower will emulate her breathing pattern until you are breathing in sync with one another. Notice whether it makes you feel uncomfortable to have eye contact; if it does, just note that eye contact can create an intimate connection, which may in itself feel threatening to you. If you can, continue breathing together and having eye contact anyway. Notice how it feels to breathe deeply, how relaxed it makes you feel, and how it feels to breathe together in this way.
- Now the leader should speed up her breathing and the follower match her breath. Notice how much more excited you tend to feel when you breath more rapidly and how it feels to breathe together in this way.

THE IMPORTANCE OF TOUCH

As we have been discussing, many survivors suffer from being cut off from their emotions, their bodies, and their sexual feelings. The following exercise can help you reconnect with all of these aspects of yourself. It can help you reclaim your natural capacity for pleasure through the use of sensual, loving touch. Perhaps most important, it can help you tear down the walls that have kept you feeling separate and alone.

The following are instructions for how you and your partner can reintroduce or introduce sensual touch to your lovemaking. This type of touch, sometimes called the "caress" technique or "sensate focus," can help you learn to touch in a very slow, sensuous, and loving way, helping you to take your focus away from the genitals and sexual arousal and instead focus on pleasuring the entire body. It is also a great way to get you out of your head and into your senses. Because this exercise is nonthreatening, it is an especially good one for couples who feel a lot of pressure to perform.

SENSATE FOCUS

Reaching out to connect with another person physically requires a vulnerability that many former victims of sexual abuse find difficult. Many have learned to put up defenses to protect themselves from further hurt. Letting down these defenses, even when they are in the presence of loved ones, can be difficult. But former victims can reclaim their natural capacity for pleasure through the use of sensual, loving touch. They can tear down the walls that have kept them feeling separate and alone.

Receiving intimate touch can help melt the armor that you may have used to protect yourself and encourage you to share your feelings of anger, fear, and pain with your partner. By daring to be vulnerable and free from rigid self-control, you can also free the flow of love between yourself and your partner.

Sensate focus was designed to help establish trust between couples and to help them find alternative ways of touching and sharing intimacy. It is a deeply relaxing, sensuous experience that can help you and your partner become more present, more open, and more loving. It is especially positive for former victims of sexual abuse who dissociate often, who are afraid of or turned off to sex, or who find themselves continually compelled to reenact the abuse. This sensate focus exercise teaches you how to

- be present and in your body
- focus on your bodily sensations instead of being in your head or in fantasy
- touch your partner in a loving, sensuous way that is guaranteed to be pleasing. This helps you stop "performing" and worrying about whether you are pleasing your partner

The term sensate focus refers to the fact that during these exercises, you focus your attention as closely as you can on your sensations, how it feels to touch and be touched. For example, whether you are the one giving the touch or receiving it, make sure that you always focus all your attention on the point where your body comes in contact with your partner's skin. If your mind wanders during the exercise, bring it back to the exact point of contact between your skin and your partner's skin.

Sensate focus teaches you an entirely different way of touching than you are used to. This way of touching, called *caressing*, has been proven to remove the pressure to perform, to allow people to touch for their own pleasure, and to help people express tenderness, caring, and gentleness. The word caress comes from the Latin *carus*, which means "dear" or "precious." Caressing is a special way of touching that enables you to communicate to your lover just how dear he or she is to you, just how precious his or her body is to you. Caressing allows you to use your hands as an extension of your heart.

Caressing is different from massage or even what is commonly called "sensual massage," because instead of manipulating the underlying muscles of the body, you focus on the skin. Caressing is a slow, sensuous touch that is much lighter than massage and is done very, very, slowly, using not only your fingertips but your entire hand and even your forearm. You caress your partner's skin with long sweeping strokes, using the flat of your fingers, palm, wrist, and forearm.

Another difference between caressing and massaging is that massage is intended solely for the pleasure or therapeutic benefit of the person receiving the massage, while caressing is done for the pleasure of the person giving the caress as well. For example, it is common to become tired while giving a massage or to become anxious because you are concerned about whether you were doing it right and pleasing your partner.

When you give your partner a caress, he or she will not be the only person experiencing physical pleasure. You will enjoy it just as much, and you won't be worrying about how well you are performing, so it will not feel as much like a task.

To understand what I mean, try the following:

- Imagine that your right hand is the "giver" and your left hand is the "receiver." Touch your left hand using only the fingertips of your right hand. Notice how this feels. Which hand feels pleasure? Most people report that their left hand, the "receiver," feels the pleasure, but the "giver" hand—the right hand—doesn't really feel anything.
- Now touch your left hand again, this time using the flat of your fingers, your palm, and the inside of your wrist instead of your fingertips. You can also include your forearm if you choose. Notice which hand feels the pleasure of the touch this time? Most people say that both hands feel pleasure, both the "giver" and the "receiver." In fact, it is difficult to tell which hand is the giver and which is the receiver.

I recommend using this caress technique in place of the typical massage as a way of deeply connecting with your partner and yourself. I suggest that you begin by caressing one another's feet, which is typically a very nonthreatening experience for most people. Remember, use only your wrist, your palm, and the flat of your fingers—not your fingertips. You and your partner will discover that this foot caress is far more satisfying and relaxing than it would be if you used your fingertips—which can create a "ticklish" reaction.

Next, either during the same time period or at another time, give and receive a back caress. Use long strokes (again with your wrist, your palm and flat of your fingers) and make sure to go extremely slowly—the slower the better.

Note: For more directions on how to complete the caress technique, read my book *Sensual Sex* or the books on sensate focus recommended in the back of the book.

You have a right to a gratifying and exciting sexual life. Our sexual organs have thousands of pleasure receptors, making it possible for us to feel intense pleasure. Unfortunately, along with many other negative effects, the sexual abuse you suffered may have robbed you of experiencing the delicious pleasure that sexual activities can provide. You have the right and the ability to take back what was taken from you.

Hopefully, the information I have shared with you in this chapter, as well as the strategies I recommend for managing and healing your trauma reactions, have helped you begin to heal the damage you sustained. On the other hand, this may be just the beginning of your healing journey. I have included a number of books in the recommended reading section in the back of the book to further help you on this journey.

CONCLUSION

Some of you have been through things so traumatic that the human mind isn't built to handle but you fight and persevere every single day and night. If that's not strength I don't know what is. You are a survivor.

—Anonymous

If you've made it this far in the book—congratulations! This hasn't been an easy book to read, because it likely brought up many painful memories and difficult emotions. I hope you feel proud of yourself for sticking with it. If you completed many of the exercises, you have even more reason to feel proud of yourself. Many of the exercises and processes offered are extremely difficult to complete and take an extra amount of determination and strength to tackle.

Throughout the book, I've discussed the various ways that survivors tend to cope with the trauma of child sexual abuse, even though these coping mechanisms may have made your life more difficult. I hope you have been able to understand why you took on these coping strategies that are sometimes destructive and that you have forgiven yourself for using them. Although there are many negative coping strategies, former victims have survived the trauma in two overall ways: taking on a victim or passive mentality to avoid further attacks and putting up a defensive wall to protect themselves from further shame. Although I hope the book has helped you in numerous ways, my strongest hope is that it has helped you if you took on either of these life strategies.

If one of the most profound results of the abuse you suffered was that you ended up feeling hopeless and helpless, my most sincere wish for you is that after reading this book, and hopefully completing the exercises, you feel more empowered. I hope you have stopped blaming yourself for the abuse and instead have come to the powerful realization that the abuse was not your fault. I hope that you have been able to connect with your righteous anger—at your abuser and anyone who enabled him or her. I hope you have been able to allow yourself to express this anger in healthy ways and that you have stopped taking out your anger on yourself, either by being self-destructive or by continuing to get involved with people who abuse you or don't show you the respect you deserve. And finally, I hope you have developed an inner sense of strength that will enable you to walk away from any person or situation that does not respect you.

If you put up a defensive wall to protect yourself from further shame, my deepest hope is that you have been able to lower that wall, if only a little. I hope you have recognized that although you may have kept yourself safe from being criticized or shamed, the price you have paid is that you have had to suffer alone, with no one to whom you can share your pain. I hope you have been able to become even the slightest bit more vulnerable in opening up with others. This kind of vulnerability can be scary, but also incredibly rewarding. Even more important, I hope that you have taken the risk of opening up to yourself—that you have allowed yourself to connect with your emotions, even the most painful ones. I hope that you have been able to offer yourself even the slightest amount of self-compassion, recognizing how difficult your life has been. And finally, I hope that you have been able to forgive yourself for the harm you may have caused others because you were in such pain.

If you have taken any of these steps, acknowledge how difficult they were and be proud of yourself for taking these risks. This can be the beginning of a whole new perspective and a whole new life for you. No one wants to be completely alone, even when it feels safer. We all long for connection with others. Take your time, but continue to take those risks.

In addition to honoring yourself by continuing to open up—to others and yourself—continue to practice self-compassion. It truly is the remedy for shame. The more compassion you can allow yourself to feel for all your suffering, the more you will be able to feel compassion for the suffering of others, and the more connected you will feel to the rest of humanity. The more self-compassion you can experience, the less defensive you will need to be and the less shame you will feel.

Pride is the opposite of shame, so I encourage you to allow yourself to be proud of how hard you have worked to heal your shame. Be proud of sticking with it, even when you wanted to quit. Be proud of admitting the truth to yourself, even when you could have remained in deep denial. Feel proud of acknowledging your pain and allowing yourself to grieve your losses. Acknowledge how difficult it was to finally allow yourself to feel and express your anger. And allow yourself to feel proud if you finally were able to tell someone. Most important, feel proud of not continuing to blame yourself but for placing the blame and responsibility where they belong.

I'm honored to have been a part of your healing journey. It has been a privilege to walk this road with you. Shame is an extremely difficult emotion to heal. I admire your strength, your determination, and your willingness to dig deep within yourself to heal that shame. Bravo!

REFERENCES, RECOMMENDED READINGS, AND RESOURCES

REFERENCES

Introduction

Hall, M., and Hall, J. "The Long-Term Effects of Childhood Sexual Abuse: Counseling Implications." Vistas Online, 2011.

Kaufman, Gershen. *Shame: The Power of Caring.* New York: Schenkman Books, 1992.

MacGinley, M., Breckenridge, J., and Mowill, J. "A Scoping Review of Adult Survivors' Experiences of Shame Following Sexual Abuse in Childhood." *Health and Social Care in the Community* 27, no. 5 (2019): 1135–46.

Chapter 1: Why Child Sexual Abuse Is So Shaming

Feiring, C., and Taska, L. S. "The Persistence of Shame Following Sexual Abuse: A Longitudinal Look at Risk and Recovery." *Child Maltreatment* 10, no. 4 (2005): 337–49.

Herman, J. L. "Postraumatic Stress Disorder as a Shame Disorder." In *Shame in the Therapy Hour*, ed. R. L. Dearing and J. P. Tangney, 261–75. American Psychological Association, 2011.

Kaufman, *Shame.*

MacGinley, Breckenridge, and Mowill, "Scoping Review."

Tapia, Natalia. "Survivors of Child Sexual Abuse and Predictors of Adult Re-victimization in the United States." *International Journal of Criminal Justice Sciences* 9, no. 1 (January–June, 2014).

Younique Foundation. "The Effects of Child Sexual Abuse: Shame and Child Abuse." https://youniquefoundation.org.

Chapter 2: The Immediate and Long-Term Effects of Shame

"Adult Manifestations of Child Sexual Abuse." American College of Obstetricians and Gynecologists, 2011.

American Psychiatric Association. *Diagnostic and Statistical Manual of Mental Disorders, Fifth Edition:* DSM-5. Washington, DC: American Psychiatric Association, 2013.

Consequences/Sexual Assault/ INSPQ. https://www.inspq.qc.ca/en/sexual-assault/under standing-sexual-assault/consequences, 2003.

Courtois, Christine. *Healing the Incest Wound: Adult Survivors in Therapy.* New York: Norton, 2010.

Finkelhor, D., and Browne, A. "The Traumatic Impact of Child Sexual Abuse: A Conceptualization." *American Journal of Orthopsychiatry*, 55 (1985): 530–41.

Herman, "Postraumatic Stress Disorder as a Shame Disorder."

Irish, Leah, Kobayashi, Ihori, and Delahanty, Douglas. "Long-Term Physical Health Consequences of Childhood Sexual Abuse: A Meta-Analytic Review." *Journal of Pediatric Psychology* 35, no. 5 (June 2010): 450–61.

Kaufman, *Shame.*

Lawson, David M. "Understanding and Treating Survivors of Incest." *Counseling Today*, March 6, 2018.

MacGinley, Breckenridge, and Mowill, "Scoping Review."

Chapter 3: Why You Must Heal Your Shame to Heal from Child Sexual Abuse

Briere, John N., and Scott, Catherine. *Principles of Trauma Therapy: A Guide to Symptoms, Evaluation, and Treatment.* Los Angeles: Sage, 2015.

Classen, C. C., Palesh, O. G., and Aggarwal, R. "Sexual Re-victimization: A Review of Empirical Literature." *Trauma, Violence, & Abuse* 4, no. 6 (2005): 103–29.

Darkness to Light. "Child Sexual Abuse Statistics: Perpetrators," 2015. www.darkness 2light.org.

Filipas, H. H., and Ullman, S. E. "Child Sexual Abuse, Coping Responses, Self-Blame, Posttraumatic Stress Disorder, and Adult Sexual Re-victimization." *Journal of Interpersonal Violence* 5, no. 21 (2006): 652–72.

Kaufman, *Shame.*

MacGinley, Breckenridge, and Mowill, "Scoping Review."

Mash, E. J., and Barkley, R. A., eds. *Assessment of Childhood Disorders*, 4th ed. New York: Guilford, 2007, 685–748.

Noll, J. G., Horowitz, L. A., Bonanno, G. A., Trickett, P. K., and Pullman, F. W. "Re-victimization and Self-Harm in Females Who Experienced Childhood Sexual Abuse: Results from a Prospective Study." *Journal of Interpersonal Violence* 12, no. 18 (2003): 1452–71.

Oshri, A., Tubman, J. G., and Burnette, M. L. "Childhood Maltreatment Histories, Alcohol and Other Drug Use Symptoms, and Sexual Risk Behavior in a Treatment Sample of Adolescents." *American Journal of Public Health* 102, no. 2 (2012): 250–57.

RAINN, www.rainn.org.

Tapia, "Survivors of Child Sexual Abuse and Predictors of Adult Re-Victimization in the United States."

van der Kolk, B. A. "The Compulsion to Repeat the Trauma: Reenactment, Revictimization and Masochism." *Psychiatric Clinics of North America*, 12 (1989): 339–41.

Chapter 4: Facing the Truth

Bank, S. P., and Kahn, M. D. *The Sibling Bond.* New York: Basic Books, 1982.

Darkness to Light, "Child Sexual Abuse Statistics."

Dorais, Michel. *Don't Tell: The Sexual Abuse of Boys*, 2nd ed. Montreal, Canada: McGill-Queen's University Press, 2008.

Finklehor, David, et al. *Children's Exposure to Violence: A Comprehensive National Survey.* Washington, DC: Department of Justice, Office of Justice Program, Office of Juvenile Justice and Delinquency Prevention, 2009.

Fogler, Jason, et al. "Betrayal and Recovery: Understanding the Trauma of Clergy Sexual Abuse." *Journal of Child Sexual Abuse* 17, nos. 3–4 (2008): 330.

John Jay College of Criminal Justice. *The Nature and Scope of Sexual Abuse by Catholic Priests and Deacons in the United States 1950–2002*. New York: City University of New York, 2004.

McMaster, Geoff. *Researchers Reveal Patterns in Sexual Abuse in Religious Settings*. Alberta, Canada: University of Alberta, 2020.

Reardon, Christina, MSW, LSW. "Innocence Lost, Faith Damaged, Trust Betrayed." *Social Work Today* 19, no. 2 (2022): 16.

Research and Advocacy, Washington Coalition of Sexual Abuse Programs 10, no. 2.

Rudd, J. M., and Herzberger, S. D. "Brother-Sister Incest/Father-Daughter Incest: A Comparison of Characteristics and Consequences." *Child Abuse and Neglect*, 23 (1999): 915–28.

Sibling Sexual Abuse: A Knowledge & Practice Overview. Centre of Expertise on Child Sexual Abuse, 2021.

Simons, Dominique A. *Adult Sex Offender Typologies*, SOMAPI Research Brief, U.S. Department of Justice, Office of Sex Offender Sentencing, Monitoring, Apprehending, Registering and Tracking, 2015.

Weihe, V. R. *Sibling Abuse: Hidden Physical, Emotional, and Sexual Trauma*. Thousand Oaks, CA: Sage, 1997.

Chapter 5: Other Reasons for Confusion: Self Doubt, Fuzzy Memories

American Psychiatric Association, *Diagnostic and Statistical Manual of Mental Disorders, Fifth Edition:* DSM-5.

Courtois. *Healing the Incest Wound.*

Finklehor, *Children's Exposure to Violence.*

Fisher, Janina. *Transforming the Living Legacy of Trauma: A Workbook for Survivors and Therapists*. Eau Claire, WI: Pesi Publishing and Media, 2021.

Freyd, Jennifer. *Betrayal Trauma: The Logic of Forgetting Childhood Abuse*. Boston: Harvard University Press, 1998.

Chapter 6: Stop Blaming Yourself

Ballantine, M. "Sibling Incest Dynamics: Therapeutic Themes and Clinical Challenges." *Clinical Social Work Journal* 40, no. 1 (2012): 56–65.

Child Family Community Australia. "The Long-Term Effects of Child Sexual Abuse: The Impact of Child Sexual Abuse on Mental Health." *Journal of Child Sexual Abuse* (January 2013).

Courtois, *Healing the Incest Wound.*

Dorais, *Don't Tell.*

Freyd, *Betrayal Trauma*.

Hanson, R. K., and Bussiere, M. T. "Predicting Relapse: A Meta-Analysis of Sexual Offender Recidivism Studies." *Journal of Consulting and Clinical Psychology*, 63 (1998): 348–62.

Jespersen, A. F., Lalumiere, M. L., and Seto, M. C. "Sexual Abuse History among Adult Sex Offenders and Non-Sex Offenders: A Meta-Analysis." *Child Abuse & Neglect*, 33 (2009): 179–92.

John Jay College Research Team, *Nature and Scope of Sexual Abuse*.

Kluft, Richard P., MD, PhD. "Ramifications of Incest," *Psychiatric Times* 27, no. 12 (2011): 2.

Lawson, "Understanding and Treating Survivors of Incest."

Porges, S. W. *The Polyvagal Theory: Neurophysiological Foundations of Emotions, Attachment, Communication, Self-Regulation*. New York: Norton, 2011.

Robinson, Bryan. "Female Offenders Driven by More Than Sex." ABC News, March 21, 2006.

Sheinberg, M., and Fraenkel, P. *The Relational Trauma of Incest: A Family-Based Approach to Treatment*. New York: Guilford, 2001.

"Sibling Incest." *Washington Coalition of Sexual Abuse Programs, Research and Advocacy* 10, no. 2.

"Sibling Sexual Abuse: A Knowledge & Practice Overview." Centre of Expertise on Child Abuse, 2021.

Simons. *Adult Sex Offender Typologies*.

Stemple, Lara, and Meyer, Ilan. "Sexual Victimization by Women Is More Common Than Previously Known." *Scientific American*, October 10, 2017.

University of Alberta, www.uaalberta.ca/folio/2020/08/researchers-reveal-patterns-of-sexual-abuse-in-religious-settings.html.

Walker, Pete. *From Surviving to Thriving*. Createspace, 2013.

Chapter 7: Acknowledge Your Pain and Grieve Your Losses

Engel, Beverly. *It Wasn't Your Fault: Freeing Yourself from the Shame of Childhood Abuse with the Power of Self-Compassion*. Oakland, CA: New Harbinger, 2015.

Germer, Christopher. *The Mindful Path to Self-Compassion*. New York: Guilford, 2009.

Neff, Kristin. *Self-Compassion: The Proven Power of Being Kind to Yourself*. New York: William Morrow, 2015.

Chapter 8: Give Yourself Permission to Be Angry

Engel, Beverly. *Breaking the Cycle of Abuse*. Hoboken, NJ: Wiley, 2005.

———. *Honor Your Anger*. Hoboken, NJ: Wiley, 2004.

———. *I'm Saying No! Standing up to Sexual Assault, Sexual Harassment and Sexual Pressure*. Berkeley, CA: She Writes Press, 2019.

———. *The Right to Innocence: Healing the Trauma of Childhood Sexual Abuse*. New York: Random House, 1989.

Hall and Hall, "The Long-Term Effects of Childhood Sexual Abuse."
Kaufman, *Shame*.
Levine, Peter. *Waking the Tiger: Healing Trauma*. New York: North Atlantic Books, 1997.

Chapter 9: Tell Someone
MacGinley, Breckenridge, and Mowill, "Scoping Review."

Chapter 10: Forgiving Yourself for the Ways You Have Harmed Others
Engel, Beverly. *The Power of Apology: Healing Steps to Transform All Your Relationships*. Hoboken, NJ: Wiley, 2001.
Neff, *Self-Compassion*.

Chapter 11: Forgiving Yourself for the Ways You Have Harmed Yourself
Behavior Modification—Goethe University Frankfurt.

Chapter 12: Avoiding Unhealthy Shame-Inducing Behaviors
Briere, John. *Treating Risky & Compulsive Behaviors in Trauma Survivors*. New York: Guilford, 2019.
Engel, *I'm Saying No!*
Levy, Michael, S. A. "Conceptualization of the Repetition Compulsion." *Psychiatry* 63, no. 1 (Spring 2000).
———. "A Helpful Way to Conceptualize and Understand Reenactments." *Journal of Psychotherapy Practice and Research* 7, no. 3 (1998): 227–35.
Mellin, Laurel. *The Solution:* New York: William Morrow, 1998.

Chapter 13: Taking the Shame Out of Your Sexual Relationships
Bourke M., and Hernandez, A. "The 'Butner Study' Redux: A Report of the Incidence of Hands-On Child Victimization by Child Pornography Offenders." *Journal of Family Violence*, 24 (2009): 183–91.
Engel, *I'm Saying No!*
———. *Sensual Sex: Arousing Your Senses and Deepening the Passion in Your Relationships*. Alameda, CA: Hunter House, 1999.
Hilton, Donald L., and Watts, Clark. "Pornography Addiction: A Neuroscience Perspective." Surgical Neurology International, February 21, 2011. https://www.ncbi.nim.nih.gov/pmc/articles/PMC 30500601.
Hogeveen, J., Inzlicht, M., and Obhi, S. S. "Power Changes How the Brain Responds to Others." *Journal of Experimental Psychology* 143, no. 2 (2014): 755–62.
Lawson, "Understanding and Treating Survivors of Incest."
Problematic Use of Pornography/Porn Addiction. https://livingwell.org.au/managing-difficulties/problematic-use-pornography/.
"The Role Alcohol Plays in Sexual Assault on College Campuses." Campus Safety, www.alcohol.org.

Segal, Elizabeth. "Power Blocks Empathy: Research Shows That People with Power Have Low Levels of Empathy." *Psychology Today*, September 23, 2019.

Simons, D., Wurtele, S. K., and Heil, P. "Childhood Victimization and Lack of Empathy as Predictors of Sexual Offending against Women and Children." *Journal of Interpersonal Violence*, 17 (2002): 1291–1305.

Solomon, Lou. "Becoming Powerful Makes You Less Empathetic." *Harvard Business Review*, April 21, 2015.

"Understanding and Treating Survivors of Incest." *Counseling Today*, 2018.

van der Kolk. "The Compulsion to Repeat the Trauma."

Young, Robin. "How Power Erodes Empathy and the Steps We Can Take to Rebuild It." *Psychology Today*, July 9, 2020.

Zaki, Jamil. *The War for Kindness: Building Empathy in a Fractured World*. New York: Crown, 2020.

Chapter 14: Replacing Shame-Inducing Sex with Healthy Sex

Engel. *Sensual Sex*.

RECOMMENDED READING

Recovery from Trauma

Briere, John. *Treating Risky and Compulsive Behavior in Trauma Survivors*. New York: Guilford, 2019.

Briere, John, and Scott, Catherine. *Principles of Trauma Therapy: A Guide to Symptoms, Evaluations and Treatment*. Los Angeles: Sage, 2015.

Fisher, Janina. *Transforming the Living Legacy of Trauma*. Eau Claire, WI: Pesi Publishing and Media, 2021.

Herman, Judith Lewis. *Trauma and Recovery: The Aftermath of Violence—From Domestic Abuse to Political Terror*. New York: Basic Books, 1997.

Levine, Peter. *Healing Trauma: A Pioneering Program for Restoring the Wisdom of Your Body*. Boulder, CO: Sounds True, 2005.

McKay, Matthew, Fanning, Patrick, et al. *Healing Emotional Pain Workbook: Process-Based CBT Tools for Moving beyond Sadness, Fear, Worry, and Shame to Discover Peace & Resilience*. Oakland, CA: New Harbinger, 2022.

Perry, Bruce D., and Winfrey, Oprah. *What Happened to You? Conversations on Trauma, Resilience, and Healing*. New York: Flatiron Books, 2021.

Schwartz, Arielle. *The Complex PTSD Workbook*. Berkeley, CA: Althea Press, 2016.

van der Kolk, Bessel A. *The Body Keeps the Score: Brain, Mind, and Body in the Healing of Trauma*. New York: Penguin, 2014.

Recovery from Childhood Abuse and Neglect

Engel, Beverly. *Healing Your Emotional Self: A Powerful Program to Help You Raise Your Self-Esteem, Quiet Your Inner Critic, and Overcome Your Shame*. Hoboken, NJ: Wiley, 2006.

———. *It Wasn't Your Fault: Freeing Yourself from the Shame of Childhood Abuse with the Power of Self-Compassion.* Oakland, CA: New Harbinger, 2015.

Recovery from Child Sexual Abuse

Bass, Ellen, and Davis, Laura. *The Courage to Heal: A Guide for Women Survivors of Child Sexual Abuse,* 2008.
Dorais, Michel. *Don't Tell: The Sexual Abuse of Boys.* McGill-Queen's University Press, 2008.
Engel, Beverly. *The Right to Innocence: Healing the Trauma of Childhood Sexual Abuse.* New York: Random House, 1989.
Hunter, Mic. *Abused Boys: The Neglected Victims of Sexual Abuse.* New York: Fawcett, 1990.
Lew, Mike. *Victims No Longer: The Classic Guide for Men Recovering from Sexual Child Abuse.* New York: Perennial, 1990.

Self-Compassion

Germer, C. *The Mindful Path to Self-Compassion: Freeing Yourself from Destructive Thoughts and Emotions.* New York: Guilford, 2009.
Neff, Kristin. *Self-Compassion: The Proven Power of Being Kind to Yourself.* New York: William Morrow, 2015.

Recovery from Codependency

Lancer, Darlene. *Conquering Shame and Codependency: 8 Steps to Freeing the True You.* Center City, MN: Hazelden, 2014.

Domestic Violence

Bancroft, Lundy. *Should I Stay or Should I Go? A Guide to Knowing if Your Relationship Can—and Should—Be Saved.* New York: Berkley, 2011.
———. *Why Does He Do That? Inside the Minds of Angry and Controlling Men.* New York: Berkley, 2002.

Emotional Abuse

Engel, Beverly. *The Emotionally Abused Woman: Overcoming Destructive Patterns and Reclaiming Yourself.* New York: Fawcett, 1990.
———. *The Emotionally Abusive Relationship: How to Stop Being Abused and How to Stop Abusing.* Hoboken, NJ: Wiley, 2002.
———. *Escaping Emotional Abuse: Healing from the Shame You Don't Deserve.* New York: Citadel, 2021.

Anger

Engel, Beverly. *Honor Your Anger: How Transforming Your Anger Style Can Change Your Life.* Hoboken, NJ: Wiley, 2004.

Healing Shame

Engel, Beverly. *It Wasn't Your Fault: Freeing Yourself from the Shame of Childhood Abuse with the Power of Self-Compassion*. Oakland, CA: New Harbinger, 2015.

Kaufman, Gershen. *Shame: The Power of Caring*. New York: Schenkman Books, 1992.

Self-Empowerment for Women

Engel, Beverly. *I'm Saying No! Standing Up against Sexual Assault, Sexual Harassment and Sexual Pressure*. Berkeley, CA: She Writes Press, 2019.

———. *Loving Him Without Losing You: How to Stop Disappearing and Start Being Yourself*. Hoboken, NJ: Wiley, 2000.

———. *The Nice Girl Syndrome: Stop Being Manipulated and Abused—and Start Standing Up for Yourself*. Hoboken, NJ: Wiley, 2008.

Healing Your Sexuality

Carnes, Patrick. *Out of the Shadows: Understanding Sexual Addiction, 3rd ed*. Center City, MN: Hazelden, 2001.

Engel, Beverly. *Raising Your Sexual Self-Esteem: How to Feel Better about Your Sexuality and Yourself*. New York: Fawcett, 1995.

———. *Sensual Sex. Arousing Your Senses and Deepening the Passion in Your Relationships*. Alameda, CA: Hunter House, 1999.

Haines, Staci. *Healing Sex: A Mind-Body Approach to Healing Sexual Trauma*. San Francisco: Cleis Press, 2007.

Maltz, Wendy. *Incest and Sexuality: A Guide to Understanding and Healing*. New York: Lexington, 1991.

———. *The Sexual Healing Journey: A Guide for Survivors of Sexual Abuse*, 3rd ed. New York: HarperCollins, 2012.

Shershun, Erika. *Healing Sexual Trauma Workbook: Somatic Skills to Help You Feel Safe in Your Body, Create Boundaries, and Live with Resilience*. Oakland, CA: New Harbinger, 2021.

Weiner, Linda, and Avery-Clark, Constance. *Sensate Focus in Sex Therapy: The Illustrated Manual*. New York: Routledge, 2017.

Weiss, Robert. *Cruise Control: Understanding Sexual Addiction in Gay Men*. Carefree, AZ: Gentle Path, 2013.

Communication Skills

Heitler, Susan, and Hirsh, Abigail. *The Power of Two Workbook: Communication Skills for a Strong & Loving Marriage*. Oakland, CA: New Harbinger Publications, 2003.

Leal, Bento C., III. *4 Essential Keys to Effective Communication*. Author, 2017.

Tawwab, Nedra Glover. *Set Boundaries, Find Peace*. New York: Tarcher/Perigee, 2021.

Sexual Predators

Duncan, Karen, A. *Female Sexual Predators: Understanding Them to Protect Our Children and Youths.* Westport, CT: Praeger, 2010.
Salter, Anna. *Predators:Pedophiles, Rapists, and Other Sex Offenders.* New York: Basic Books, 2003.

RESOURCES

Hotlines

Rape, Abuse & Incest National Network, (800) 656-HOPE (800) 656-4673.
Childhelp, (800) 4-A-CHILD.

Websites

Darkness to Light, Darkness2light.org.
National Sexual Violence Resource Center (NSVRC), www.nsvrc.org.
Rape, Abuse & Incest National Network (RAINN), www.rainn.org.
Survivors of Incest Anonymous (SIA), www.siawso.org.
Survivors Network of Those Abused by Priests (SNAP), www.snapnetwork.org.

INDEX

PRAISE FOR *FREEDOM AT LAST*

"Beverly Engel's *Freedom at Last* nails it! Like no other book on sexual trauma, she focuses on the core issue—shame. Compassionate, thorough, and personal, her book takes former victims gently by the hand and guides them through a step-by-step healing process. Therapy for sexual abuse that omits healing shame is incomplete. This workbook can lead you home."—Darlene Lancer, LMFT, author of *Conquering Shame & Codependency*

"Shame is pervasive among survivors of sexual trauma, and especially profound for survivors of childhood sexual abuse. Beverly Engel has written a comprehensive and accessible book filled with journal prompts and engaging exercises that skillfully guide and support readers in freeing themselves from the shame brought on by children sexual abuse. A transformative read for survivors as they navigate the healing journey."—Erika Shershun, LMFT, author of *Healing Sexual Trauma Workbook: Somatic Skills to Help You Feel Safe in Your Body, Create Boundaries, & Live with Resilience*

"Beverly Engel provides a healing and transformative book for sexual abuse survivors. From a deep understanding of the pain, she illuminates the different stages of recovery and offers a clear path for survivors to regain their life after trauma. *Freedom at Last: Healing the Shame of Childhood Sexual Abuse* gives voice to sexual assault survivors and shows how they can heal through validation. This is the one, indispensable book that survivors need most." —Matthew McKay, PhD, coauthor of *Healing Emotional Pain Workbook*

"Beverly Engel's newest book, *Freedom at Last*, turns the spotlight directly onto shame, that most elusive and disturbing of all emotions. Shame is like a wound made on the inside by an unseen hand. Engel pulls back the curtain surrounding sexual abuse, revealing an ever-growing cancer of shame within the self. This book is not only a journey into shame but, equally important, a journey out of shame through learning self-compassion and self-forgiveness." —Gershen Kaufman, PhD, author of *Shame: The Power of Caring*